CW00801872

Peter Lloyd join
in the Sydney television newsroom for three
years before moving to Britain to work for the
BBC and British Sky News.

Peter was appointed the South Asia corre-
spondent for the ABC in mid 2002. Based in
New Delhi, he covered the South Asia nations
of India, Pakistan, Afghanistan, Sri Lanka,
Bangladesh, Nepal, Bhutan and the Maldives.
From 2002 to mid 2006 he was based in
Bangkok reporting on South East Asian
affairs in Thailand, Burma, Laos, Cambodia,
Vietnam, Malaysia, Brunei, Singapore and the
Philippines. His compelling reports on the
Bali bombings and later the Tsunami disaster
earned several Walkley Award nominations.

INSIDE STORY

PETER LLOYD

ALLEN&UNWIN
SYDNEY•MELBOURNE•AUCKLAND•LONDON

Allen & Unwin
83 Alexander Street
Crows Nest NSW 2065
Australia
Phone: (61 2) 8425 0100
Fax: (61 2) 9906 2218
Email: info@allenandunwin.com
Web: www.allenandunwin.com

Cataloguing-in-Publication details are available from the
National Library of Australia
www.trove.nla.gov.au

ISBN 978 1 74237 905 0

Typeset in Garamond by Midland Typesetters, Australia
Printed and bound in Australia by The SOS Print + Media Group

10 9 8 7 6 5 4 3 2 1

Contents

ONE

Downfall

Two young men are at my flanks. A third is stepping from the shadows to block my escape. *I'm being mugged,* I think. I'm looking around, bewildered, processing this unexpected turn of events. *I'm being mugged in the low-crime capital of Asia.*

These assailants are shorter than me—all three are Chinese, dressed in jeans and T-shirts. The one to my left has gravity-defying hair—the style you see on young fashionistas in Singapore. *A life support system for hair product,* I think.

Yet something is not quite right about this scene. They don't look that threatening. A mugger is supposed to be armed or menacing and these three look as dangerous as actuaries. *Where are the weapons?* I'm thinking. *Why aren't they making any demands?* They're in far more peril than me, because they're breaking the golden rule in Singapore: hands off the foreigners (it's bad for business). I may lose my wallet but, in Lee Kuan Yew's cold utopia, thieves are scarified with bamboo rods and jailed for years for this kind of outrage.

Time to end this nonsense. Flushed with indignation, I am about to get aggressive, to start pushing and shoving. The idiomatic, artless and unequivocally Australian denunciation 'Piss off, fuckwits!' is rising fast in my throat. It's a tried and trusted put-down, guaranteed to scatter pests the world over. Its potency is as much in the tone as in the telling.

I'm opening my mouth to unload my tirade when the interloper in front of me steps forward to set me straight. 'My name is Detective Jack Teng, from Singapore Police, Central Narcotics Bureau.' He's showing me an identity badge. 'You're under arrest.'

He's a cop. They are all cops. I'm panicking. I'm not being mugged. I am being arrested.

To the right: a policeman seizes the mobile phone from my hand with the instruction, 'Don't move! We need you to co-operate.'

To the left: Fashionista Hair is patting me down, pushing his hands against my pockets. He's looking back at Teng, who is asking, 'Are you armed?'

I gape. Words aren't coming out.

'Are. You. Armed?' repeats Teng.

'Do you speak English?' asks the policeman holding my phone.

'Yes. I. Speak. English,' I stutter. '*Not* armed,' I add, shaking both my hands loosely. 'I'm Australian,' I declare, as if national identity is a shield against suspicion.

Jack Teng: 'Are you carrying drugs?'

'No,' I stutter. 'No drugs.'

The policemen at my flanks have released my arms so they can thrust their hands deep into my pockets simultaneously. Just as quickly they withdraw a few banknotes and a receipt for a tall caramel macchiatto at Starbucks, the sum total of their trawl.

A pause.

I'm stunned.

A minute ago I was minding my own business, standing on a Singapore street in front of a convenience store. Now I'm that most dreadful cliché, 'helping police with their inquiries'. I can feel adrenalin charging around my body like something monstrous and urgent trying to find the exit. I'm sweating profusely. Adrenalin is the most primeval hormone—it is what helps the body decide between 'fight' or 'flight'. I'm doing neither—I'm submitting to circumstance.

This is mortifying. A crowd is gathering, off to the right. They're throwing dagger-like stares in my directon. A bemused onlooker, an older Chinese man with a wispy moustache, is stepping in for a closer look. 'Hey,' says Teng, 'step away!'

Obedience is contagious. The rubbernecker fades into the dark.

I am terrified. I'm thinking, *I've never been arrested before.*

Sweat beads are sliding down my neck, making my shirt sticky. Maybe they will let me go, now they haven't found anything.

My hands feel wet and greasy. Can I pay a fine? Of course not—this isn't Thailand or Indonesia, where you can pay a fine and be on your way.

These thoughts and sensations are tearing around, competing for my attention. To the right, I see handcuffs. 'Please,' says the policeman, 'don't struggle. They will only get tighter.'

Handcuffs! They're not going to let me go. I have seen these tools of the police trade many times before but never felt them, never had them wielded against me. I discover they are cold and heavy, uncomfortably tight. Handcuffs are not fun or sensual or erotic. People who get off on them surely could not have experienced being arrested.

My head is spinning. From no handcuffs to handcuffs. From free to not free. Each step worse than the last.

I'm in the back seat of a black sedan. Detective Teng has announced to me that he is an assistant superintendent, or 'A/S-P', and that I am required to answer all of his questions or face additional charges for failure to comply. I've asked when I can talk to a lawyer, but he says that I have to answer police questions first. This seems unfair, but I'm silent. This is not the time or place to demand rights that I suspect do not exist in Singapore.

'What is your name?'

'Where are you from?'

'Do you live in Singapore?'

I'm conscious that this is, in all but name, a police state, so everything Teng says is going through a filter in my head that is sifting for some kind of a trick question. Police—here and elsewhere—are in the business of suspicion, so he is probably finding the stuttering pauses before each response dubious. Suspicion reinforces itself by prompting suspicious behaviour.

Awkward silences. He's staring back at me, waiting for me to speak. So I do.

'I have drugs—but not here,' I'm confessing. 'They are in my room.'

Why have I just done that? I am not sure where this is going, but now is not the time to lie. I'm sensing big trouble looming—it's as though a hungry serpent is twisting and tightening around my torso. Fatigue is wearing me down. And I'm a rotten liar.

'They're at a hospital close by,' I explain. 'I've been staying there because I picked up an eye infection in Bali,' I say, pointing to my eye. 'I got sick in Bali, and they sent me here for treatment.'

$$\bullet \; \bullet \; \bullet \; \bullet \; \bullet$$

I AM BEING LED in handcuffs through the hospital lobby. The phrase 'walk of shame' is running through my head as I pass the doormen and porters, receptionists and nurses, who probably recognise me as a patient. I'm feeling ashamed—hyper-aware of the public gaze—and wondering if anyone realises yet who I am and what this arrest means.

I'm trying to avoid eye contact, to lower my profile. It's easy to do. Anyone who has lived in India, as I have, develops the ability to stare through crowds, in order to avoid the beggars and pleaders trying to part you and your money. It is the self-preservation technique called the Thousand Mile Stare.

We're in my room. I'm sitting on a small couch, being closely watched by the policeman whose hair I found so amusing. Both of the younger policemen are a little too self-consciously attired in street clothes. They've really tried to look 'street'. It must be the technique of the drugs agency to encourage undercover operatives to appear as much as possible like authentic drug users. I guess that's how they entrap people here.

Jack Teng is older, probably in his mid to late thirties. The younger cops are no more than twenty-five years old, and seem to be having lapses of maturity. In between one staring menacingly at me and the other searching my suitcase, they've moved to fits of giggling and bantering in Mandarin. Teng is sitting at a desk, taking notes and observing.

'What is this?' he asks, holding up a transparent plastic bag. There is a small amount of white crystalline powder inside. I tell him for the third time that it's ice—methamphetamine. I'd taken them straight to it after we arrived.

'How much do you earn?' asks the policeman guarding me. I am puzzled. I look to the other two and back again. I tell him. He snorts, and rattles off some more commentary in Mandarin. In response, the other policeman hees and haws. The boss of this operation, Detective Teng, is ignoring the bantering.

'What do you do—what is your job?' The snorter is digging for information.

This is the one question that I was hoping to avoid. Of course I can't. Of course they were always going to ask me. This is really not something that I want to reveal. This is where the serpent around my body goes in for the kill.

'I am a journalist.'

They're all looking at me now, my declaration having captured their riveted attention.

'What paper do you write for?'

That's a universal assumption—that all journalists are newspaper writers. Normally it irks me. Tonight, I have no liberty to be irked.

'I don't write for a newspaper. I report for radio and television.'

They look at each other, and back to me. This time it is Jack Teng who is taking an interest. 'Where?' he asks.

'Australia.' Deep breath. 'I work for the Australian Broadcasting Corporation.'

They are exchanging more odd looks now. Something has just happened—I have revealed something sensational. I am not a garden-variety arrest. I am news, and they know it.

•••••

AT THE POLICE STATION. I have been escorted to the men's room and instructed to pee into two small beakers. I get to choose one to surrender for laboratory analysis, and one to discard in a big black bin full of other people's arrest paraphernalia—piss-filled jars, scrunched-up paper towels.

'Can I see a lawyer now?' I ask.

'No. Cannot,' replies the fingerprint officer, without offering any explanation. He points to a chair in the corner of the office. 'Go sit.'

I am in the detectives' office. The desks are imposing—government-issue gunmetal grey. They are eerily familiar to me—as ugly and institutional as the desks in the first newsroom I worked in at the ABC in the 1980s. The chairs are familiar too, scuffed or broken after years of careless use. There are matching gunmetal filing cabinets pushed up to every wall.

There are too many lights on, or there is too much wattage in these bulbs. It is brightness beyond daylight, and everyone shuffling around silently in this room looks pallid.

More cops have been passing by, asking the same questions over and over again. It could be a process of double-checking my story, probing for inconsistencies. Or it could be the officers taking turns at making suspects sweat it out. Whatever the motive, I reply with the same truthful responses about my identity.

But it isn't making them change their tone. They listen and respond with what seems to me unnecessary scepticism. So I start replying with a tone of exasperation: 'Yes—I am Australian.' 'No—I do not live here.' 'Yes—I really do live in India.' 'Yes—I really do work for the ABC.'

The atmosphere of suspicion in a police station produces a remarkable level of paranoia. At this rate, 'Would you like a cup of tea?' will sound to me like 'Where did you hide the body?' I make a mental note not to suspend disbelief.

Anything could happen now. I feel like I have lost control of my life, and the shots are being called in another room. It is dawning on me that this may not be a private matter.

•••••

ANOTHER ROOM, THIS ONE inside the emergency department of Changi General Hospital.

It took four policemen to escort me here in a minivan—two up front, and two in the back. I wonder if terrorists get this much attention. One escort officer asked me the popular question du jour, 'How much do you earn?' It was the third time. The irrelevance of this question is irritating, so I am now giving wildly differing answers. At first I'd told the unvarnished truth. Nobody was that impressed. But since I was trapped in some sort of payday groundhog day, I began putting my foot on the exaggerator, granting myself pay rises fit for a movie star. Nobody has challenged the lie so far.

They're putting me back into a hospital. I am fantasising about this experience ending, just as it is getting irreversibly worse. Here in casualty, the nurse doing the admission paperwork is cold and formal, refusing to hold my gaze. I think she deliberately tried to strangle my arm with the blood pressure cuff. *She is waving the thermometer at me,* I'm thinking, *like a knife.*

Now I'm shuffling along a long cream-coloured corridor. It's midnight. I'm wearing ankle shackles and handcuffs. This is overkill. When the police finally took off the metal handcuffs at the station, I thought they were going to relax a bit. But they keep telling me that they have 'procedures' every time they do something shitty, like making me piss into a beaker or strapping me up in restraints like a mentally ill person.

These new handcuffs and ankle shackles are not the metallic kind— they are black and made of super-tough fabric, like seatbelts. By binding my legs in this fashion I am hobbled and moving at the speed of a road-safety-conscious octogenarian. There are police officers at either side, lightly holding my arms. I think they are far more concerned about me falling flat on my face than escaping.

I am thinking about Steve McQueen and Dustin Hoffman as prisoners in *Papillon*. I remember men in that film shackled to balls and chain—the cruelty and violence, the deprivation and noble deaths. The book on which the film was based is by Henri Charrière. Before he was famous as an author, Charrière was infamous for killing someone and doing a lot of escaping and re-escaping from horrendous French garrison prisons. Old Henri gave new life to the proverb of the desperate: that old chestnut, 'Where there's life, there's hope.' I know it's a cliché. But right now, that's all I've got.

I have arrived at the ward for prisoners. Who knew that such places existed? There are two sets of heavy bombproof metallic doors that we pause before until somebody, somewhere—the unseen

7

operator of the locks—can satisfy himself that it is safe for them to be opened. Until tonight I was being put up at a luxurious private hospital with a 'come and go' policy that gave me lots of freedom to dine out and shop. For all intents and purposes, it was a hotel offering prescription drugs.

Changi General Hospital prison ward is not quite at the same standard. Staff have shoot-to-kill authority. I scan the room. Men in blue PJs occupy beds around the room. They're all very old and frail. And they're all handcuffed to their beds.

Oh fuck. They're going to handcuff me to my bed as well, like a dog.

'This is Lloyd, Peter Gerard,' says one of my escorts. I'm being delivered to jailors in blue uniforms. 'He was arrested tonight. Australian national. Speaks English. Detained on drugs charges.'

The one in blue nods in acknowledgement. 'Okay, Lloyd Peter Gerard, go there.' He is pointing at the nearest empty bed. I pause, trying to listen to the thickly accented instructions and to process their meaning. But apparently this is a little too much pausing.

'Get to the bed, eh. Quickly.'

My jailor is barking and growling and bellowing at me in that strange version of English they call Singlish. I am instructed to remove my clothes, put on the light blue PJs of the inmate and get into bed, pronto.

I'm feeling like I have arrived in the basement of Singapore, a place visitors do not get to see. And I am being fed to the pigs.

I'm on the bed, watching myself be handcuffed around the right ankle. The guard is attaching the other cuff to the bed. I'm like a dog, chained up for the night. I ask permission to use the bathroom. 'Not at night,' he says before handing me a wine-bottle-shaped plastic container. I recognise it immediately. This is the Comfort 100—the must-have portable pisser used by Thai commuters in the eighties and nineties, when Bangkok city traffic jams were so bad you needed to have somewhere to go when you were on the go.

'Prisoners can shower in the morning, but only from 0500 to 0600.' Another blue-uniformed nanny-state operative has arrived at my bedside to set me straight about bathroom 'privileges'. 'If you want the toilet after that, you need an escort. There are no escorts to the toilet after five o'clock. From 5pm to the next 5am, you have to stay in the bed and use the bottle.'

Why do they call them 'privileges'? I wonder. If you want to pee at night, you lie sidesaddle and aim for the Comfort 100. But no one is offering advice about how to deal with the next and obvious bodily excretion dilemma. It must be presumed that my bowel will co-operatively fall into line. I can't help but agree with that sentiment.

An emaciated Chinese man is hurling abuse, seemingly at these officers. He is wild-eyed and agitated and angry, like a dog straining at the leash. *If he is under sedation, they need to reconsider the dosage.*

I've made accidental eye contact with him. 'What you want, you fucking mother-fucking fuck? Fuck you. Fuck you. Fuck you, mister, ang mo.' Ang mo is the local Singapore slang for a white man.

In the beds opposite there are more prisoner-patients, broken-down-looking old Chinese men. They're stirring and studying me, hawking, spitting and exchanging reviews.

I lie back and stare at the ceiling. I notice the paint is peeling. A gecko is scampering in search of shadows. In spite of all this compelling drama, I am gripped with exhaustion. I am experiencing a strange yet familiar sensation of falling backwards through space and time. It scares me because I know what is coming next. I cannot stop the fall, and I cannot avoid its destination.

I'm going to surrender to the sleep I have come to dread. *I am at that place again. It is a place I have seen many, many times before. Here, the dead outnumber the living. Here, the dead are all that I see. Here, I know the dead won't ever let me go.*

TWO
Living nightmare

'OPEN MOUTH, MISTER!'

I'm grasping at the sheets, jackknifing back to life. 'Huh, what?'

'Open mouth.' A nurse is shaking me awake, shoving my shoulder like a rowdy drinker pushing towards the bar. She opens her mouth, imitating the demand, as if I am deaf or dumb and not catching on. 'Now, eh!' she bawls.

A menacing guard, standing just behind her, is staring hard my way—an enforcer ready to pounce on wayward patients. 'Temperature, uh?' he says.

I wipe my mouth, discreetly checking for drool. Then I do as instructed, and open my mouth for the thermometer.

They seem not to notice the nightmare. People are trapped and burning to death. It's horrific. It scares the shit out of me. I am always so tired when I wake up after these dreams, short-changed of sleep.

Orhan Pamuk reckons our dreams are our second existence. The Turkish writer believes we live two concurrent lives. If that's true, my second life is a misery. My dreams—my nightmares—are full of pain and suffering. They spring from actual events that I have seen and reported on over the last few years. Some of them are re-runs of events I was involved with. Some are just way-out weird, abstract and horrifying. I play the role of a spectator, watching people suffering. I feel as though I'm being held hostage at a fringe film festival that shows only one kind of film—archives of horror, unearthed from my troubled subconscious.

Being awake isn't much fun either. I really am a hostage now, in a living nightmare where I am imprisoned and chained to a bed. The other prisoners stare at me like a new exhibition just arrived at the zoo.

'Okay. Temperature okay.' She's taken back the thermometer.

'What happens now?' I ask her.

'Eat!'

'No, I mean how long will I be here?'

'Not up to me, lah.' The nurse is pointing at a man leaning against a wall across the room. 'Up to them.' I haven't seen him before. He's in civilian clothes, but wearing a police identity badge around his neck. He must be from the drug squad, sent to keep an eye on the prize. 'You celebrity, ah?'

'What?'

'Famous man, they say,' she's chuckling. 'Maybe infamous, ah?'

I notice that her teeth are startlingly yellow. *Well, if I am a celebrity, sister, then get me the hell out of here,* I think.

It is early on Thursday, the eighteenth of July. Soft early light is filtering through a small window above my bed. If I sit up and lean forward, and twist my body over and to the right, I can see a little bit of the outside world. I probably look like I'm doing some sort of 'positive thinking' yoga stretch. That'd be the day—I'm about as flexible as a fallen log.

I can hear the lilt of far-off voices and the hum of traffic, and I can see a little bit of grey sky, but the eaves of the rooftop obscure the view. I must be on the top floor. The outside world seems a million miles away.

I look around the room. The walls are institutional white and completely bare, with not a clock, calendar or poster to be seen. It is as if, by decree, decor was deemed an extravagance for prisoners. Clocks are redundant as a prisoner is captive to another's schedule. I'm looking at the floor. It is as bare and white as the walls. It is hard to see where one finishes and the other begins. Anthropomorphically speaking, they could take turns playing each other's supporting role, just to relieve the boredom.

Here comes trouble. It is the burly guard: 'Makan.' He hoists a polystyrene takeaway box onto the roller-table and pulls it up the bed.

'Food?' I ask.

'Yes, lah.'

I take breakfast—rice with kangkung. Kangkung is a kind of water spinach used in restaurants and food stalls all over Asia. It's a staple because it is so easy to prepare, its hollow stems cooking as quickly as the leaves. Thais serve it with chilli and garlic and a splash of salty fish sauce, or shrimp paste. It is a favourite dish of mine, but of course no one here knows that. The prisoners pause to watch the spectacle of me hungrily devouring the meal. It looks like a bread-and-circus moment, with me as the circus.

Last night's dinner plan was interrupted by my arrest, so I haven't eaten for quite a while. This kangkung is pretty dull, with barely a chilli to be seen. I have a private chuckle that I still have a critical palate, even in such a monumental crisis. That must be a good sign. I look up and give a toothy grin with each mouthful, deliberately trying to disappoint my audience. *Now, that's entertainment,* I think.

When breakfast is over, I hail the same guard. 'Can I use the bathroom?'

'Why?'

What a question. Does 'Can I use the bathroom?' really need detailed explanation?

'Shit or shower?'

'Well, er, both.'

'Okay. Wait, lah.'

That verbal tick again—*lah*. Singaporeans append *lah* to statements and sentences out of habit, with no form of rules for when or where it appears. *Lah* is to languages what the appendix is to the human body—functionally redundant and occasionally irritating.

I suppose it could be argued that it lends a certain flourish of cadence to the otherwise rat-a-tat-tat monotony of spoken English at the arse-end of the peninsula. I've noticed that Chinese Singaporeans, when in the company of other Chinese Singaporeans, have a tendency to race to the finish of a sentence, as though coughing up something distasteful. It is the human equivalent of cats expelling hairballs.

When speaking to a foreigner they generally ease up, to allow us to catch the words they are mowing down like machine gunners at the Eastern Front.

Better-educated locals speak plain and understandable English with no difficulty at all, but I haven't come across any of those Singaporeans in the last twelve hours. Instead I'm on the receiving end of Singlish. It is a buffet dialect—a bit of this, and a bit of that. A mongrel form of English where syntax is twisted, definite articles abandoned and verbs stand alone as complete sentences, it is hard to keep up with because it is hard to understand. The rather strange impression forming here seems to be that I am non-English-speaking, or deaf, or extremely dimwitted.

The guard is back, and he's brought keys. 'I don't want any trouble,' he says as he unlocks my ankle. 'You give trouble?' It is not a rhetorical question. He cocks his eyebrow demandingly.

'No,' I respond.

This man fixes me with a menacing *do not fuck with me* stare. I am so obedient that I nod confirmation, words being an unnecessary part of the exchange.

I keep surprising myself at how meekly I am submitting to authority. He is the first person to make eye contact since I got here. It's funny how you only notice basic civilities after they're gone. This not-looking-at-me caper is making me feel like a non-person. I'm beginning to wonder whether the training manual encourages this act of depersonalisation.

'Hands!' the new guard instructs, holding his own up, as if in prayer. It is another demonstration for Stupid.

'Is that necessary?' I ask, nodding to the hand gesture. 'I'm going to need mine, right?'

'S-O-P.'

'S-O-P?'

'Standard operating procedure. All prisoners must be handcuffed at all times when under escort to the bathroom.'

'Ah, an escort. That *will* be nice.' He gives me a puzzled look, but my sarcasm bounces right off. That's probably for the best, in the circumstances.

'Rules. Must be obeyed, lah.'

I'm handcuffed. Under supervision by two guards, I swing my legs to the floor and stand up. But I've moved too fast, and I'm falling off balance. One grabs my arm and saves me from falling sideways to the floor. The other chides me like a child. 'Ah easy, ah! Go slowly, lah.'

I am shuffling as I walk, as if the leg restraint is still attached. That experience has been imprinted and it's influencing my motor skill. This is in turn draining my confidence and I notice that I am shaking. Being upright all of a sudden reinforces my sensation of fatigue, dragging my spirits down like the pull of a heavy anchor.

We're in a small orange-tiled room with a toilet bowl. Against the wall to the right is a length of hose and a single tap head. I think: *Holy shit, is this the bathroom in a major public hospital in a first-world country?*

'Toilet,' announces the guard, 'and shower.' As if *these* fittings require introduction or explanation. My left hand is uncuffed. I watch the now-empty half of the cuff manoeuvred and locked around a handrail positioned parallel to the toilet bowl. The 'dangerous dog' is now handcuffed at the toilet.

My escort stands back and folds his arms, expectantly. 'Okay. Now you go.'

'In front of you?'

'S-O-P.'

I slump forward in an act of surrender. I keep my head bowed, trying to hide my tears in my chest. I can't remember the burn of so much humiliation.

I have to get out of here, I think.

• • • • •

I'M BACK IN BED, staring at the ceiling. I'm feeling pretty raw and sorry for myself, having just had a layer of dignity peeled away. Being in custody is merely the commencement of a series of consecutive punishments. First you are denied liberty, then privacy and courtesy and, ultimately, respect. Privilege is not absent by accident. Someone has thought carefully about what to deny, and when to deny it. Strip privilege from the privileged, and that's a punishment. Deny dignity to the dignified, and that's another punishment. Expose the proud to humiliation, and that's a punishment again. It's a spiral staircase that goes only one way, and that is down. The lower you get shoved, the darker your world becomes. Nobody can make that back up to you when it is over. It is the price of admission for the criminally accused.

I wonder if the guard enjoyed my humiliation—whether that's a bonus in an otherwise monotonous job. Perhaps he is a sadistic bastard who enjoys bringing people down a peg or two—a slayer of tall poppies. Or maybe he's not. After all, he did turn his back when I did an ungainly one-armed strip-tease to take a shower. And some 'shower' that was—a blast of cold water from a garden hose.

I've had a lot of weird and wonderful bathing experiences during my time in Asia, but none of them has cured my love of the long, hot shower. I think there must be two types of people in this world: the functionalist bathers who soak, soap and rinse; and people like me who do it because they must and because the cocoon of warm water feels good.

But in our present era of carbon footprint consciousness, this type of showering is a guilty pleasure. We're not supposed to hang around and just enjoy the moment. I would really like to see the honest show of hands in support if the price of a slightly greener planet were a permanent cold shower. Perhaps the presidents of the top polluters—the United States, China and India—could kick things off as a gesture of leadership and sacrifice.

It is a relief to be thinking about something so far-fetched right now, something so removed from this living nightmare. It is much better than dwelling on the moment, the rank humiliation of shitting for an audience. Tell me, do I get a sentencing discount for mortification? I am going to try to go back to sleep. I need to escape from this place. *I am so tired.*

• • • • •

'MISTER!' IT'S HER—the persistent nurse with the bony-fingered wake-up call. 'You must wake up now.' I uncurl my body and roll over.

Through my tears I can see her, the nurse with the yellow fangs. 'IO here.'

'Who?' I'm foggy. 'IO?'

'Investigating Officer—IO.' She sighs. 'He wants you in five minutes, okay, lah?'

She's gone. I'm exhausted, still. This has got to stop. I'm having a nightmare as soon as I go to sleep. That one was from the Boxing Day tsunami, back in 2004.

Joseph and Ivana Giardina were the first people I spoke to who had been caught in the tsunami. The Melbourne couple had been standing on Patong Beach, Phuket, when the tsunami arrived. I remember Ivana's harrowing description—how 'everybody started running and panicking, and the water just came over. It just . . . it just filled up. There was furniture everywhere hitting us, and a jeep just floated by.' She had an incredulous look on her face, as if to say, *Can you believe it? A floating jeep? Who would have thought?* Ivana recounted seeing more strange sights: 'The pier with the boats attached just floated down the beach.'

Joseph and Ivana's ten-year-old, Paul, was a child living with Down syndrome. Paul and his parents were separated in the confusion. Joseph told me that the last time they saw him was when the wall of water smashed into them. Now, as they lay in hospital with a patchwork of cuts and bruises and attached to intravenous drips, Ivana and Joseph confronted a deluge of a different kind, waves of pessimism and then hope about the fate of their missing son.

Then the room went very quiet. Ivana began rocking backwards and forwards, sobbing with raw grief. I have never heard such deep, volcanic weeping. When I think about that sound, all the hairs on my forearms stand to attention. I feel a deep fellowship with Ivana and Joseph—Paul was not my son, but I am a father and my son, like theirs, is disabled. It was no stretch to imagine our roles in reverse. I was stationed in Bangkok, and the island of Phuket was my holiday playground too. Except for a different plan that Christmas, it could have been my family strolling along Patong Beach on Boxing Day.

Grief is a contagion—hang around it long enough and you catch it. I caught some of Ivana's that day, and carried it for years. Since Benazir

Bhutto died, I've been seeing a lot of Ivana. But I need a break—I can't keep this up. It's too much. I'm so tired. I feel like I'm drowning in dreams.

The nurse is back. 'Hurry now!'

Fuck, I'm thinking. *Will you ever give me a moment's peace?*

I've been pushed up the corridor in a wheelchair. I've lost the will to protest, to insist that I am not an invalid. I am worn out, so I don't speak.

We enter what looks like a private room in a regular hospital, but there are no beds. The room is empty, save for a low desk and behind it a man sitting, sphinx-like, with his arms folded across his chest. 'Hello, Peter. I am your IO, Jeff Lee.'

I look up.

'Do you understand?'

I nod.

'Can I get you a glass of water?'

I am crying again. I am tired and terrified.

'Did you manage to get some sleep?' Lee is dispensing token courtesies; but they're stone cold and mechanical, and I feel like a bug trapped in a big, fat web.

'I am really tired,' I explain. 'I have been having these nightmares lately, you see.'

I cannot tell if Lee does 'see'. His expression is deadpan. Thin and casually dressed in jeans and a polo shirt, he is moving his chair closer. A spider setting up to strike. He is wearing sunglasses, even though we are inside. These specs are dazzlingly mirrored, rock-star style. When I sit forward and peer into this inscrutable face I see my own disconcerted expression squinting back. He leans forward, removing his glasses. The metaphoric gloves look like they're off too.

'Okay. I have some questions.' He is pulling out a pen, clicking the top to push down the nib, like a bureaucrat firing the starter's gun. 'Let's go through last night again.'

Last night. I arrived at a food centre, expecting to meet an acquaintance. What I did not know was that my friend had been arrested, a few hours earlier, in possession of drugs. He told police I had sold the drugs to him a week earlier at my hotel. They, in turn, contacted me, via text message, using his phone. The meeting was a set-up. It was an entrapment.

'Peter, you are going to be charged with three offences.'

My head snaps up, my attention captured. I'm still with Lee. He's been talking for a while but I haven't been concentrating. Mini-nightmares keep intruding, like flash frames and explosions. It is the last days of 2007 in Pakistan and the Opposition Leader, Benazir Bhutto, is campaigning in the elections; she forces her body through a rooftop hatch and puts herself in an assassin's line of sight. It is a warm Boxing Day morning in Thailand in 2004 and hundreds of people stand and watch and wait as the unusual spectacle of a receding tide turns back on itself, delivering a rushing, inescapable and biblical onslaught. I keep seeing that inferno and poor Ivana, crying at the tsunami.

I'm holding it together, I think, but I haven't followed anything Lee has been saying until now. It is as though his voice has been turned down low. I know that he has been talking, but it's a whisper compared to the noise in my head.

'Charged?' I ask. How did we get to 'charged'? I'm searching my mind, thinking, *A minute ago a glass of water was being pushed across the table. Now he's got important-looking papers arrayed in front of him.* 'I don't understand.' I'm paying attention, now. 'Three charges? Are they all for possession?'

He's ignoring me. 'Peter Gerard Lloyd,' Lee is looking down, reading, his voice a police-speak monotone, 'you are charged that you, on the ninth day of July 2008, at about 7pm to 8pm, at the York Hotel, Singapore, did traffic in a controlled drug.' Lee continues on and on about subsection this, paragraph that, but my head is swimming. He's charging me with drug trafficking. I'm thinking, *This is fucking out of control.* His voice is a whisper, drowned out by my panic. I can feel adrenalin charging around my chest, slamming into my skin. It's that sensation again—something monstrous still trying to find the exit. My heart is pounding.

Lee looks up when he's finished. 'Trafficking?' I ask. 'Jeff—*trafficking*?' I'm begging now. 'I am not a drug trafficker. This is crazy. I am no drug trafficker. This is a mistake, can't you see?'

'Peter.' He sits back, folding his arms. 'Someone we have arrested says you sold him drugs. We caught you in possession of drugs. See, lah? Why would he lie?'

'I don't know, Jeff.' I'm fighting for my life now. 'He's probably protecting his source—the person who did sell him drugs. I don't know. I hardly know this guy. We've had drinks, been to the same party, and last night he wanted to meet for dinner. He's the one who gave me the phone number of the guy who I did buy drugs from. Maybe he bought his drugs from the same guy? I don't know. I'm not from here. I am not, and never have been, a drug trafficker. Why would I admit to having stuff—I volunteered that, remember?—and then lie about selling it? I have a job, and it pays pretty well. Why would I suddenly go into business selling drugs in a place like Singapore? It is madness, Jeff. It doesn't make any sense. This guy is lying to you.'

'Peter,' Lee is giving me that moving-right-along look, 'you need to get a DC. Get bail.'

'DC?' I'm confused. 'What's that?'

Lee sighs, tiring of my ignorance of jargon. 'Defence Counsel, a lawyer.'

'What are the penalties?' I'm gathering myself up, and I need to know how big a hole I'm in.

'For trafficking,' Lee is looking down, reading, 'five years minimum and five strokes.'

'Five years?' I feel stunned, like I have just been punched hard in the face. 'And five strokes?'

'Yes, five years minimum.'

He's said it. I've said it. And he's said it again. But I can't quite get my head around this piece of information. *I could be going to jail for five years. Five years! That's sixty months. How many days is that? What is 365 times five? Okay, well five threes are fifteen. One thousand, five hundred days. Wait on, that's not right. There's five times sixty-odd too, and that's another three hundred. That's one thousand eight hundred days. So 1800 days in jail. In Singapore. Fuck me! I'm fucked!*

Lee is staring ahead, seemingly waiting for me to do the sums. I'm thinking, *Does everybody do this desperate arithmatic?*

'And, ah, the . . .' I am stuttering. 'And the other charges?'

'There is no minimum sentence for possession or consumption.' Lee keeps looking down, reading it. He must know this stuff off by heart—*why does he keep doing that*? 'First timers usually get around one year, for each offence.'

Holy shit! I feel like my body is dissolving. Any minute now I am going to be a puddle on the floor.

Lee is scribbling something on the papers before him. He's left-handed, like me. Most of us lefties look like we have shockingly arthritic hands when we write—all cack-handed. 'Sign now, ah!' Lee is pushing the pen at me. 'You must sign these, to acknowledge that you understand these charges. Okay, lah?'

As I am signing, I notice Jeff Lee has appended the time of day to each charge sheet: it is 5.27pm.

I'm really on someone else's schedule now.

THREE
Swimming with sharks

'THERE SEEMS TO BE a security problem with your Facebook profile.' It's Emma Tilston, a consular officer from the Australian High Commission in Singapore. She's been ushered into the room to join Jeff Lee and me. 'It seems the media in Sydney have used it to obtain pictures of your family.'

She's hesitating. The way you do when you have saved the worst for last. 'They have pictures . . .' She's baulking—this must be really bad. 'They have pictures of you and your partner, Mazlee.'

I slide my jaw from side to side, pushing my tongue hard against my front teeth. It's a habitual physical stalling tactic, something I do when I'm thinking hard about how to respond to a surprising twist in a crisis. Usually it is someone else's crisis, not mine.

'They're already up, live on their websites,' Emma adds.

I slump forward, running my hands through my hair, hard and searching. That's my default position for covering up panic. *Mazlee's picture is on the internet? He has nothing to do with this. He is a private person. He's not even here. He will be mortified.*

'People . . .' I'm looking up again. I'm speaking slowly—these words taste particularly bitter. 'They *know* about this?'

Emma is studying me, surprised at this spectacular naivety. So am I. *Of course they know. Did you really think this could be a secret? Catch up!* But that's the problem—I haven't been thinking straight for weeks now; I haven't been thinking much at all. I've been running, and now I'm at the precipice.

All that's left is the fall.

'How bad is it?' I ask her, but I don't really need the answer. This is a major sensation. Big-time correspondent busted for drugs in Singapore. It would be a feeding frenzy out there. My blood is in the water, and white pointers are coming my way. I can almost feel chunks of flesh being stripped off my carcass. 'They will eat me alive.'

'We're getting a lot of calls, yes.'

'What are they saying?'

'Not much, so far. They have reported that you have been arrested. They know that you are being held on suspicion of trafficking.'

'That's a lie,' I say.

Lee shifts in his chair, but his face does not betray opposition.

'Okay, well, we need to get you out of here,' Emma continues. I get the impression she's done this before. 'The ABC is sending someone from the legal department to sort out a lawyer for a bail hearing, as soon as possible.'

I'm numb, blinking, thinking. Not thinking. Emma steps into the void. 'First thing, Facebook. We could shut it down, if you give me the password and authorise me to do it.' Thank God someone is thinking straight.

'Yes, do it, please.' I scribble the password down. 'Who had the pictures first?'

'News Limited.'

I raise my head to the ceiling, mentally examining the list of names on my Facebook 'friends' list. The security settings were the highest possible. Only friends can see my photos. Only one of my friends works for News Limited. Looking at Emma, I say, 'I think I know which "friend" did this.'

• • • • •

'WAKE UP! IT'S TIME TO GO!' It's the policeman who was in the corner yesterday. 'Put your clothes on!'

It's Friday night and I'm being roused from a sleep unusually undisturbed by nightmares. I'm relieved that I am not in the middle of some psychological turmoil, so I want to go back for more. It was a safe place, for once. But the cop is not going away.

'Where am I going?' I'm sitting up. It's late—we ate dinner hours ago. 'Am I being transferred?'

'You will see,' he says mysteriously, handing me back the board shorts and black T-shirt I was wearing when I was arrested. They have a stale odour—something funkier than perspiration. Fear perhaps. This must be what fear smells like.

We're driving. I'm wedged in the middle of the back seat of a dark sedan, with burly detectives sitting on either side. There is a skinnier and younger cop behind the wheel, staring at me in the rear-vision mirror, casting fearful looks like he's ferrying Hannibal Lecter around town. They're bantering about a social event coming up on the weekend, and gossiping viciously about who is coming and who is not.

They think that favours have been bestowed by the invitations, and ruthlessly denied through exclusion. It's a classic snapshot of office politics banter, a revealing cauldron of banalities and speculation—barely disguised what's-wrong-with-me paranoia tangled with naked and frustrated ambition. All this exertion is over a seat at the big table and the chance to break bread with higher-ups, who are probably bliss-fully unaware of the firestorm of rivalries they've ignited.

I'm wearing two seatbelts tonight—one belonging to the car, and one courtesy of the police. My handcuff is this seatbelt material. I wonder if they invented this contraption in Singapore, or whether they bought it online from one of those American law-and-order sites. I know that is possible because I had to look it up once for a story about DIY law and order. There's one website called Handcuffs Online in the US. It sells all manner of handcuffs, but I don't recall any being made from seatbelts.

I remember Handcuffs Online had these testimonials from suppos-edly satisfied customers. There was something unintentionally funny about policemen writing in to say they had been looking for a back-up pair of handcuffs, for when they were 'off duty, and might need them'. I had a sense that the distinction between law and order and fetish was a little blurry at the Handcuffs Online checkout. The writers of the stageplay *Avenue Q* were right in observing that 'the internet is for porn'. It is amazing what you can buy with a computer these days. All you need is a credit card and a little imagination.

'Here we are,' announces my escort. 'Changi.'

We've arrived at the outermost security checkpoint of the sprawling prison complex known to the world simply as Changi. It's at the eastern end of the island, next to the airport of the same name.

The original jail was British-built back in the 1930s, an era when the British Empire had its guns trained seaward, warding off a feared naval invasion. It was back in the time when no one seriously considered that an army of Asian invaders cycling in from the north could overwhelm the Kingdom's defences in a matter of hours. Back then, inglorious defeat was for the steaming hordes and subjects, not for the great civilisers from Europe's mightiest kingdom. The Japanese took over Changi prison during the wartime occupation, detaining 3000 civilian prisoners in a facility intended for a mere 600. Military prisoners of war were housed next door in a British barracks. The suffering of the 50 000 inmates held there, mostly British and Australian, has become legend—a kind of mini-holocaust at the hands of jailors whose cruelty was in turns strange and truly terrifying.

In a move that was entirely in step with the functionalist philosophy of Singapore's post-independence authoritarian regime, both sites were all but bulldozed into oblivion by the turn of the millennium, to make way for a modern, purpose-built penal complex. All that remains of the original jail are the main entry gates, unearthed and transported to a more convenient location for easy display to passing tour buses. It's a delicious thought that some of those leisure buses may be transporting incontinent old Japanese, casting a guilty eye over the scene of their crimes en route to the all-you-can-eat buffet.

Moving the original gates kept faith with Lee Kuan Yew's obsessive adherence to facadism during the rush to modernise. Facades, as the name suggests, provide the illusion of preservation with none of the substance. For a meddler and bully like Lee, necessity always triumphed over the howls of protest from limp-wristed conservationists. In the case of the Changi prison redevelopment, necessity was a matter of arithmetic and regime logic. Tough-love rulers have a tendency to lock up their subjects, so Lee's Singapore needed a really big slammer. The entire complex, when completed, will have room for 23 000 inmates. In the last few years the total prison population has hovered well below that number—around the 13 000 mark—but the penal maniacs who run the city-state have clearly planned for a stunning collapse in civil obedience.

This is not my first trip to Changi prison. I've been here before, originally as a tourist and then a few times as a reporter. But on those happier occasions I was on the preferred side of the high perimeter security fence—a fearless spectator giving no serious thought to the conditions or characters that lay within. This time I'm the customer—shivering and fearful as I am delivered into the belly of the beast. This time the guards in the high watchtowers have their sniper rifles trained on the escort vehicle arriving at the checkpoint. I'm crossing a physical, floodlit boundary that separates the free and the not-free.

It is a psychological threshold too, a personal Rubicon. Behind me lies a life unblemished by accusations of criminal behaviour. Before me lies captivity, disgrace and shame—and that's even before the permanent stain of conviction. It's the next step in what we journalists poetically call the Fall from Grace.

• • • • •

ISOLATION. THIS IS NOT what I expected. I imagined a six-by-four, with bars and shadows. Instead this is a cavernous room, with a cathedral-like, four-metre-high ceiling, lined with a promiscuous number of long and thin and ugly fluorescent tubes. It might be the middle of the night outside, but inside this containment cell it is the middle of an artificially permanent day.

A security camera winking in the corner of the roof confirms my suspicion that I must be under round-the-clock surveillance. A cleaning cupboard–sized room, just out of camera range, contains a low white ceramic toilet bowl with no seat or moving part of any kind. A steel shower nozzle, a few centimetres in length and the width of a twenty-cent coin, is protruding from the wall. The cell walls are spare, save for the huge blade fans whirling and oscillating. The fans are way beyond reach, deliberately installed in a place and manner that prevents them being used in a conspiracy to end one's life.

The entire room looks like it was conceived and constructed to be suicide-proof. I must be on suicide watch. *Why do I feel insulted by that discovery?* I'm thinking. My situation may be desperate, but I am not. I've had a sleep tonight and I'm feeling much better. Putting me on suicide watch is a provocation to my contrarian sensibilities, an opportunity to prove my jailors wrong. I'm feeling a little jaunty that I haven't completely lost it after my delivery into solitude.

A pair of prison officers, who are treating me with civility and kindness, receive me. 'Lloyd Peter Gerard,' they intone, using the Chinese form, where family and thus family name come before all else. Their curiosity about which of my three given names represented the family piqued profound sadness in me with my realisation that my family had, by now, been told something terrible and shocking. I am trying to exile such thoughts to the shadowlands.

One of the officers, Iqbal, says he likes Australia very much because it is beautiful and the climate is good and the people peaceful and tolerant. The other guard who brought me to this vast cell issued me with one pillow and one blanket, and told me that I should try to get some sleep. There are at least a dozen identical empty beds here, each with a hard plastic mattress. I'm making this selection carefully. It is the first exercise of free choice since arrest.

· · · · ·

'WAKE UP! WAKE UP, Lloyd Peter Gerard!'

I'm panting for breath, seizing the mattress, while my legs wheel.

'Lloyd! Stand to attention at the end of your bed—an officer is coming to see you.' It's a disembodied voice, coming from the ceiling. It must be an announcer from the control room supervising my cell. The heavy metal door is rolling open, with a grinding electric sound.

It's Iqbal. 'Are you all right? We are watching you on the camera— it looked like you were screaming. Are you having a bad dream?' I'm silent, nodding. 'Your legs were spinning like you were riding a bike, my friend.'

He tries to lighten the moment, but I'm winded, rendered speechless by this recurring nightmare. It isn't one of the way-out and weird ones. It's something that really happened to me in a mortuary in a rundown hospital in Karachi, Pakistan's wild southern port city.

We'd been filming a sequence in the aftermath of a suicide bombing. It was an attack on the motorcade carrying former Prime Minister Benazir Bhutto, two months before she was assassinated. It was a bloodbath like the Bali bombing, with at least 140 people killed and 500 injured. We went to the hospital where most of the dead and injured had been taken. A doctor, outraged by the worst atrocity ever committed in Pakistan, insisted on taking us to film the mortuary. He wanted the world to see the consequences of the bombing, and to bring shame on the bombers and their families. The mortuary floor was slippery with sticky black blood and gore, and I blundered and lost my footing . . .

In the nightmare, my legs are spinning like the Road Runner in a Warner Bros cartoon as I try to avoid falling face first into a pile of dismembered limbs and torsos. I wake up screaming, and running. That's the first time someone has seen it happening to me. Now I'm sitting on the floor, crying uncontrollably.

• • • • •

SATURDAY MORNING.

'This will be breakfast every day.' It's a prisoner—my first face-to-face encounter. He's handing me slices of bread, stuck together with red jam. He's terrifyingly scrawny and outrageously camp. 'My name is Raymond. And yours?'

Solicitous too. *Horny room service,* I think. *This is just what I don't need right now.*

'Peter.'

'Well, Peter. What you need to do is run back over there,' he's pointing to my bed, 'and get that mug they gave you when you came in. You get tea or coffee served here at the door every morning at half past seven.'

A guard is supervising Raymond. He's pretending not to notice the one-way flirting. Raymond is one of those gay boys who can make any outfit look camp just by putting it on. The prisoners' uniform is a blue pair of shorts and a white shirt. Nothing, I imagine, could be *less* sexy. But, in the hands of Raymond, this combination looks like a back-to-basics costume for a recession-era Sydney Mardi Gras. The shorty-short pants are pulled up so far he's going to need surgery to bring them down again. The T-shirt is too small by far, cling-wrapping his unsightly bony torso.

'I'll be just next door if you need anything,' he adds sourly as the door, to my relief, rolls shut again. *Three cheers for the temple of solitude.*

I've been awake since morning bell. There was this ding-a-ling sound over the public address system, followed by a thick-accented man instructing all prisoners to stand by for morning muster. We have to be properly dressed (no bare chests) and standing to attention, army style, at the end of our bed.

Iqbal briefed me about this routine last night. They do it again at midday, and once more in the evening. One of the staff comes around to make a visual check that all prisoners are present and accounted for. It beats me why they bother, given that I'm under a surveillance camera. The escape feat I could pull off here would need to start with my becoming invisible.

It is too much wishful thinking. I'd better lie down and stare at the ceiling.

• • • • •

SUNDAY AFTERNOON. I've just finished standing to attention yet again for the muster check. I'm up like Pavlov's proverbial dog every time; I'm a quick student—a model prisoner complying with the demands of my jailors.

Now there is an odd sound catching my attention, like something sliding across the floor. I get up from the bed and go looking for the source. This is *quite* odd. A parcel is being slid under a narrow gap between my door and the floor. Across the hallway there is an identically large room, occupied by several prisoners. Pages torn from a magazine and rolled into a telescope shape are behind the parcel, shoving it my way. I look through my door's glass peephole, and across the narrow corridor separating these two rooms I see a heavily tattooed man behind glass, grinning and waving.

He's pointing down, gesturing me to open the parcel. I do as instructed, bending down discreetly so the supervisors monitoring me with the camera don't see. It's extra rations of bread.

I stand up, and see the muscled guy grinning back, giving me the thumbs up. 'What's this going to cost me?' I say. He can't possibly hear me, but he has an apparent gift for lip-reading. 'Nothing,' he mouths back, and then gives me a manly wink. He's straight from prisoner central casting—Popeye with preposterously rippling muscles and sailors' tattoos.

I step back and look up at the camera, wondering if this transaction is authorised, or whether I'm trading in contraband. I'm more worried about whether acceptance is consent for some future sexual transaction. I retreat to my bed to consider my next move. I've got to figure this out before the arrival of nudge-nudge Raymond with the evening tray of ('I do hope you like big portions, Peter') double entendres.

I can't help seeing the resemblance between Raymond (Chinese and rake thin) and the British king of camp, Kenneth Williams (British and rake thin, of *Carry On* films fame). If I were casting the remake of *Carry On Matron,* I'd be begging Raymond to audition that unforgettable line: 'Matron, I'm a man! I'm *all* man and I can prove it!' Come to think of it, Williams served on the peninsula in the British Army in World War Two. Perhaps Williams is a long-lost link in the distaff line of Raymond's family. That would explain a great deal of *his* carry on.

The door is opening and it's Staff Sergeant Iqbal, back for the night shift. 'Come with me,' he says.

I'm handcuffed and led up the corridor.

'I have to handcuff all prisoners,' he explains as we walk, 'whenever you are under escort from the cell to the nursing station.' He feels the need to explain, but I've already surrendered to the idea that I do as I'm told now.

'Hello, Peter.' It's a male nurse, with a strangely American accent. He must be from the Philippines. 'I'm Dan. I just need to check your BP and temperature. We do that with every new arrival.'

Iqbal points to a chair, where I'm to sit for the examination. He pulls up a seat in front of me.

'You're quite famous, eh?' asks Dan. 'It says so in the paper.'

'Oh? I'm in the news?' I deadpan.

Dan chuckles. 'Oh boy, are you in the news.' He's wrapping the blood pressure cuff around my arm, 'Okay, hold still. This machine is sensitive.' He's punching a button on the control device, and the cuff inflates.

Iqbal taps my knee, like a salesman ringing a doorbell. He's got something to say. 'You're a gay?'

I've noticed that it sounds like *ghee* when locals say that word.

'Yes.' I confirm my ghee-ness.

'But it says that you have a wife, and children?' Iqbal raises his left forearm, flicking his wrist open to face me, like I'm about to hand him a ball.

'Was married. Now not. She's my best friend. My kids are still my kids—being gay has nothing to do with how I feel about them.'

'How could this be?'

I shrug. 'Who knows, Iqbal—life happens, eh?'

'Were you always gay?'

'No. But I met someone a few years ago, and my wife and I were already separated because of our work. My life changed that year. A friend became something more than that. Until that point I was happily married. And I still would be—if it wasn't for the whole "ghee" thing.'

'I am a Muslim.' Iqbal is sitting back. 'For us, this is forbidden.' He pauses before adding, 'Officially.'

'I'm a Catholic,' says Dan, removing the cuff. 'We're not allowed to do it either. Officially. BP excellent.'

'So am I,' I explain. 'But you can't help who you are—or who you become—can you? Who is to say sexual orientation is a lifelong state of being? People change.'

They're both nodding, agreeing.

I seize the moment to implicate the police for a piece of foolishness.

'The policeman who arrested me said there weren't any gays in Singapore until foreigners started coming here.'

Dan is snorting derision. 'He told you gay was "imported"?'

'Basically.'

Iqbal: 'Was he Chinese?'

'Yes. Why?'

'They always say that. Very conservative people, the Chinese. Don't like foreigners. Always blame outsiders for trouble. It's just their way.' Iqbal is shaking his head in mild disgust.

I think I'm in a safe place, so I keep going. 'I did think of telling the cops to go to Neil Road, to visit Singapore's gay bars to have a look at the number of gay Chinese out on the town, but I thought better of that.'

'Good idea,' says Dan.

Iqbal is silent for a moment. Then he taps my knee. 'If you are a good man, then Allah, he forgives. He forgives us all. Are you a good man?'

'I try to be.' I'm perplexed at this sudden turn to spiritualism.

'Are you honest?'

'Yes, I think people would say that about me.'

Iqbal is looking thoughtfully at the floor, pinching his fingers to his nose. 'Did you do this?' We're not talking about religion now.

'Did I traffic drugs? No, Iqbal—it's a lie. I did not do that. It is true that I had a small amount for myself. But that is all that happened. I thought it would help me.'

Iqbal seizes my hand. He is intense. 'My friend, then you must fight.'

'You have to get a good lawyer, fast,' adds Dan.

'Listen,' Iqbal has turned around and closed the door. It's just the three of us. 'This charge. It is very bad, Peter. They put you in here for five years, at the least.'

'And they cane you too.' It's Dan, waving the BP cuff at me.

'This caning,' Iqbal is waving his finger under my nose to get my attention back. 'You must know that it is not like being a naughty schoolboy. When they cane you in prison, they tear holes in your flesh. I've seen this punishment given to grown men—bigger than you, strong—but they cry and beg for mercy. Five strokes, Peter. This is not something light. You will be scarred for life.'

He's scaring me now. I have not allowed myself to think about these charges. It is too much. Such thoughts are in that dark corner where I store stuff I don't want to think about.

'He's right.' Dan is holding out a thermometer. 'You have to fight the trafficking charge—at least fight that. I have to go to the caning room sometime. We're not allowed to give the prisoners any treatment. They have lacerations all over their buttocks.' I open wide, and he puts the thermometer in; without pausing, he continues. 'You know what we do for them? We put iodine on the wound to stop the infection. If they ask for it, we give them a pill for pain relief. That's it. Then they go back to their cells and lie face down for two weeks while the scab forms and the skin heals. It's not pretty.'

Dan withdraws the thermometer: 'Thirty-six point six. You're a well man.'

Iqbal is sitting back, his arms folded. 'You have seen many things in your job, yes? Bad things?'

'Yes,' I reply.

'They make you sad?'

'Yes.'

'Why do you do this job?'

I shrug. 'It's all I've ever wanted to do. It's important. At least it is to me.'

'It's not doing you any good, man.' It's Dan.

'You could say that.'

'If you did not do this,' it's Iqbal, tapping on my knee again, 'then you must fight. You understand?'

I'm looking at Iqbal—confusion must be written on my face. He explains. 'I'm not from Singapore. Neither is Dan—he's from Manila. I'm from Johor Bahru, across the border in Malaysia. This is a job. I don't have to "believe" in Singapore.' His hands are up: he's doing the aerial inverted commas. 'Not like the locals.'

Leaning forward, conspiratorially, Iqbal whispers, 'The Chinese.

They can be *cruel*.' Now he's waggling a finger in my face again. 'Inshallah, you get bail. And get a good lawyer.'

Dan is nodding. 'He's right. Some people belong here; some don't. Stay away for as long as you can.'

'Because I'm gay?'

'Because you're not well. You need to get well.'

I'm surprised by Dan's comment, puzzled. He sees my confusion and nods in Iqbal's direction. 'He told me about the nightmares. You can get help for that on the outside. You can see someone.'

I'm crying. This is unexpected kindness and candour.

• • • • •

MONDAY MORNING AND I am still in the observation room.

There is a tapping sound at the small glass observation window in the door. It's Popeye the Sailor Man, waving at me. *Here we go,* I think as I get up off the mattress and go to the door. 'Okay?' he asks, holding his thumb up. He must be on his way to the yard for exercise privileges that I am not yet allowed. He is standing in the corridor.

'Yes, okay,' I confirm.

I'm waiting for a question about whether I enjoyed the bread. But he takes me by surprise. 'How many kilos?'

'What?'

'How many kg did you do?'

I'm shaking my head. 'Not kilos. This much,' I say as I hold up my pinky finger, pointing at the nail.

Popeye reels back in disgust. Evidently I have failed to impress. He's walking away. *I guess I won't be getting any extra rations then,* I think.

I'm swimming with sharks.

FOUR

Bail-out

I'M PUTTING ON A salmon-pink jumpsuit, the kind worn by wretched al-Qaeda hostages in Iraq just before they meet the blade. Shortly I will face judgement too, but of a far less fanatical kind. It's the day of my bail hearing. The jumpsuit is the official uniform of inmates in Singapore when travelling beyond the prison gates. Salmon pink is intended to be conspicuous, the opposite of camouflage.

'Stevie Wonder could see me in this,' I tell the chubby, cheerful guard supervising my change of outfit.

'Is he a friend of yours?' he asks.

I'm biting my lip here. 'Yes, I suppose he is.' *Let's leave it there,* I think. *I'm in enough trouble.*

'Put your things in that clothing basket against the wall and wait for further instructions,' he says. 'With any luck you won't be needing those clothes again.' I'm thinking, *Now who's doing the funny stuff?*

I was arrested seven days ago. I have a Singaporean lawyer, Tan Jeeming, hired by the ABC to get me out of jail. Jeeming came to see me a few days ago, to explain the legal manoeuvres underway to get me out as fast as possible. Singapore has strict laws governing bail. The money has to come from a local, so it is not possible for my family to wire the money from overseas.

Jeeming's engagingly cheerful and upbeat and reassuring, despite the dire circumstances. He had me thinking of Peter Ustinov, portly and theatrical as Hercule Poirot. When portly Jeeming talks, his voice is big too—it booms and bounces off the walls, reverberating self-confidence and, one hopes, courtroom authority.

Between explanations about the legal process he paused to ask, 'And, are you okay? Are they treating you well?' During our first meeting he was employing idiomatic Australian expressions, to try to build a bond between us: 'I'm a mate.' To my relief he speaks plain English, not Singlish. He left me feeling hopeful. I'm swinging at the end of a rope, dangling over a cliff. It makes me feel good to know people are trying to pull me back up.

After three days in the large isolation room, I was transferred across the island to a new jail, the Queenstown Remand Prison, a colonial-era relic. There are no beds to sleep on here. Another privilege denied. In QRP I have been sleeping on the floor, with only a roll-up rattan mat for comfort. I've been told to expect this after my conviction. It's assumed here already that I will be convicted and jailed, before a single day in court.

The guard is back, along with two auxiliary policemen from CISCO, the private escort and guard company subcontracted by Singapore Prison Service to transport inmates from jail to court and back again. CISCO began life as part of the Singapore police force, before being hived off in the 1970s as guns for hire. CISCO stands for Commercial and Industrial Security Operation and is a good example of how the ruling People's Action Party maintains absolute power in Singapore by commanding and controlling the corporate world.

CISCO is a government-linked corporation, or GLC. The People's Action Party government holds a controlling stake in GLCs through a government holding company called Temasek Holdings. The notoriously secretive Temasek Holdings has a board of directors that reads like a who's who of the Singapore elite—chief among them is its CEO, Ho Ching, the wife of Prime Minister Lee Hsien Loong and thus daughter-in-law of Lee Kuan Yew. In Singapore, GLC managers are just as elite and clubby and familiar to each other as those at the top of Temasek Holdings.

This is not to suggest a lack of competence. GLCs produce most of the country's GDP, and the three biggest—Singapore Airlines, SingTel (the multinational telephone company that owns a controlling stake in

Optus in Australia) and MediaCorp—have well-deserved international reputations. These corporate cash cows deliver rivers of income to their government shareholder. But I cannot imagine any staff member being blind to the system's intrinsically political nature. Management appointees are carefully screened for both their competence and their regime loyalty. The best minds get to run GLCs, and their future is paved with rich benefits and privileges for as long as they conform, comply and kowtow to the status quo. Singapore Inc.'s founder, Lee Kuan Yew, wouldn't have it any other way.

'Okay, Lloyd Peter Gerard, face the wall.' He's a burly CISCO operative, of Indian extraction. 'Hands behind your back.'

Most of the CISCO workers I have seen are Malay or Indian. Singapore's ethnic minorities tend to dominate the low-skilled workforce. Chinese are outrageously privileged by the education system created under Lee Kuan Yew and as a result have become pickier and prouder about career choice. Another CISCO guard, also Indian, is at my feet, attaching cuffs. He's already put a pair around my wrists. A length of chain tethers these two sets of cuffs. It is uncomfortable and uneasy and quite deliberate.

'Okay. Let's go. Slowly, lah,' he says, as if I have a choice.

As I shuffle duck-footedly towards the door, I think, *Looks like entrée, waddles like main course.*

• • • • •

I'M STANDING IN THE open air for the first time in a week, blinking involuntarily as my eyes adjust to natural light. The atmosphere is moist and fresh, and I feel the caress of a light breeze. After a week inside a bleak and windowless detention cell, I'm back at the frontier of normal life. I see a lawn of lush green and, above it, a palette of soft blues and gentle greys and cottony-whites. Heightened too is my sense of smell—at a table somewhere beyond my view I detect some of my favourite kitchen aromas: chilli, garlic and lime.

'Name?' My reverie is over. A snippety guard is snapping his fingers, like an obnoxious diner. 'Prisoner. What is your name?'

'Lloyd, Peter Gerard.' (It pays to say my name the way he understands it.)

'You are going to bail court—understand?'

'Yes.'

'Yes, sir.'

'Yes, *sir.*'

'Complaints!'

He is astonishingly cranky. This graceless command is surely not meant to invite answers. This feels like protocol—the prison service establishing an alibi, should it be called on later to account for mistreatment. The last thing this angry crank wants to hear are complaints about the diabolical rice and rubbish combinations at lunch and dinner; the tyrannical old bag in the infirmary with the yapping-mutt voice, shrieking hysterically when I had the temerity to wash my hands without first seeking her kind permission; or the despicable meanness of making prisoners sleep on the floor with nothing but a thin mat between them and the concrete, where cockroaches muster and scavenge by night.

'No sir.' I'm fixing him with my angelic, altar-boy smile. 'I have absolutely *nothing* to say.'

He's staring back, incensed by my show of politeness. Hissing, 'Go now!'

CISCO officers escort me across the compound to a mid-sized prison truck, ushering me up the rear stairs, instructing me to sit in a caged passenger section. It is the same type of pen you transport animals in.

'I THOUGHT YOU HAD THEM!' There's a commotion outside.

'No! I GAVE THEM BACK TO YOU!'

'I haven't got them.'

'Yes, lah—BEFORE, LAH.' There's heat in this disembodied exchange. 'You have them, lah.'

A pause.

'The doors are locked.'

'*Apasal kau bodoh sekali?*' I hear—'How can you be so stupid?'

I pivot around and peer through a crack in the security grille. I can see what they are looking for—the keys are still in the ignition.

During a ten-minute interlude of revealing ugliness, *l'affaire de la clef* is blown out of all proportion. I witness a score of Chinese prison guards descend like ravenous vultures sensing carrion, feasting on the misstep, reminding the hapless duo, in triplicate, that they've been 'incompetent, lah' and 'failed to follow procedures, lah'. It is a public confrontation—a town square naming and shaming ceremony—and I can hear every single demeaning pejorative. It is as though the error is a motif for the accusation of ingrained stupidity and laziness that hangs, Damocles-style, over Indians and Malays. Minorities in Singapore cultivate an aura of deference to the majority race, and for good reason, for the Chinese seem to enjoy seizing the opportunity to shit on less entitled citizens.

At last we're on the move. Peering through a crack in the outer layer of the prison van's armour, I see a bright and busy world—a mosaic of cars jostling with blue taxis and red buses in light rain; houses and condos and lush tropical gardens; and everywhere, a meandering stream of people in a state of unselfconscious liberty. This blissful personal freedom, I vow, will not be taken for granted by me again.

Prison was, by comparison, a slow lane of long silences and sepia-like dullness, a village of crushing uniformity, where shadows seem to seize and suffocate light. And yet, a prison is a kind of sanctuary. Routine and rules replace mental chaos and temptation. At first the monotonous schedule revolted me. After a day or two I accepted it. After a week I was reassured by it. When life is stormy, prison seems like a safe port. Now that I'm heading back into the world, I feel a rising sense of dread. I will have to confront my family, my friends and my employer. I will have to confront the media, and bear the taunts and shame and ridicule. And, hardest of all, I will have to confront my demons, no longer a secret that I can conceal.

The vehicle has pulled up in the basement of the Subordinate Court, in the Chinatown district. Sheepish now, after the public haranguing, my CISCO guards command me to exit the transport van.

'Easy, lah,' says the first. 'Take these steps carefully.'

And his companion: 'Don't want you to fall over, eh?'

I shuffle into the custody of the policemen running the reception centre. A thick document file is handed over. It has followed wherever

I go and contains the obligatory mug shot, up against a white wall with a tape measure to indicate my height, and copies of the documents relating to my case. I've only been a 'case' for a week, but the file is already bulging and I have noticed that police and prison officials seem gladdened at the sight of so much paperwork. Presumably this paper trail provides reassuring evidence of the smooth functioning of process and procedure, the twin pillars of Singapore existence.

'You must wait for your case to be called,' advises the officer in charge. He has a pleasant, nice-to-see-you sort of demeanour. 'Please follow the officer.'

The basement of the Subordinate Court is a maze of passageways and holding cells, a busy transport hub for commuters of the criminal kind. The atmosphere is schizophrenic. Some compartments are packed to the rafters, like catacombs for the newly departed—their occupants are ex-civilians, people who have just been sentenced in courtrooms upstairs. In other compartments are bawdy and cheerful men, dressed like me in salmon-pink jumpsuits, anticipating being bailed out. It is like muck-up day.

I'm locked in a cell by myself, segregated again from the other commuters. I sink to the floor and rest my head back against the wall, fearful about the looming prospect of freedom and all that that means.

· · · · ·

'WAKE UP! TIME TO GO!' A policeman is standing over me, a puzzled expression on his face. 'What fire? Were you dreaming?'

I had been. 'How long have I been here?' I ask.

'Maybe one hour.'

I get up off the floor, unsteady and dispirited after another screening at the horror film festival. Two policemen are at my sides, ushering me along the passages and up a series of staircases that twist and turn and disorientate. A door opens and I shuffle through, not realising until the last moment that I am in the jaws of a brightly lit public courtroom.

I have been inside many courtrooms as a reporter, but this time I am the subject of scrutinous eyeballing—from the magistrate at his high table, from the lawyers at the bar and from the keen-eyed observers from the media. I hear a hubbub to the left, and murmurs. First impressions are being sketched. I'm determined not to give anything to the mob, so I find a point on the wall above the magistrate's head and fix a steady gaze.

It is a lie, of course, to disguise the inner turmoil of the moment—the flush of horror that my demeanour is being picked over for the slightest hint of distress. I cannot show joy or happiness or relief, because hostile reporters could construe that as contempt for these proceedings. I will not break down and weep, because that would reveal that I am a wreck. And I cannot be caught in eye contact with Mazlee, because that would surely bring down the curtain on this bravura act of composure.

'All rise! This court is now in session.'

The prosecution is going first, setting out stringent bail conditions. Freedom is conditional on my posting $60 000 bail, and agreeing to report to the police every Monday, Wednesday and Friday.

I can sneak a peek at the crowd in the gallery, but not yet. I must wait until the sharks' attention is distracted. I'll do it surreptitiously.

'Your Worship, Tan Jeeming for Mr Lloyd.' It is Jeeming, standing to address the magistrate. 'I am advised that bail can be posted today by a friend of Mr Lloyd, a Singapore national.'

'Who is this person?' The magistrate sounds suspicious. 'I want to speak to them.'

'Yes, Your Worship.' Jeeming is turning around, signalling to the gallery.

To my left, movement. It is Mazlee, my partner, moving towards the witness microphone. I catch his eye and he casts a pitiable look back my way, but blanches. This is our quota for public acknowledgement—one fleeting look is all that either of us can afford. He looks like he could lose it.

I return my gaze to the magistrate—not out of respect, but necessity, knowing that I could lose it too.

Leaning forward, the magistrate begins grilling Mazlee. 'Who are you?'

'Mohamed Mazlee bin Abdul Malik, Your Worship.' His voice is low but steady.

'And this is your money?'

'Yes.'

'Mr Mazlee, I will advise you that you are under oath. You must be truthful. So I will ask you a second time: the money for Mr Lloyd's bail—is it yours?'

Steadier now, Mazlee replies, 'Yes, sir.'

It was a bad time to be an Australian seeking a sympathetic bail hearing in Singapore. A year earlier, another Aussie facing marijuana trafficking charges had posted $100 000 bail and then promptly disappeared. The suspect was an Adelaide musician, Michael Karras, who'd been arrested in possession of cannabis after police searched his apartment in East Singapore. Karras's mother had posted the bail, a week after his arrest. After failing to appear for a pre-trial hearing, Karras was deemed to have jumped bail.

Karras had been charged with possessing 495 grams of the drug. Five more grams and his matter would have been far more serious—a capital punishment case, where suspects are never granted bail. The magistrate in my hearing was determined to make Mazlee aware that my conduct was now his responsibility.

'If Mr Lloyd tries to abscond, you have not just the right but, as his bailor, a duty of responsibility to make a citizen's arrest. Do you understand?'

'Yes, sir.'

'I hope you do. I am holding you personally responsible.'

Turning to me, 'And, Mr Lloyd, I hope you understand the seriousness of this matter. It would be a very grave error on your part to subvert the conditions of bail. Do you understand?'

'Yes, Your Worship.'

'Very well.' He's signing documents. 'Bail in the amount of $60 000 is hereby granted. Mr Lloyd, you must attend the Central Narcotics Bureau office on Mondays, Wednesdays and Fridays.'

I sneak a peek. The gallery of reporters includes Eddie Meyer from Channel Ten. We used to sit next to each other when I was with the Ten Network. He's a good reporter, compassionate and not given to hysterical reporting. I'm safe with Eddie. To the far left, I see Geoff Parry from the Seven Network. I've never met him, but he has had a tough-guy reputation for tabloid, attack dog–style reporting ever since the notorious occasion when he cornered Perth lawyer Penny Easton in her garage in the days leading up to her suicide. I'm probably not safe with Parry. One row back I see Brett McLeod, a reporter for Channel Nine based in Melbourne. I don't know him either but, judging by his reports, he's a straight shooter (a coded description the media gives to objective reporters who present a fair and accurate account of events).

Across to the right: the grim features of the bearded head of News at the ABC, John Cameron. If you are in favour with Cameron, he signs his emails 'Camo'. If your relationship is more distant, he signs off as 'John Cameron'. I used to get 'Camo' emails. Next to Camo is the ABC's Greg Jennett, a reporter normally based at Parliament House in Canberra. *Why is he here?* I'm thinking. I don't know him very well—perhaps that's the reason he has been assigned this story. I don't envy the poor bastard. This is a shit-eating assignment for any ABC reporter. Jennett is another straight shooter.

Sitting next to Jennett is a friend, Tim Palmer. Tim and I became friends when he was based in Jakarta and I was covering the rest of Southeast Asia from Bangkok. We both carry the scars of too much trauma reporting. I always thought he'd fall apart first. He's been back in Australia for a few years and we haven't seen each other over that time, until now.

• • • • •

I AM IN THE FOYER of the Subordinate Court. It's after five o'clock and the building is emptying. I've just been released from chains and handcuffs, given a pair of shorts and T-shirt by the police, and sent up a flight of stairs to freedom. It all happened in an instant. One minute I'm a prisoner of the state, the next a shabbily attired citizen wandering up innocuous-looking stairs that lead back to freedom.

To my left, Mazlee is stepping from the shadows.

'No time to talk.' His tone is urgent and businesslike. This is what Mazlee is like in public—excessively formal, lest anyone recognise that he is my lover. 'We're going to get you out of here.' Handing me a plastic bag. 'Go change! Bathroom's over there,' he says, pointing.

In the bathroom I catch myself in the mirror, shockingly drawn and pale. I've lost four kilograms in a week. I look ill. I change into my own shorts and T-shirt, and dispose of the police-issued clothing in a rubbish bin. In the bag are a baseball cap and a cheap pair of dark sunglasses, like items seized from a paedophile. I think, *No disguises. I'm going out the front door with dignity, head held high.*

Outside again, walking towards the exit with Mazlee.

'I'm sorry—no hats and glasses, Maz,' I explain. 'That only feeds The Beast.' He's puzzled, but I don't have time to explain that The Beast is the media. 'I'm going down with my head up.'

'No. We're not going out the front door,' he explains as we detour to more stairs.

John Cameron is there, and so is Jeff Lee, my police nemesis. I think, *Fuck. I'm being arrested, again.*

My terror must be apparent to Camo. 'Don't worry. The police are going to get us out of here.'

FIVE
Pandora's box

WE'RE IN THE POLICE CAR, speeding away from the court.

'My role here is to support you. I'm not here to do anything other than get you out of jail and get you to a lawyer.' It's Camo, explaining why he is in Singapore. 'I don't want to impose myself. I'm here for whatever help you need.'

Here's my boss, walking a tightrope. He's a compassionate man who is clearly very worried for me, but he's also part of a giant corporation that will have to deal with me, harshly I fear. But I'm grateful that he is here—part Camo, part John Cameron.

I nod in his direction, but I can't quite get words out yet. I'm sitting in the back seat, between Camo and Mazlee. If I look over at Mazlee, I know that I will not be able to hold my composure; so I stare ahead at the traffic, pretending that there is nothing more routine than being chauffeured around Singapore by two top investigators from the Central Narcotics Bureau.

'Peter,' says Jeff Lee, leaning back from the passenger seat, 'we wanted to give you an opportunity to avoid the media. Australian media can be tough, eh? No need to see them today, okay. We take you to the hotel that Mazlee has found. Private. No one will know where you are.'

I look back to Camo, puzzled by this smooth-talking malarkey. I'm sensing a law-and-order red carpet being rolled out—the cops are under orders to be nice. I wonder to myself, *What is the price of nice, Jeff Lee?*

My right knee brushes up against Mazlee's leg. He pushes back. I hold my breath and push back too. An exchange of signals, a lovers' morse code—*I love you* and an urgent response, *I love you too*.

Our relationship is new—we have been together less than a year. And here I am testing his commitment, burning through credit I have not earned.

Camo breaks the silent tension by telling me how Tim Palmer's trousers had burst open. Camera crews had recorded him walking into court with fluorescent-coloured underwear exposed. It had been a matter of lively debate as to whether flashing undies at a Singapore magistrate's hearing amounted to indecent exposure or to contempt of court. Or both.

• • • • •

THE HOTEL IS IN A quiet side street, a block from the offices of Tan Jeeming. Tim Palmer was already here when we arrived. He and I embrace awkwardly, the way men do when they find themselves unconsciously abandoning social conditioning, the unspoken rule that blokes don't hug.

Camo, Tim and Mazlee represent the three corners of my life—work, friends and family—so I'm prompted to unburden myself in one go: 'I've been having nightmares since the beginning of the year. Bad ones. I haven't told anybody. I have been trying to deal with this myself. That's what the ice was for.'

'We thought that it must have been something like that.' Camo is going first. 'There are some very good people in the field that we can get in touch with and get you help.'

Tim sits down to my right, sensing my mortification at this public fall from grace. 'We are all in the gutter,' he says, quoting Oscar Wilde, 'but some of us are looking at the stars.'

I laugh for the first time in a week. 'Had to quote a fag who went to jail, eh?'

'Good to see you've still got a sense of humour,' he says.

We're drinking beers and talking about everything else but the elephant I have introduced into the room. Its presence has been acknowledged, but none of us wants to talk about it now. Nobody wants to climb aboard the giant pachyderm and go for a ride, for nobody knows where that journey ends.

Camo is making an exit. 'I'll leave you three to it. I'm up the corridor if you need me.' He's walking the tightrope, colleague/boss. 'There is a meeting at Jeeming's office tomorrow. We can go over what happens next when we are there.'

Mazlee is also leaving, to get clothes for the night and to buy food. Alone now, Tim and I begin a discussion that I've wanted to have all year. I have picked up the phone a dozen times, but never finished dialling.

'I have kept this to myself because, every time I reach for the phone, I think about what you have told me about the Middle East—about suicide bombings. And then I tell myself that my own experience doesn't compare. I tell myself to get over it. I tell myself to shut up and stop being such a wimp.'

'Peter, that *is* crazy.'

'And that's a surprise? I must be nuts. This—this fucking Singapore disaster—this is not me.'

'You're not nuts.'

'I thought I could deal with it. I was—for a long time.'

'How many correspondents have seen what you have seen? How many cops or soldiers have, for that matter? Think about it: the Bali bombings, the tsunami for weeks on end, then another Bali bombing, the bombings in Jakarta . . . then you go and move to India and start covering the Afghan war. The Karachi bombing was another Bali—and you just kept on going. Peter, something had to give.'

I'm nodding.

Tim's phone is ringing. He answers it, and hands it to me.

'Petey. It's me.' Kirsty—my ex-wife. She's distraught. This is our first conversation since I was arrested.

I take the phone to the bedroom and listen to the referred pain caused by my downfall. She's been living for the past few months in Jakarta, working as the Communications Chief for UNICEF. But that life has suddenly unravelled. Hounded by the media, she's unable to take the kids to school or go to the office or operate a normal life. Her phone has not stopped ringing, with reporters seeking comments and reaction.

The tables have turned—on all of us. Kirsty has decided to return to Australia, to the support of her family and friends. Life in Jakarta is over for her. 'I'm so sorry that I'm not there for you, but I have to put the boys first.' She's terrified for me, and for what might come next.

Those who know Kirsty and me can understand how it is possible for us to remain best friends after the end of our marriage. We'd been something akin to soul mates for much longer than we'd been married, and we were determined to remain on good terms—not just for the sake of our children, but because we still loved each other. Our investment in each other's lives extends well beyond the remit of documents of marriage or other legal declarations. For better or for worse, we're stuck with each other for as long as we both shall live. This was the 'worse' part coming sooner than either of us could have predicted.

'You're doing the right thing,' I reassure her. 'I want you to look after the boys first. Forget about me, here. Tim is here. Mazlee is here. I'll be okay. I don't want you to worry about anything. It'll be okay,' I lie.

As soon as she hangs up, there is another call waiting: my mother. Now I'm the one seeking solace. It is a short and painful conversation, during which an eighty-year-old woman has to soothe her grown son as if he were a wounded infant. There is less in the substance of such a conversation than there is in its very existence—her calling me is enough to say *I love you*.

Another call. This one is for Tim—he takes it in the corner, out of earshot.

'That was Camo.' Tim is back on the sofa, curling his hair with his fingers, the way he does when he is thinking. 'What have you done to Geoff Parry?' he asks.

'Nothing. I've never met him.'

Laughing, Tim says, 'He is going nuts about you. He has been on the phone to Camo, screaming about how outrageous it is that "the criminal drug user" has been protected from a "perp walk" in front of the cameras by his boss.'

'A "perp walk"? What is this—an episode of *Law & Order*? Camo had nothing to do with that—the cops came up with that idea.'

'That's what Camo told Parry, but he doesn't care. He says he is going to make you pay for it. He was swearing and yelling at Camo—who hung up on him. And then Parry is calling back for more. Are you sure you've never met?'

'Positive. I worked at Channel Seven, but never in the same office as Parry. Plus, I think I'd remember someone like that.'

'Wow!' says Tim. 'Imagine if he knew you! Then he really might hate you.'

We're both laughing now.

• • • • •

MAZLEE IS BACK. And behind him in the doorway is my sister, Cathy. She's flown in from Sydney to represent the family.

'Oh, Petey,' she says, stepping into the room and hugging me. 'No more secrets.'

'Yeah,' I say, falling into her embrace.

She's my elder by five years, and has dropped everything to get on a plane and come to Singapore and rescue me from myself. She too knew nothing about the trauma that was tearing my life apart, such was my proficiency at disguising the truth. The physical isolation of living alone in India was not only contributing to the condition, but enabling me to continue living with it. As long as nobody witnessed my disorder, I could go on pretending that it did not exist. It was the perfect arrangement for an alpha male mind in a state of denial.

She hugs Mazlee too, like a long-lost friend. Yet this is the first time they have met face to face.

'Cathy and I have been in touch a lot since the arrest,' explains Mazlee. 'We've gotten to know each other very well—thanks to you, mister!'

The details of my arrest are public knowledge. What I'm now hearing is the details of how other people found out.

Cathy: 'I was in my gym clothes. I had just got back home. The phone goes, and I answer it. It's your boss, Tony Hill, and he says, "Cathy, Peter has been arrested in Singapore. It's going to be on the midday news." And it is like in the movies—I slide down the wall and hit the floor.'

Mazlee and I look at each other, silent.

Cathy continues. 'Then I had to get into the car and drive out to Mum's place, and wait for Tony Hill to arrive there to tell Mum the story too.'

'How did she take it?'

'Better than I expected. She's tough.'

'True,' I say.

'So,' says Cathy, sizing up the battle ahead, 'what's next?'

'We're going to the lawyer's office tomorrow,' I say. 'He wants to meet before the first court appearance on Friday.'

Mazlee interrupts. 'You need to sleep first, Cathy. We all do.'

I think there is censure in Mazlee's tone. I think I'm going to get hauled over the coals as soon as we're alone. I cannot blame him—this guy has a lot of reasons to be angry with me tonight. I've known him for almost a year. I have been having nightmares for seven months, but I have never trusted him with that information. He has no idea how reassuring his presence has become. I don't have the dreams when we are together—Mazlee is my sanctuary, my safe place. When I'm with him, I don't have another private, tortured existence. We are in another world.

So now I have brought those worlds together. I have come to his home city and bought drugs without his knowledge, and then been caught red-handed. I have dragged his good name into the limelight of my sordid personal collapse. He is going to be tarnished—people are going to assume he knew, or was involved. He did not, and he was not. His employer—Singapore Airlines—has a zero-tolerance attitude to drug use. He is going to fall under suspicion because of our association. This relationship is costing him and he has a right to be angry, but tonight I'm not ready for it.

'I'll see you for breakfast,' says Cathy, leaving for her room up the corridor.

Alone now, Mazlee and I hug. There is a heavy silence, so I fill it by talking and apologising.

'It's okay,' he says. 'It's okay. Don't worry about it. It will be okay. You need to get some rest.'

I surrender. I'm in bed a moment later, curling around Mazlee's body. I'm wondering what my private struggle may have brought between us. I have been dishonest—I have kept a dark secret—and Mazlee will never forgive me for not trusting him.

This is going to haunt me—this question of trust. But there is a simple explanation. I did not trust Mazlee with the truth because I was afraid that he would leave me. I did not trust my friends or family with the truth because I thought that they would think less of me. And I did not trust my employer with the truth because I feared they would demote me.

Hours later I'm awake, my legs spinning in a wheel. I look at the clock—5am. This is the first nightmare I have experienced when Mazlee has been beside me. My two worlds have become one.

SIX
Ben from Bali

IT WAS A CLOUDY MID-WEEK day in tropical Bali when I saw him. He was probably in his twenties, at a rough guess. Tallish, fit and tanned, with dark, wavy hair and a blank, expressionless face. He seemed perfectly relaxed in that all-too-familiar sun-seeking pose. Had we been at the beach, or lounging poolside, I would not have taken any notice. But we weren't at the beach. We were at a mortuary. And, like the rest of the bodies collected and haphazardly deposited here and there across the burning-hot courtyard, he too was quite dead.

Even now, so many years after, I cannot tell you his name, nor where he came from, nor even if he was aged in his twenties. And really, what is the point of being apprised of such a singular biographical detail as his age? We are never so old as when we are dead and death, George Herbert reminds us, 'keeps no calendar'. I admit to knowing no more about the provenance of this young dead man than I do about that of any of the other young dead men and women from those bleak days. All that I can tell you, with certainty, is that years later this *particular* corpse came back to haunt me, night after night. These nocturnal encounters made him become somehow familiar, like a long-forgotten friend who had drifted back into the stream of my life.

It seems somehow indecent, in telling this story, to continue referring to *the body* or *the corpse*. Whatever his origin, this man in the morgue deserves to be remembered as someone more than just another cadaver. He had travelled so far and for so long, only for his journey to end like this—dead and disposed on a summer holiday. He deserves dignity and identity—he does not deserve to be known merely as a number hastily scribbled on a tag hooked around his big toe. He deserves a name. So I will call the man in the morgue *Ben*—Ben, from Bali.

What drew my attention to Ben was the apparent lack of violence surrounding his death. This is something that made him stand out in that stench-filled crowd. Ben did not appear to have a scratch on him and so the contrast with all of the other dead bodies could not have been starker. The corpses lying around Ben made no secret of the dreadfulness of their ending—there were gaping wounds, disfiguring injuries, dismemberment and hideous burns. Ben's quiet repose in that mortuary looked easy compared to these others, who were frozen and stiff and anguished in rigor mortis.

There were hundreds of bodies in the courtyard, so scale made this contrast that much more apparent. The scene was a mosaic. The stiffening of so many limbs—some scorched and blackened from the explosion or the fire; some awkward and upright, in a declarative pose— created a mosaic depicting the apocalypse. The end of days could look like this. One imagines that, at the last moment, these wretched people raised their limbs skyward in a last petrified appeal for a mercifully swift death.

But Ben was different. Ben was without such rigid gestures. And so a mystery was born. Thus I was presented with an imponderable puzzle: had this Ben been distant from the blast and the ravaging fire, but not distant enough to escape the toxic smoke that billowed out from the ruins? Had he been unconscious, incapable of legging it, and given up for dead by the panic-stricken mob making for the exits? Or had death just got to him faster and more neatly? How had Ben died?

The bleak possibilities were distracting, and not just to me. 'He must have been killed by the smoke,' suggested David Leland, my cameraman. 'Maybe someone dragged him outside, but then realised that he was already dead from smoke inhalation.'

'Yeah. That's it,' said another media bystander. 'He couldn't have been inside during the explosion and not be physically injured —no way.'

It never occurred to me then that Ben would later make a kind of comeback and engage with me *mano a mano*, so to speak. But when those strange and vivid nightmares finally arrived, Ben exhibited a truly memorable quality—he could talk. Let me repeat that. Ben—the dead young man in the morgue—spoke. This is not a metaphor. Nor is it a parable. In my dreams, Ben is the talkative kind of dead person— voluble and confident, and determined to put me in my place.

This disturbing state of affairs—this condition of sleep inter-rupted—became horrific and frightening, and ultimately exhausting. After all, the dead are not supposed to express opinions, at least not to the living. The talking dead are a phenomenon of faith and fiction. Yet there he was in my nightmare: Ben from Bali, the talking corpse.

I began experiencing these nightmare episodes in early 2008, a very long time after the real-life event that brought us together. That episode, the Bali bombings, remains the worst terrorist atrocity to ever befall the Australian community. And it unfolded on the Indonesia resort island of Bali on the sultry, hot night of 12 October 2002.

• • • • •

IT IS AGAINST THE RULES to enter a crime scene unless you have a role in the investigation. This is especially so after a heinous act of international terrorism. Police forensic experts will tell you that this has the possible effect of contaminating evidence and making their delicate work impossibly difficult.

But that is now. Back in 2002 in Indonesia such law enforcement etiquette was not required, or at least not enforced. Back then police at crime scenes pulled up a chair, brewed themselves a cup of tea and got on with the job at hand: complaining bitterly to each other about their dull gate-keeping assignment. For the media at that time, the most important maxim of international reporting still applied: a confident white camera crew in a developing country can go a long way without being stopped or questioned.

This is an unattractive truth in my profession. But, as a freshly minted correspondent, I found wielding such power and influence compellingly attractive. It may be argued, sometimes justifiably, that using the mystical presence of a television camera to achieve Access All Areas is outright bullying, or even faintly racist. But at this time I did not pause for any kind of self-examination. Here was a huge catastrophe, and I was a reporter in a hurry.

'Hello, friend, come—come through,' said one of the policemen guarding the scene of the bombing. We were on Jalan Legian—the bustling commercial heartland of the Kuta Beach district. Bars and clubs sit cheek by jowl with restaurants and shops selling T-shirts and trinkets. The territory might be Indonesian, but for decades Kuta has been virtually Australian-occupied.

For many Aussies, Bali is their first, and perhaps only, foray overseas. It is easy to get to, its weather is year-round tropical, its prices are low and the locals—the majority are of the Hindu faith—tolerate the boozing and cavorting of decadent westerners. All in all, Bali is bacchanalia for backpackers. But this bawdy tradition did not have universal approval. In 2002 a handful of men linked to the extreme Islamic organisation known as Jemaah Islamiah (JI) were inspired to curb Bali's decadence by carrying out a dramatic act of violence. Their target was Jalan Legian.

On any Saturday night, the street teems with crowds of westerners eating, drinking and dancing. Just after 11pm on the night of 12 October, a bomb hidden in a backpack exploded inside a popular watering hole, Paddy's Bar. The blast killed the man wearing the backpack, a suicide operative. Injured and uninjured patrons ran into the street, some in the direction of the Sari Club across the street. Around ten to fifteen seconds later a second, much more powerful 1000-kilogram car bomb in a white Mitsubishi van bearing the livery of the Häagen-Dazs ice-cream company exploded in front of the Sari Club. The explosion left a one-metre-deep crater. A third bomb was then detonated in the street in front of the American consulate. This bomb caused only minor damage, but it had an inexplicable and disgusting bonus feature—the bombmaker had packed the device with excrement.

The Jalan Legian car bomb literally blew up the Sari Club, setting off a massive fire. Cars and bikes were set alight, becoming a wall of flame and debris that blocked the escape of revellers. Glass windows shattered for hundreds of metres in every direction. The walking wounded tried to help people sitting stunned and bloodied in the road. They tried to help the unconscious, and they tried to comfort the dying. There was no emergency response of ambulances and fire engines. Instead, civilian cars and pick-up trucks and taxis ferried the injured and dead to hospital.

I had been asleep at the time of the bombings—four hours flying time away in Bangkok. The middle-of-the-night phone call came from an assignment editor in Sydney making frantic efforts to get as many reporters and cameras on planes to the scene as fast as possible: 'You've got to get to Bali. There's been a massive nightclub explosion. Lots of Aussies are dead.' The number of dead was already in the high double figures, and the speed with which hospitals were releasing the tally of dead and injured to CNN suggested the number of people killed would rise well into the hundreds. That was the extent of my briefing, with the question of cause and motive still uncertain.

In the first few hours, there was just as much speculation that there had been some terrible accident, like a gas leak and explosion, as an act of terrorism. I did not need to know. Being woken up in the middle of the night was the dream start to an assignment, a magnificent curtain-raiser that tells you three important things: It must be big. It must be bad. And it must involve me. This is one of the guilty secrets of journalism: for us to have a really good day, someone else must have a very bad one.

During a crisis, reporters tend to swim in the opposite direction to the rest of the crowd: in the direction of danger, mayhem and chaos. Professionally it makes perfect sense, since reporters need to look closer at the horrors of life in order for them to become convincing and reliable storytellers. According to this thesis, one might conclude that risk-takers would make better disaster reporters. I'll say only that many reporters on the disaster beat are risk-takers. The reliability of their work is another question altogether. At the personal level a clinician might observe that such behaviour suggests the pathology of a certain reckless personality type. I'm somewhere in the middle—risk-averse, but willing to travel to find the edge of the envelope. To go just far enough, to get a good look at the world.

That Sunday, as the Bangkok-based danger reporters settled into the forward cabin of the Thai Airways plane, regular passengers coming aboard were only just catching up on events. Many had no idea about what had happened the night before in Bali, and learned the gory detail of the disaster from the travelling media. I related the sketchy details to a Japanese couple dressed in matching plaid outfits, like a couple of golf course tragics.

'Ah, yers. I see. Yers,' the man said in response.

Neither he nor his wife possessed outstanding English skills, but they seemed to get the gist of it. As I carried on to my seat the man came after me, tapping at my shoulder. He bowed low and thanked me very much before turning around, grabbing his partner by the elbow and shoving her back out the door.

This was no real surprise. The Japanese are known to be amongst the most skittish of world travellers. Anytime, anywhere, when something out of the ordinary happens, they are generally the first nation to react by cancelling plans. As a nation, the Japanese are uniquely averse to unscheduled drama. But a smallish number of other holidaymakers from France, Britain and Thailand were so mortified by our sketchy tales that they also did a mid-cabin U-turn, exiting the aircraft and demanding their luggage be offloaded.

Take-off was delayed as the Thai ground staff obliged. It was a convenient delay for the dozens of reporters stuck at the standby desk. The exodus of holidaymakers who had lost their stomach for Bali emptied the forward cabin of the plane. This was a fortunate turn of events for my competitors from the *Australian* newspaper, CNN and the BBC, who had not, like us, managed to get a confirmed seat. Thai Airways Flight 431 was that day's only direct flight to disaster.

Four hours later, when we landed at Denpasar International Airport, the arriving media pack had to swim against the human tide trying to escape Bali. The Island of the Gods had lost some of its heavenly appeal. It seemed like the entire island's tourist population had decided to leave en masse. The airport concourse was teeming with sweating, desperate and determined families, whose holiday buzz had been killed off by the multiple suicide bombings.

But many holidaymakers did choose to stay. They became known pejoratively as the Bali Stayers. Their demographic profile was unsurprising: mostly young, single and seemingly not too bothered by someone else's tragedy, despite its uncomfortably close proximity. I didn't object to their choice until seeing a few dozen prats from the UK falling down drunk on the very street where the bombs had gone off. This struck me as grossly insensitive and yobbish. Locals, however, held their collective noses and greeted the decision of the Stayers with enthusiasm and relief. Tourism operators were quick to assess that a terrorist atrocity on this scale would be followed by an economic collapse that would touch almost every family on this tourism-dependent island.

• • • • •

SUNDAY EVENING, AFTER DUSK. On Jalan Legian there was still heat rising from the crater where the car bomb had exploded. David Leland, kicked over a blackened object and speculated that it 'looked like a piece of carburettor'.

'Really? You can tell that?'

Truthfully, he couldn't. But I learned from episodes like this over many years that David was the great ruminator, with a remarkable talent to cogitate without hesitation on topics far and wide for which he held no obvious qualification. He's hugely entertaining company, with an encyclopaedic level of recall for personalities and news events, stretching back over the past two decades. 'Mr Corporate Memory' doesn't have a very catchy ring, so instead 'The Ruminator' became his nickname.

Shards of glass littered the road. I could tell we were approaching ground zero from the state of shopfront windows: the closer we got the more shops had lost windows, blown out by the force of the blasts. I had no difficulty finding the seat of the car bomb blast because of the sizeable crater. The two-storey Sari nightclub was no longer standing in any meaningful sense. There were blackened girders and beams and the odd piece of discernible debris, but the club had to all intents and purposes been eviscerated. David pointed to the twisted wreckage of what seemed to be a vehicle chassis: 'That's got to be the car,' he declared.

The police officer who had waved us under the limp crime-scene tape watched us with indifference. Apparently it did not register as irregular that a pair of foreigners was scratching around at ground zero of the deadliest terrorist attack ever perpetrated in Indonesia. Neither of us picked up anything, of course, nor did we remove anything from the scene.

'What do you think?' I asked David. Not for a point of view about the epic cruelty of terrorism, or man's inhumanity to man. No, my question was more precisely about whether there was anything to be gained in remaining.

'No deal,' he replied. 'Too dark.'

What he meant was that it was too dark to film anything meaningful with the camera equipment we had. A night-vision lens would have made the scene green and mysterious, and frankly a little bit creepy. We didn't carry such equipment, so the dilemma of whether to use it or not was eliminated. Having had a good look for ourselves, we lost interest fast.

Next stop was Sanglah Hospital. The most important rule for covering the aftermath of disasters is: head to casualty. Chaos and drama are everywhere there, and the camera loves them both. Sanglah has the look and feel of a place that grew during fits and spurts of urgent necessity throughout the Suharto era, but without any real master plan. It's a mishmash campus: sprawling, long, white, single-storey huts planted around a few low-rise admin blocks.

The role Sanglah played on 12 October was probably never conceived, for there is no evidence that the hospital ever had a 'master plan' to cope with a crisis on a scale such as this. The emergency rooms at Denpasar's biggest hospital looked like outback Australian artist Kevin 'Pro' Hart had thrown a tantrum with buckets of blood, like in that famous TV ad he did for carpet stain remover. But Bali was not a film set and the pools of sticky red liquid were nothing as benign as the spaghetti, tomato sauce and jam Hart had hurled.

David and I hovered in the corner, like nervous teenagers at our first school dance. We were waiting for someone in charge to invite us to come in, or send us packing. I had no idea what would happen. This was my first encounter with an Indonesian hospital.

'You want to come in?' asked a doctor, approaching us from a triage corner.

'Yes—is that possible?' I said, as he eyed the camera. 'Australia,' I added, hopefully.

It usually helped not to be American. On occasions like this, David knew to keep his mouth shut. He may have been in Asia for years and years, but he still sounded like a bullhorn blasting out from his hometown, Boston, when he spoke.

'Australia!' said the doctor with surprise. 'Then you must come. Most of these people are from your country.'

After exploring a few nondescript rooms we found Jen Fitzgerald, an Australian nurse, pitched back against the wall in one of the treatment rooms where the floor was still thick with blood—she had momentarily fallen asleep on her feet. From Perth, she had been holidaying in Bali and had responded to the emergency in little more than her swimsuit. She explained, 'Most of the patients had legs ripped off, like this gentleman here.' She then pointed to a man lying on a stretcher just behind us.

In all likelihood high on a painkiller like morphine, the morbidly pale man was staring up at the ceiling as if studying it for imperfection. Both of his legs had been blown off, just above the knees. His breathing seemed shallow and, for a moment, I wondered whether he had died as we were speaking. I hadn't noticed him when I walked into the room but now that I had I was behaving cowardly, refusing to look him directly in the eye. What does anyone say to a stranger shivering between life and death? I knew that nothing could be more hackneyed than the 'it will be okay' kind of reassurance, especially when we both understood perfectly well that it probably wouldn't be. The urge to turn on my heels and retreat from the ER was overwhelming. I felt now that I did not belong here.

Then a morbid thought pushed its way to the surface. There is an old tale—as black as they come, and wildly inappropriate at this moment—about an ABC reporter who had attended a similar scene involving a legless man at a railway station in Sydney. Some time before this tragic event, the reporter had been severely criticised by his superiors for failing to discover that a man who had won the lottery was also celebrating no less auspicious a day than his birthday. Not to be caught out twice, the reporter fearlessly asked the train accident victim whether today was his birthday.

What kind of reporter am I? Not the kind who asks dying men stupid, meaningless questions. I could not bring myself to ask the name of the man with no legs, let alone inquire as to whether this was a propitious day for him. I did not want the burden of knowing the identity of someone who might die at any moment, possibly while I was in the room. Knowing a full name would only make his death that much harder to forget.

Yet there is another, less romantic truth behind this lapse of professional curiosity: I did not *need* to know. On his behalf, Jen Fitzgerald had asked that we keep his face out of our report. In a more conscious state a few hours earlier, he had apparently begged her: 'Don't let my mum see me like this.'

• • • • •

PEOPLE OFTEN ASK ME how I coped in Bali. At the time, and for some years afterwards, I would have said that I managed somehow. But that is a lie, or perhaps more kindly described as a massive self-deception. The truth is I did not cope very well at all, but I did an excellent job of disguising it.

On reflection, I can identify the place and time when I began not coping. It was during that first night in the Sanglah Hospital ward, when I met Val. 'That's my granddaughter,' said Val, pointing at a sick-looking teenager. 'And that's my other granddaughter over there,' she added. Stunned, I asked her to repeat those words. I thought I had misunderstood, but I hadn't.

This was a tragedy that had struck deeply into one family—and there was more to come. I can trace the roots of shock and revulsion to that moment. I was clutching a handheld microphone—my grip was so tight that my fingers curled around the mike stem and dug into the palm of my hand. I looked down and saw blood, but, instead of releasing my hand, I dug harder and deeper, searching for a reaction. I wanted to feel my pain. I wanted to feel anything that distracted my attention from my reeling sense of horror. I looked at Val and asked myself over and over one simple question: what in God's name is this frail old woman doing here?

Val had been enjoying a peaceful sun-and-fun holiday with her extended family of kids and grandkids. Now she was holding a bedside vigil and fretting publicly over their welfare with a strange reporter wanting to know what 'it' was like. That was when Val shot me a look that I have never forgotten. It was pure bewilderment—the woman was simply lost for words. I felt a huge sense of inadequacy and self-consciousness that I had even asked for an interview, like a home invader or a peeping Tom. Val was looking at me, searching for some sort of insight on how to respond. Val could not see what my fingers were doing around that microphone. Val had no clue that all my instincts were to grab hold of her and hug her tightly and reassure her that it was going to be okay. If only I could have. If only I'd known that this was even true. The urge to quit and run—which had begun back in the emergency room—boiled inside.

Then Val's story got even more disturbing. Val was explaining that another patient in the ward was her daughter, Leanne. Leanne's partner had been at the Sari Club too. But he was not on the ward. He was 'missing', she said.

'Missing?' I inquired, hinting at the horror behind the euphemism.

Val saw through me immediately. 'I think we say we're still looking, and don't give up hope.' Casting a challenging eye my way she said it again, as much for me as for her, I imagined. 'You can't give up hope. We just hope for the best.'

Val hit me with 'hope' three times. I felt every blow. Over the years I have heard many expressions of 'hope' during moments of personal crisis and catastrophe, and so the word tends to land on me like a hammer blow. It is a rhetorical veil we apply when reality is too brutal and confronting. George Herbert said 'hope is the poor man's bread', but in Bali hope was a meal that I could not stomach without feeling heavy and sad. Having been to the Sari Club already, I knew that there was no 'hope' of someone being pulled alive from its ruins.

HERE IS A TYPICAL working day in Bali at this time. We would usually be up at dawn for a series of story-planning conference calls with editors in Sydney. That was followed by a breakfast round-table meeting with the producer, cameraman and local fixer. The 'fixer' is an expression used to describe a locally engaged journalist who acts as translator and guide. The quality of the fixer and their contact book can make or break a reporter working in a foreign environment. In Bali we were fortunate to have the services of a genial man named Dharma, who happened to be the best fixer on the island. I have no doubt that Dharma's presence on the team made all the difference to the quality of my reports from Bali during this disaster, and in the years of Bali-based coverage that followed.

Daily story planning in a crisis like Bali is a bit like being a kid preparing for Christmas—you start out in the morning with a fresh wish list of the things you want to achieve, people you want to interview and filming opportunities that will support the story. Perhaps you might even think of something that no one else has considered. You imagine a big, fat, shiny package wrapped in those magic words: *exclusive*. Then reality and circumstance conspire like a budget-conscious parent. All of a sudden the rich and fat wish list has been pared back to a bare-boned skeleton of a few basic interviews and sequences that can be achieved in the limited time available. With luck, a few of your favourite wish-list items will still be possible. Some days Santa delivers a sack full of goodies, and some days Scrooge intervenes and shits on everything.

Good reporters learn to make their luck, mostly by looking after the basics. The most important basic lesson of news-gathering is the early start. Time is the mortal enemy of the television reporter working to a same-day deadline. If you give yourself more time, you create opportunities to get out filming and interviewing more people, hopefully before anyone else.

Time zone was a huge problem in Bali. My daily deadline was three o'clock. This was when our edited stories had to be relayed via satellite to head office, in time for the first round of broadcasts back in

Australia. Working backwards, that meant we had to finish filming by lunchtime, to allow enough time to edit the story in the hotel room. This in turn meant that we effectively had from sun-up to midday to do all of the creative and physical heavy lifting: to decide on the day's news angles; to identify, locate and interview the most appropriate people; to film sequences; to consider and construct the narrative; to shot-list the video tapes; to write the script and submit it to the Sydney-based editors for approval. Most of this work was done inside a moving vehicle, often on rough terrain, in hot, stuffy and unpleasant conditions. The team, crammed inside one van, all have a role to play—producer, camera, fixer, even the driver—and most will voice their opinion, but ultimately the reporter is in charge and makes the final decisions about what to do and when. There is nothing remotely glamorous about producing daily television reports—it's hard and unrelenting, and physically and mentally draining work.

• • • • •

AFTER THE BOMBINGS, bodies from the explosions were brought to the morgue at the rear of Sanglah Hospital. This small whitewashed cottage was equipped to accommodate perhaps a dozen bodies. When those spaces were taken up, hospital orderlies carefully deposited corpses in the narrow corridors. Then the dead spilled out onto the covered verandah. When the verandah overflowed, exhausted staff ran out of easy choices. That's when burned and dismembered bodies were discarded in the open-air courtyard.

After first light on the Sunday morning, the temperature began climbing rapidly into the low thirties. A foul stench hung in the air. An overcrowding crisis was unfolding. By sundown Bali's hot, humid and sunny conditions had set off an irreversible chain of putrefaction. Remains began decomposing and dissolving, and disappearing into gutters and drains.

It was a race against time. A call went out to transport companies operating refrigeration trucks large enough to hold scores of bodies. Some truck owners who made big money hauling seafood and fresh produce around Bali expressed deep reluctance. For some it was a matter of superstition and fear—they had no stomach for storing dead bodies in food lorries. Others made a commercial judgement that there was nothing to be gained from an open-ended commitment to an emergency operation of this kind. And no one wanted trucks with easily recognised corporate logos emblazoned on the side to be seen on television. They had a point: who amongst us would be the first to volunteer to eat seafood sold from a vehicle that had stored rotting human flesh?

While the haggling went on behind the scenes, mortuary workers and volunteers did everything they could imagine to help slow down decomposition. They formed human bucket brigades to fetch and carry and spread ice, or dry ice, or buckets of water. Some took turns holding up open umbrellas—anything that provided a moment of shelter.

As this was happening, relatives and friends began trickling into the morgue, conducting a gruesome body-by-body search for a missing person. On the Sunday, facial recognition was still possible for some victims. But not all. Other bodies were identified by items of clothing or jewellery. Successes were few and far between. The next morning, it was harder still.

A man who called himself Cole came in search of two teenage surfers from the New South Wales south coast. The boys had not been heard from. 'I've been here, sifting out all the information I can find. I've also viewed a few bodies. It's not nice viewing,' he said. It was a typically Australian understatement—two days of looking at rancid bodies, and still no luck finding the bodies of the missing boys. It did not matter, since no one was allowed to remove a body without far more formality than a visual identification. When word got around that there was a big mountain of red tape, the atmosphere of grief turned into something a little more ugly.

By late on Monday the fourteenth, inside the small office at the morgue, a group of Australian forensics experts who had flown in were quietly getting down to work on the largest disaster-victim identification project undertaken since the 11 September 2001 attacks in the United States. These were gatekeepers of the dead, and reluctant masters of the red tape. Their work would be both time-consuming and labour-intensive. Strict international protocols called for matching of fingerprint and dental records and DNA samples before a set of human remains could be formally identified and released for burial. The operation began amid an atmosphere poisoned by grief, misunderstanding and frustration.

For the media, the morgue became an indispensable platform from which to tell the story of what happened after the bombings. Back home in Australia a chorus of outrage was growing at the official line that, no matter how many bodies had been visually identified, none were going to be released until after the completion of internationally recognised protocols. I can tell you that none of us in the media *wanted* to be there. But you simply had to be there to stay up-to-date with the unfolding forensics effort.

It was quite unique that the aftermath of the bombings was thus playing out in broad daylight. In the west, very little of this sort of compelling human drama ever plays out in public, but in Bali there was nowhere to hide. In one convenient location were the victims, the walking wounded, the relatives and friends searching for missing people and the well-intentioned forensics professionals and government officials trying to establish order amid absolute chaos.

But there was a heavy personal price to be paid for this access. Shutting one's eyes does nothing to eliminate the omnipresence of death. What you don't see, you still smell; it gets into your head via your olfactory system. And death has a particular stench that is beyond comparison to any odour known to humankind. In my travels, the closest I have come to it in nature is the pungent fragrance of the tropical durian fruit. At the morgue in Bali, this odour defied our efforts to block it out by applying menthol balm to our upper lip and wearing facemasks. Nothing could keep that insidious reek at bay.

By the Tuesday the call for volunteers at the pitifully understaffed morgue was producing some macabre consequences. David and I did a double take as a group of local schoolgirls in full uniform marched into the yard in silent single file. Protective masks covered their mouths, but their bulging watery eyes betrayed their horror. Several retched and gagged and turned away, but none headed for the exit, as one might expect.

Two and a half days of ripening had seen bodies break down to such an extent that, when attempts were made to move a few of the corpses, limbs began separating from torsos. I was mortified to see these teens in the courtyard. The instincts of a reporter—to ask why and listen objectively to the answer—should have governed my reaction. But that did not happen. Instead I was gripped by parental outrage and indignation, and the overwhelming urge to eject them. So I attempted just that.

Confronting the tallest of the young girls, I summoned up all my white, middle-class, pompous outrage. 'What is the meaning of this? Where are your parents? Who is in charge? You shouldn't be here. You must leave immediately.'

The response punctured my preposterous presumption and set me straight. 'We're here with our parents' blessing. We offer help. Australia need help.'

'Your parents know that you're here?' I spluttered in disbelief. 'Really?'

'Yes, mister.'

That did not make the exercise any less distressing. The youngest of the group, twelve-year-old Arlin Utami, was quite literally lost for words during an exchange broadcast on the ABC that night: 'I can't really say anything, really scary . . . I can't feel so many friends, people could die in my place and nobody can believe it happened in our island, in our country.' I, too, was lost for words that teenage girls were being called upon to lift and carry bodies. It struck a deep chord of revulsion, no matter that they had their parents' well-meaning, but horribly misguided, permission.

$$\bullet \ \bullet \ \bullet \ \bullet \ \bullet$$

AFTER A FEW DAYS at the mortuary, observing all of the comings and goings, David and I had developed a morbid curiosity about the one corpse with no apparent sign of injury. It was, of course, the body of the man I now call Ben.

We were tired and numb from so much horror and so much grief. Neither of us speculated about Ben with any sense of disrespect. We had been talking amongst ourselves about a possible cause of death, never knowing that our amateur guesswork was unnecessary. The schoolgirls were about to provide the answer.

It was Tuesday afternoon. As David filmed from a discreet distance, four girls each took a limb in hand and raised Ben up—a sculpture of post-mortem completeness in a field of human parts. But suddenly unsupported, his head lolled back and a fist-sized chunk of hair and skull fell away. David and I were both stunned. Ben had sustained a massive and probably fatal injury to the back of his head. The wound had not been apparent while his body was lying still and face up. The mystery of how Ben died was over.

It was a dispiriting revelation that our guy was just like every other corpse—broken and dead. I had invested in the most forlorn emotion imaginable, hope, and it had made me a fool. So appalled was I by the horror of the morgue that I had almost convinced myself that a miracle was possible. A romantic notion had planted itself, an absurd and impossible notion of a happy ending. I had imagined myself bearing witness to a miracle in Bali. I had choreographed the event in my imagination: Lazarus-like, a man wakes from a coma and rises, days after being declared as dead and then discarded.

I had fallen for the foolishness and desperation of passively hoping for that miracle. I had convinced myself that it was possible—against all the available evidence before my eyes—that there could actually be an interruption of the laws of nature.

After that disappointing day, I slipped quietly into a state of despair that lingered in the shadows for years and years.

SEVEN
Black Friday

THERE ARE DAYS WHEN you need an alarm clock to give you a push out of bed, and days when you don't. Your first day in court as a criminal defendant is a no-alarm morning. I have been awake since five o'clock, fretting.

I had a preview of the media attention I can expect a day ago, when I attended the pre-court meeting called at Jeeming's office. Getting inside the office had been relatively easy. The only media crew on the street had been from Channel Ten, Eddie Meyer looking terrified at the prospect of having to doorstop a former colleague. He did the decent thing, I suppose, posing as benign a question as he could possibly ask: 'Peter,' he'd stuttered, 'how are you feeling?'

The subsequent meeting was a bit of a blur. Jeeming had convened it in a small glass-panelled conference room on the second-floor office space he occupies in Chinatown. Most of the chairs around the table were wonky-legged, broken-backed or otherwise misshapen. Jeeming said it was from the burden of his generous proportions. He had talked in a conspiratorial whisper about the legal process, and made a speech about how he would do his very best but 'the law is very strict' and there weren't 'a lot of avenues for the defence'. At this meeting he reminded me less of Hercule Poirot and more of a salesman, simultaneously making a pitch and pre-paring an alibi for a high-priced failure. A new lawyer, Jeeming had said, will be joining the defence case, and he is a former prosecutor.

Everyone seemed to agree that that sort of a lawyer would be good for me, but their consensus made me more certain than ever that my prospects are extremely grim. Surely two lawyers means I'm in double trouble.

Then everyone's attention had turned to the media camped outside. The rest of the pack, who had been hunting for me elsewhere around the city, had by now joined Eddie on the footpath. The television stations had banded together in a pool arrangement—as soon as one located me, the others would be summoned. If you've ever seen a David Attenborough nature film about hungry lions or tigers, you would know how it works.

However, I was now sitting up, focusing on something I do understand. 'I have to say something to them,' I announced. 'I am on the taxpayer's dime after all.'

'Not you,' Tim said. 'You are in no condition to talk for yourself.'

There had been a murmur of discussion before Tim offered to be spokesman. I'd insisted on him saying that I had been treated well by the police. I wasn't thinking straight about much, but I knew that we could head off extreme shock-jock reaction. Commercial radio is a place where the happily ill-informed, paranoid and xenophobic feed on a steady diet of tabloid nonsense and conspiracy theories. 'The last thing I need is talkback radio criticising the authorities or feeding anti-Singaporean sentiment,' I said.

Camo took two phone calls from Greg Jennett—the first seeking directions to Jeeming's office, and the second apologising for being late and asking if we could delay leaving for fifteen minutes. Not for the first time, the ABC was in danger of missing the story.

We killed time by choreographing the departure. By text messaging, Tim forewarned the media pack that he would be making a statement on my behalf. A taxi driver, Johnny, who worked for Jeeming regularly, would be waiting downstairs. Cathy and I were to leave first. Then Tim was to follow, and hold an impromptu doorstop. This would give Cathy and me time to escape.

It seemed straightforward to me. But Mazlee and Cathy were looking terrified, so I gave them a quick lesson in media: 'I understand better than most how the media operates. It is a beast and, like all beasts, it needs to be fed. If you starve it, the beast is less powerful. On a day like this, taming the beast simply requires silence. Don't respond to it. Don't let it provoke you. Keep your head up, and your mouth closed. That's how to survive a walk for the cameras.'

Maz was puzzled by this. 'But what if they ask a question?'

Tim stepped in to explain. 'Just because someone poses a question doesn't mean you are required to answer it. Remember—don't say a word. Keep walking. *You* are in charge.'

I cannot remember how many times I have given this sort of advice, free of charge, to people who work in public affairs. Many have never worked as a reporter, and fewer still in the cut-throat world of television news. When they find themselves suddenly and unexpectedly pitched into a crisis, they're usually all at sea trying to figure out what, if anything, they ought to say. 'Remember to follow the rule of the three M's,' I counselled. 'Pick your message, pick your medium and pick your moment. If you aren't completely sure about all three, say nothing and keep your head down.'

After the meeting broke up, I followed my own advice. I walked into the street and headed straight for the taxi. The commotion around me was like being in a light aircraft buffeted by a storm—it was bumpy, but brief. To the media I was a man in flight, frustrating their efforts to get to the story.

As we drove off, Tim stood in the road preparing to address the media. A taxi commissioned by News Limited to follow mine nudged forward at Tim, beeping the horn. It was a game of chicken. Tim blinked first and stepped out of the way, making room for the taxi to speed off. As he held court for the television crews, the pursuing taxi made rapid gains on us.

'We can lose him, boss,' said Johnny the driver, putting his foot to the floor and breaking through the traffic. For the next half an hour he ferried my sister and me at breakneck speeds through the city of Singapore, trying to shake off the tail.

'This is like James Bond,' said my sister, betraying the thrill of the moment.

'Crazy stuff,' I replied sternly, and yet at the same time excited by one simple desire: to win.

Finally, Johnny drove into a high-rise car park and headed down a circular driveway. 'I can lose them in here—I know this garage.' Sure enough, the tail disappeared.

When we pulled up at the hotel, our driver was grinning from ear to ear: 'Best fare I've had in ages, boss.' He handed over his card and offered to be on standby tomorrow.

'I think that's enough excitement for a while, Johnny. But thanks anyway.'

• • • • •

NOW I'M IN THE HOTEL ROOM, dressing for the next round, arriving at court. Mazlee is getting ready too, but we're not saying much. It's as if the elephant in the room is sucking out the air needed to carry on conversation.

First appearances in court are fairly routine and uneventful. I've covered enough of them to know that, for the media, they are often 'all-process, no-outcome' affairs. The real fun for journalists is in trying to extract comments from the accused as they arrive or depart. That's what makes or breaks a court story in the eyes of the editors back at the office. Sometimes the accused is emotional, or talkative, or behaves bizarrely by running or wearing a silly disguise or thumping a cameraman. People like that make a reporter's day.

People like that are called 'good television'. Alan Bond was one of them. During one of his many court appearances in the 1990s, an ABC crew was stalking the former billionaire entrepreneur. Reporter Paul Barry politely presented Bond with a business card. Bond stopped in mid-stride, threw the card to the ground and stomped on it ostentatiously, before continuing down the street. It was a great moment in Alan Bond pomposity. However, had Bond looked closer at the card, he would have noted that it bore the name of Stuart Goodman, Paul Barry's producer. The card-giving episode was a set-up from beginning to end—Goodman never dreamed that it would produce such a golden moment of TV.

Today, I'm determined not to say a word, or behave in a way that will allow the media to characterise me. And I'll not be accepting any business cards.

Our hotel room has suddenly become crowded. Cathy is here now. Mazlee has asked his friends, Bruce and Daryl, to drive him to the court and they're winding him up into a frantic state. Bruce is getting anxious about the minutiae of transport details. 'We can drop you at the front, or we can go to the car park and walk across the street. What are you going to do if they ask you questions, Mazlee?' asks Bruce.

'He's does not have to say anything.' I'm now giving another lesson in Media 101 to Bruce and Daryl. 'Just because someone from the media asks you a question, doesn't mean you have to answer it.'

'Yeah? I suppose that's right,' says Daryl. He's just started to think about the power of silence.

'I'm going to go in a separate car, with Cathy,' I remind them. I don't really care about the transport arrangements, but everyone is getting excited about them.

'Walk fast, Mazlee,' advises Bruce.

'Mazlee, just walk normally.' I'm contradicting Bruce now. 'Don't act weird or run or cover your head. That stuff attracts the media's attention. Remember what I said about it being a beast. Don't feed it. Starve it!'

· · · · ·

THE TAXI IS PULLING up at court. 'Here goes,' I say to Cathy. 'Just follow me and head for the door.'

Under normal circumstances it would take, perhaps, ten seconds to get from taxi to courthouse door. But when you are surrounded by a bevy of cameras and thrusting microphones and reporters, the pace is a little slower. I know a lot of questions are being posed but I'm tuned out, and all I hear is white noise.

A court officer has my arm.

'Follow me to the door,' he says, but I can see over his head and the heads of the camera crews and I know that we are all moving in the direction of a large glass window. Just as I pivot to turn away, a heavy-set Chinese cameraman walking backwards in front of me (always a bad idea) falls over, backwards.

'Oh shit,' I hear, as the other cameramen jostle and twostep to avoid being dragged down too.

I've spent twenty years watching my own cameraman's back, so this response is instinctive: I reach down and hold the fallen cameraman's hand as he rights himself and stands up, brushing off the dust and humiliation of taking such a public fall.

'You okay?' I ask him, rhetorically. 'Let's give him some space,' I instruct the others, as though I am someone who might still be obeyed.

We're inside the court building. The morning session is just about to begin and the foyer is being crisscrossed by lawyers and defendants and relatives and friends. It's like standing at a railway concourse, watching people come and go on long and difficult journeys. It's easy to pick who's who around the courts. The suits are almost always the lawyers. They don't look stressed. They've been here before and they will be here again—this is their terrain.

The guys with exposed tattoos and dressed in smart civilian clothes are the crooks. Perhaps I ought to qualify that remark and call them 'alleged crooks'. These men are attired in what one might describe as 'Sunday best'—even in a multi-religious society where Sunday is mostly of no special significance. They are nervous and fidgety and trying to scrub up for 'appearance's sake'. Today I'm one of them. I'm dressed in black trousers and a checked shirt. I am relieved to say that I do not have an exposed tattoo, or a packet of cigarettes in hand. I fancy myself as an uptown crook—more schmuck than sinister. The shirt I am wearing hasn't been ironed properly because housekeeping couldn't find an iron and ironing board. I'm a bit ruffled looking. Probably nobody has noticed.

I can feel the preliminary cross-examination of nearby reporters. They've followed me into the court building and are standing at what they imagine is a discreet distance. I can see them in the periphery— they're talking to each other, sizing me up, assessing my mood and composure, and calculating when or whether to approach me and ask questions. I know this because I do exactly the same thing. Often times a single reporter, usually from a press agency or a newspaper, will be the first to approach the accused in the foyer. Radio and television reporters stand back, because they have very little to gain from an encounter they cannot record and film; also, if this initial approach goes badly, it spoils their chances later on.

'Pete! Jesus!' It's a reporter—and a friend. Sarah Stewart from the Agence France-Presse news agency. 'What a mess! If there is anything I can do, please tell me. I'm not here to report on you. I was in town for an ASEAN meeting. I'm just here for moral support.'

Before I can respond I'm being whisked away along a corridor, Jeeming at my side and whispering, 'Pete, be careful what you say to these reporters—I don't think you should be talking to them today.'

'Some of them are friends, Jeeming. They're here *for* me, not against me.'

He's looking at me like I'm a bit dim. 'Still, you never know. And I don't want to give the prosecution anything to complain about, eh?'

'Okay.'

'You need to be in court now—let's go.'

I'm wading through a crowded public gallery. A court official is summoning me with his finger. He wants me to come and sit in a special gallery for accused people.

I'm the only man here without an exposed tattoo. I'm the only foreigner. I'm the only person making an appearance who has brought along a curious crowd of twenty reporters. Even the crooks are fascinated. The man to my left is jabbing my side with his finger.

'You the reporter?'

'Yes.'

He's laughing, 'Big case, bad for you, lah.'

'Thanks for your support.'

'No problem,' he winks.

'Lloyd Peter Gerard.' It's an official voice, booming over the speakers. The court officer is summoning me to a microphone, from where I am to address the court.

Jeeming is on his feet, announcing himself to the magistrate. There are two men at the prosecution table, conferring with each other. A woman is at my side reading the charges to me, in a low murmur. I'm already charged with trafficking and possession, but the prosecution is changing the details, reducing the weight of the drug substantially after laboratory analysis for purity levels.

'*Lloyd Peter Gerard, you are charged that you, on the ninth day of July 2008, at about 7pm to 8pm, at York Hotel, Singapore, did traffic in a controlled drug specified in Class A of the First Schedule to the Misuse of Drugs Act, Chapter 185, to wit, by giving one packet of 0.19 gram of crystalline substance, which was analysed and found to contain 0.15 gram of methamphetamine, to Saini bin Saidi, at $100, at the said place, without authorisation under the said Act or the Regulations made thereunder and you have thereby committed an offence under Section 5(1)(a) of the Misuse of Drugs Act, Chapter 185, and punishable under Section 33(1) of the aforesaid Act.* Do you understand?'

'Yes.'

'*Amended Charge 2. That you, on the sixteenth day of July, at about 9pm, at Mount Elizabeth Hospital, did have in your possession a Class A controlled drug listed in the First Schedule to the Misuse of Drugs Act, Chapter 185, to wit, one packet containing 0.51 gram of crystalline substance, which was analysed and found to contain 0.41 gram of methamphetamine, without any authorisation under the said Act or the Regulations made thereunder and you have thereby committed an offence under Section 8(a) and punishable under Section 33(1) of the Misuse of Drugs Act, Chapter 185.* Do you understand?'

'Yes.'

'Now, Lloyd Peter Gerard, I will read three more charges. *You are charged that you on or about the sixteenth day of July 2008, in Singapore, did consume a specified drug listed in the Fourth Schedule to the Misuse of Drugs Act, Chapter 185, to wit, methamphetamine, without authorisation under the said Act or the Regulations made thereunder and you have thereby committed an offence under Section 8(b)(ii) of the Misuse of Drugs Act, Chapter 185, and punishable under Section 33(1) of the said Act.* Do you understand?'

'Yes.'

'Fourth charge. *That you on the sixteenth day of July 2008, at about 9pm, at Mount Elizabeth Hospital, did have in your possession utensils used in connection with the consumption of a Class A controlled drug listed in the First Schedule to the Misuse of Drugs Act, Chapter 185, to wit, two tubes, one bottle and two tubes attached to a rubber stopper, which were examined and found to be stained with methamphetamine, without any authorisation under the said Act or the Regulations made thereunder and you have thereby committed an offence under Section 9 and punishable under Section 33(1) of the Misuse of Drugs Act, Chapter 185.* Do you understand?'

'Yes.'

'Fifth charge. *That you did have in your possession utensils used in connection with the consumption of a Class A controlled drug listed in the First Schedule to the Misuse of Drugs Act, Chapter 185, to wit, one tube, which was examined and found to be stained with ketamine, without any authorisation under the said Act or the Regulations made thereunder and you have thereby committed an offence under Section 9 and punishable under Section 33(1) of the Misuse of Drugs Act, Chapter 185.* Do you understand?'

'Yes.'

Consumption has been confirmed by laboratory analysis. The pre-owned glass pipe that the dealer gave me was stained with a drug called ketamine, so I'm charged with possession of that drug too. And I'm also charged with possessing the implements. That's a crime in Singapore as well.

I knew this was coming but the media didn't, so there is a flurry of excitement in the gallery. Two charges have suddenly become five. I can see, from the corner of my eye, reporters heading for the doorway, going outside to file updated reports via mobile phone. The headline that will appear over my picture just got that much bigger.

• • • • •

I'M STANDING OUTSIDE the courtroom in a huddle with Jeeming. He's introducing the new suit. 'Peter, this is Hamidul Haq, he's the former prosecutor who I want to work with on this case.'

'How do you do,' says Haq, shaking my hand.

'Well, I'm okay, under the circumstances.'

'Peter, we're going to work very hard on this case,' Haq reassures me. 'This is just day one. Things change, okay.'

'We're getting a lot of requests for comment from the media,' Jeeming says. He is staring at me. 'What are your instructions? I think I can say something innocuous as we leave, just to keep them at bay.'

'Don't talk,' I advise, not for the first time. 'Jeeming, trust me—the moment you give a motherhood statement, you open the door to follow-up questions. And I can tell you that they will be questions that you won't want to answer, like, "Did he do it?" Or, "When is your client going to plead guilty?" '

'Are you sure?'

'Believe me. They will hit you with when-did-you-stop-beating-your-wife questions. The Australian media does this better than anyone in the world, and I'm one of them.'

'Excuse me.' We are being interrupted by a reporter. 'I am from the Associated Press, can we get a comment from you?'

I'm looking over his shoulder. There are more reporters hovering in a neat line in the background. It's like sitting at an airport at night-time and watching the aircraft lined up on the horizon, waiting their turn to land.

'No, I'm not talking.' I'm trying to keep up the taciturn appearance, without being rude. 'But thanks, anyway.'

Another tap on the shoulder. I look down to see Emma Tilston from the Australian High Commission. She's tottering on high heels, dressed in a grey power suit. Her lips are beaded with sweat. I'm thinking, *What have you got to be nervous about? I'm the one facing charges.*

'Peter, I have been asked to give you this letter.' *Ah, something is afoot. No wonder she's worried.*

'What is it?'

'It is from the Foreign Minister. It is an instruction for you to surrender your second passport.'

'So the cops think I'm going to run for it, eh?'

'I cannot comment on any communications between the Singapore police and the government. I can only tell you that you have to comply with this instruction. Do you have the second passport with you?'

'No.'

'Where is it?'

'It's in the office in New Delhi.'

'Well, the ABC has to hand it over to the High Commission in New Delhi as soon as possible.'

'What's the hurry?'

'The government has agreed to a request from Singapore to seize the passport. That's all I can tell you.'

'So the Aussies think I'm going to do a runner?'

'Peter. This is not my call. I'm just the messenger.'

'It's okay, Emma. Relax. They can have my passport. I'm not running away. That'd be the dumbest thing I could do right now.'

The police were pretty excited about the existence of a second passport. I told them about it the night that I was arrested—they reacted like I had just confessed to having a Swiss bank account. However, the truth is pretty mundane. A lot of business travellers who have to submit passports for visa stamps operate on multiple passports. Some have three. I maintain two, like a number of correspondents. The system works best in places like the Middle East, when reporters based in Jerusalem want to visit anti-Israel Arab states.

But now that I'm facing serious charges, everything about my life looks suspicious. During the search of my bags at the hospital on the night of my arrest the police recovered half a dozen syringes. The needles were from an ABC-issued medical kit, stand-bys in case of a medical emergency in some developing-world hospital with suspect safety procedures. Initially the cops thought they were implements of a junkie.

Making light of the moment, I had said, 'I have bandages in there too, but that doesn't make me an Egyptian mummy.'

'We will be the judge of that,' had come the stony reply.

EIGHT
The memory of having no memory

IT'S THE NIGHT OF THE Olympic Games opening ceremony in Beijing, 8 August 2008. I'm sitting on the lounge inside Mazlee's twenty-fourth floor apartment, off Upper Thomson Road in central Singapore. I can see the setting sun through the balcony doors, but I've promised him that I won't go out there when I'm staying here alone. He is afraid that I might jump.

My second court appearance was scheduled for last Friday, 1 August, but the hearing was postponed. Unbeknown to most, I was by then a patient in the psychiatric wing of the Mount Elizabeth Hospital.

Media interest in my case collapsed after my first court appearance. Reporters realised pretty fast that I was not giving interviews, so editors called them back home. Lurking around Singapore, staying in five-star hotels and producing nothing of substance day after day is a pretty big incentive for an editor to pull the plug on an assignment like this. The only reporter to persist was Caroline Marcus from the *Sun-Herald* newspaper. She submitted a series of written questions to me, via Tim Palmer. I was reluctant to respond, but enough people around me thought that it might be time to set some of the record straight.

I had, meantime, discovered a strange coincidence. The demand by the Foreign Minister, Stephen Smith, for my second passport to be surrendered came a day after the News Limited–owned Sydney *Daily Telegraph* published an absurd op-ed piece from a media chancer named Chris Smith. Smith implied that he knew me personally and described me flatteringly as 'Peter Lloyd, a well-read journalist'. Smith suggested I ought to commit a crime to deal with my situation: 'My advice is to run, Peter, run,' he said, 'because there's a ball and chain with your name on it.'

Smith has more talent for drama than reportage. He wrongly identified Singapore as a state where convicts wear balls and chains (that state is Thailand, a little further north). But his article, of course, caused me considerable grief—the Singapore police spoke to me after its publication and quizzed me about my intentions. *Are you going to try to run?* they wanted to know. Smith may well have put ideas into the head of Stephen Smith, but the permanently paranoid Singapore government did not need encouragement—it pressured Australia to recover my passport in case I had a change of mind.

• • • • •

ON MOST WEEKENDS Jared Wong can be found photographing weddings and birthday celebrations for rich Chinese families in Singapore. But on 26 July he was taking snaps of me at Robertson Quay on Singapore's renovated waterway for the next day's story in the *Sun-Herald*. Caroline Marcus had done what I would do in the same situation—assembled half a dozen hard-hitting questions, and then padded them out with a series of softballs and Dorothy Dixers to try to cushion the impact. I responded to some and ignored others, following my own advice: pick the message, pick the medium and pick the moment. This was the result, in part:

> ABC foreign correspondent Peter Lloyd has vowed to stay in Singapore to face drug charges that could lead to him being jailed for 20 years. While there have been calls for him to run, Lloyd, 41, told the *Sun-Herald* yesterday: 'I've never ever considered attempting to flee. I will remain in Singapore.'
>
> In his first interview since being charged with trafficking and possessing drugs he revealed he had been suffering traumatic flashbacks and nightmares after covering the region's tragedies, such as the Bali bombings and the tsunami. These had left him too afraid to sleep,

a phobia which peaked in the two months leading up to his July 16 arrest, he said.

Lloyd—who separated from wife Kirsty McIvor six months ago and declared himself gay—faces a maximum sentence of 20 years and 15 strokes of the rattan cane for allegedly selling 0.15 grams of ice for $76 to a Singaporean man at the York Hotel on July 9.

Police also allegedly found 0.41 grams of the methamphetamine on him, along with utensils bearing traces of ice and the veterinary drug Special K, when he was arrested at Mount Elizabeth Hospital a week later. He was based in New Delhi but was in Singapore to seek treatment for an eye infection. Yesterday he said he did not have a wild or risk-taking personality and the infection was 'in no way connected with drugs'.

Lloyd's partner, Malay-Singaporean Mohamed Mazlee bin Abdul Malik, posted $S60,000 ($45,000) bail for him to walk free on Wednesday. During Lloyd's next court appearance, on Friday, Mr Malik appeared upset, clutching the hand of Lloyd's sister, Cathy Mulcahy.

Lloyd thanked media and ABC colleagues such as Tim Palmer. Mr Palmer said in Singapore: 'Peter's been through some of the toughest experiences anyone could face: that's not just over weeks or months, but over years. He's seen more death, injury, violence and grief than many soldiers or paramedics would see in a career. I'm not saying that any of that has led to anything that might or might not have happened but, in understanding Peter's recent past, it's obviously a huge factor.'

A legal source said prosecutors were 'scraping the bottom of the barrel' to find new charges to make an example of Lloyd. 'Recreational drugs are not accepted and anything to do with it [and the Singapore Government] will come down like a ton of bricks,' the source said.

Some commentators have suggested Lloyd should jump bail and run. The legal source said if he did he would never be able to return to Australia due to an extradition agreement between the countries. 'If I were to jump, I would not go to a country with a treaty. I should go to Indonesia or Thailand. I have seen some people do it,' he said.

I'm in no position to be objective about this article, but it did contain one small mistake—about how long Kirsty and I had been separated (out by more than a year). After the foolishness of the Chris Smith story and this piece by Marcus, I decided to stop reading any more reports. In a storm you focus on staying afloat and heading for safe port. No one has time to read commentaries.

• • • • •

THE NEXT DAY I had to report to the police at 11.30am. This is my new routine, three times a week. When you are a reporter covering a court case and you hear bail conditions being set, the only part of the proceedings that you really focus on is whether the accused is free or not and the amount of bail. The part about reporting to police goes in one ear and out the other. I've never considered whether it is an imposition or not. When you are mentally ill, it is a major life event.

Sarah Stewart, my friend from AFP news agency, volunteered to escort me to the police station and keep me company. At the Central Narcotics Bureau headquarters building in the Cantonment district security is strict, akin to entering an airport departure terminal.

'Are you going to be okay?' she asks.

'Hope so.' I'm shaking. In fact, what I cannot shake off is the dreaded feeling that the police are going to re-arrest me once I'm inside. I have no reason to suspect this, but I am petrified.

'I'm here to see Jeff Lee, please,' I say to the man stationed behind the glass wall at reception.

'Take a seat,' he says.

For such an official workplace, many CNB workers seem under-dressed in their low-rider jeans and T-shirts. Save for the identity badges they look like students, moviegoers or the unemployed. Then the penny dropped. Singapore operates more undercover drugs police per capita than just about any other country in the world. These cops are a convincing lot: they're dressed in street clothes, display tattoos that imply liberal-mindedness or perhaps gang membership, and the majority are from the most socially marginalised ethnic groups, Malays and Indians. The noticeably better-dressed and more command-ing police by rank passing by are, of course, Chinese. Doubtless the minority races in Singapore do all the really dirty undercover work. I am reminded of the CISCO fiasco when I was leaving jail.

'Hello, Peter.' It's Jeff Lee. 'Come here, lah. You must sign papers, okay.'

'Okay.' I'm almost too frightened of Lee to speak. He leads me to a small desk in the foyer. He has a file, with my name on top.

'Okay, all you do is sign your name and today's date. Then you go. See you Wednesday.'

I do as I'm told and watch in shock as Lee walks away, having left me a free man.

'Let's get out of here,' says Sarah, grabbing my hand and leading me away.

$$\bullet\ \bullet\ \bullet\ \bullet\ \bullet$$

AFTER REPORTING TO THE police I catch a train up the island to Serangoon Gardens, to the home of my psychologist, Karen Gosling. I'm still getting used to the idea that I *have* a psychologist. Saying those words—*I have a psychologist*—feels in itself like an admission of colossal weakness.

Up until now, I saw myself as bulletproof. Now I am not certain about who I am, or what I stand for. Nightmares are still haunting me. I'm sleep-deprived and sleep-phobic. The realisation that I am quite this imperfect is still sinking in. Here is the central contradiction of my life: I strive to be perfect and come up imperfect every time. Perfect/Imperfect. That's asking for trouble.

The first session took place last Friday afternoon and it was pretty exhausting. Within a few minutes of taking a seat on her lounge, between Mazlee and my sister, I had an 'episode'. I cannot remember what I said or what I described, but Karen told me afterwards that I had 'vagued' out and begun talking about saving dead people from a fire or an explosion. The clinical term Karen used was dissociation—she said that I disappeared from the conversation, re-emerging five or eight minutes later with no recall of having dissociated.

This is my second session with Karen. We clearly have a lot of work to do.

'Hello, Mr Lloyd. Would you like a coffee or tea today?'

'Coffee, I think. Or tea. You decide.'

'All right, coffee it is.' She's amused by my indecisiveness.

'Okay.'

'Gingernut biscuit?'

'This is going to be easy, Karen. Keep feeding me my favourite biscuits and I'll tell you anything you want.'

She's laughing at my crappy joke, and I'm at ease in her company. I feel immediately safe with her; that she's an Australian in Singapore practising psychology seems too good to be true. We've struck up the comfortable rapport that Australians so easily do in each other's company. The idiomatic vocabulary, the black in-jokes, the teasing, the irony and the mockery are second nature.

She operates out of the basement of a two-storey townhouse in a posh Singapore suburb. The room is comfortably decorated with couches and other soft furnishings that make this feel more like a living room than a clinician's premises.

Karen has picked up fast that I am a visually stimulated person who learns more easily when things are drawn or demonstrated. So she's up at the whiteboard, pen in hand, like a teacher with one eager pupil. She's doing a presentation on memory—how we receive information in the brain, and how the brain sorts and stores memory. We arrive fairly quickly at a Penny-drop Moment: it turns out that my nightmare analogy, of being taken hostage at a horror-movie festival, is more apt a description than I had realised. My nightmares are springing forth from a part of the brain that retains bad memories and is suffering from a dramatic case of stimulus overload.

'These dissociations,' I ask. 'I'm curious—can they last for a while?'

'Why?'

'Because there are parts of the last year that I just don't remember.'

'Such as?'

'Well, it began after the assassination attempt on Benazir Bhutto,' I explain. 'I can't remember the end of that assignment. We followed her around after the attack, but I'm not sure where.' I'm distressed at saying all this, but I press on. Leaning forward in the chair for emphasis, I say it slowly: 'Karen, I don't know *how* I left Pakistan.'

'Are there other things you cannot remember?'

'Yes.'

'What are they?'

'The end of other tough assignments. I know how they started—I mean, I remember getting there—but I can't remember the end.'

'Can you remember which ones?'

'Afghanistan, just before Christmas—we'd been embedded with the diggers for a week or two, but I don't remember leaving. And Pakistan in February, after Benazir was killed—we went back for the election, but I cannot remember leaving. I was travelling with Mark Willacy— he's a corro who likes a beer or fifty—but still that wouldn't account for my memory being so shot. What I can tell you about that assignment is that I was pretty jumpy about being blown up. We had to go to the polling stations dressed in flak jackets. We had to limit the amount of time we spent on the street, because we were worried about suicide attacks. I was smoking two packets a day, and sleeping with the curtains drawn all the time. I was certain the windows were going to explode. I just don't remember leaving.'

'It sounds like there is a pattern here—every time you feel threatened, your mind switches off. Or stops remembering the experience of being threatened. To put it in journo speak—it is like your mind has hit the erase button.' I'm silent. 'Does this upset you?'

'The memory of having no memory?'

'Yes, I suppose you could call it that.' Karen is chuckling at my play on words.

'Yes.' I'm feeling exposed, and wounded by airing my troubles. 'It does upset me.' I'm clutching a throw cushion. I'm crying. 'Karen, I don't remember buying drugs.'

NINE
Tsunami

'SIR. YOU HAVE A VERY lucky face,' said the man in the turban, 'and I would like to tell you why.'

'Is it because I am about to ignore you?' I parried to the strangely out of place Sikh hustler on my way to the Starbucks outlet at the end of my street, Soi Somkid, in the steaming central district of Bangkok.

It was Boxing Day 2004 and I was in Bangkok, in a dreamy holiday torpor. I had not switched on the television to monitor CNN and BBC World, or logged on to my computer to see what top stories were appearing online on ABC. I had not dialled up the foreign desk in Sydney for a briefing, or even spoken to our Jakarta correspondent, Tim Palmer. Such 'short calls' usually lasted half an hour or longer, lingering on work-related topics briefly before rocketing to the outer edges of the known social universe. Tim and I have a friendship based on our equal capacity for hyper-tangential discussion.

No, this was emphatically a No Work Day, for Kirsty and I were about to embark on a road trip—we were taking our sons, Jack and Tom, to the local Dream World fun park, the Big Mango's tepid answer to Disneyland. But first I had to get a tall caramel macchiato and some iced latte frappe nonsense for the grown-ups, plus a couple of muffins. These signature purchases announced the commencement of any excursion from our Bangkok home.

The momentous events unfolding a few hundred kilometres to the south had yet to encroach on our plan. I was oblivious to the slight rocking sensation that had already been experienced by dwellers in many Bangkok buildings after the undersea mega-thrust earthquake epicentred off the west coast of Sumatra.

That had happened at 8am Bangkok time, when most of the city's occupants were still dozing. Our two-storeyed home was built on soft ground next to a canal, and even medium-sized vehicles driving past created a vibration that could be felt when you were lying in bed. I had become so used to the sensation that I was no longer especially conscious of it. I had probably mistakenly registered the tremors of the Sumatra earthquake—the second largest earthquake ever recorded on a seismograph—as a passing delivery van. And so, while the entire planet vibrated by as much as one centimetre, Peter Lloyd continued sleeping like a baby.

A short while later—when the resulting tsunami inundated coastal Aceh, in Indonesia, with waves up to thirty metres high—I was still padding softly around the house, rousing, feeding and dressing children. And, as the first of 230 000 lives, stretching across fourteen countries, were snuffed out, the happy cadence of our quiet life in Bangkok was continuing, uninterrupted.

• • • • •

'THERE'S BEEN A HUGE earthquake off Sumatra. I think it might be big in Aceh.' It was Tim Palmer on the mobile phone from Jakarta. I was driving down the motorway towards Dream World when he called.

Disasters keep an inconvenient timetable. They tend to happen when you least expect them, when you are the least prepared and, as was the case a day after Christmas, the least motivated to respond. *Aceh—that's not my problem*, I thought, as I continued along my way.

There would be others that day that misread, misunderstood or rejected outright the scale of the disaster and the urgent need to respond. One renowned correspondent, not from the ABC, famously remarked that, 'I'm not going to Phuket for a bunch of wet tourists.'

The second telephone call came from Mark Laban, a producer and cameraman from the Asiaworks production company. He was on the island of Phuket, staying with his parents in their retirement home located on a headland south of Patong Beach. 'Peter, something weird is going on here. I think the beach at Patong just got hammered by a big wave.' Mark was putting two and two together before I did. 'I think it might have been caused by that earthquake off Sumatra.'

The third phone call was mine, to the foreign desk in Sydney. I put the duty producer on speakerphone as he read reports of damage in Aceh, and the initial reports of a deluge of some kind striking the islands along the Andaman coast of Thailand. Phuket hotel operators were reporting damage to property and injuries to tourists at beach resorts.

'I think you better turn around,' said Kirsty. 'This sounds big.'

• • • • •

'SPEND WHAT YOU HAVE TO,' said the producer in Sydney. 'We need to get there fast.' ABC News department managers, being conscious of the organisation's limited and public funding, are reluctant to smash open the piggy bank. But this was no ordinary event and, on this Sunday afternoon, they were swinging the hammer. I didn't need any encouragement, but getting to the story wasn't going to be easy.

Phuket airport is located twenty-five metres above sea level, yet the lowest-lying portion of the 3000-metre long runway had been swamped by the tsunami, leaving debris strewn for a hundred metres down the asphalt. The Airports Authority of Thailand had ordered the suspension of flights, effectively closing the airport.

I anticipated the closure would be short-lived, since an emergency on this scale requires a functioning airport for relief operations to commence. Others had the same idea. My cameraman, David Leland, and I pooled together with colleagues from the Canadian Broadcasting Corporation and Associated Press to charter our own eleven-seat plane. The moment the Airport Authority declared Phuket International open for business again, our pilot would pull back the chocks and start up the number-one engine.

• • • • •

PHUKET AIRPORT WAS CHAOTIC. Our charter flight touched down at the same time as a Thai Airways flight delivering holidaymakers who had yet to break their schedule.

From a government charter plane emerged Thailand's top forensic scientist, Dr Porntip Rojanasunan. Porntip was instantly recognisable because of her funky punk-style hairdo. Over the years she had become a legend for her gutsy pursuit of justice for victims of violence carried out by Thai security forces. She was, as ever, outspoken as the CBC's Michael McAuliffe and I trotted along beside her.

'How bad is it?'

'Very bad,' she deadpanned.

'We hear there could be a hundred or more dead.'

'No. It is more. Maybe thousands,' she replied, before pushing her cart into the eerie darkness. 'Sorry, I must go now.'

Taxi drivers were spooked. David pushed a huge baggage cart with fourteen pieces of television equipment while Michael and I tried, unsuccessfully, to hire a taxi van driver.

'*Mai dai.* Cannot,' they said, over and over.

One driver offered a more detailed explanation: 'We won't go over the mountain into Patong. We are afraid of spirits of the dead.'

Thai people tend to be very superstitious, particularly about death. Professional drivers in Thailand are acutely sensitive, which is why they buy garlands of jasmine and hang them from the mirror—to appease the spirit guardian believed to protect the vehicle and its passengers. There was no amount of jasmine in Phuket that would convince these drivers to take us where we wanted to go. As a compromise, one man would take us as far as the main hospital, safely located in the middle of the island and far away from the beaches.

• • • • •

BEDS IN THE EMERGENCY ROOM were filled with bloodied, scratched and wounded westerners dressed in garishly coloured swimwear. It was an incongruous mix—holiday meets horror. There was a strange silence in the room—patients too sick and too shocked to utter more than a whispered response, and doctors and nurses so focused that they needed to say only what was necessary. Saving words was a way of saving the energy needed to stay alert.

It was a medical emergency unprecedented in Thailand. The deputy director of the hospital, Kongkiat Kespechara, told me that broken bones were the most common injury. 'About fifty per cent have a fracture. This is a big problem, because they need some operation.' Reinforcements were being sent from Bangkok, he said, because the number of people needing treatment was rising fast.

It was in a treatment room nearby that I found Joseph and Ivana Giardina. He had a burst lung and she had cuts and abrasions, but the couple's only thoughts were for their missing sixteen-year-old Down syndrome son, Paul.

Ivana told me how it began. 'We were at the Sea View hotel in Patong, in the restaurant having breakfast, and everybody was really curious of what was happening, so they've gone to the beach. They've crossed the road to get a closer look, and we're all watching. We just went outside the restaurant—just outside, not across the road to the beach. And then . . . the water was coming, everybody started running and panicking, and the water just came over, it just . . . it just filled up. There was furniture everywhere hitting us, and . . .' Ivana was in a state of shock as she described the frustration of not being able to reach out and save Paul. 'I couldn't get to my son, because I had the tables from outside and the chairs had gone in between us. But my husband, Joe, had Paul . . . But Paul, being stubborn, he was calling me . . . Then they just went. They just all went.'

That was the last time they saw Paul—earlier that day, during the tsunami's assault on the curious crowd on the main Patong Beach. Twelve hours later, Paul was amongst the hundreds of holidaymakers and locals officially listed as 'missing'. Just like Bali, the word 'missing' was to become a morbid euphemism in the days ahead.

•••••

THE TSUNAMI DID MORE than kill and injure. It wreaked havoc on communications infrastructure. Roads were blocked. Telephone lines knocked down. Mobile phone services simply stopped working.

This sent the twenty-first century news media back to the equivalent of the communications stone age—the time before mobile phones, the era when brands like Nokia and Blackberry and iPhone were vague dreams in the minds of pointy-headed inventors.

The effect of this was a cloak of isolation. It also perverted the assumption by our listeners and viewers that those of us at the coalface during a disaster are always the best informed. With the tsunami, nothing could have been further from the truth. We knew with certainty only what we could see and hear, and on the first night that was precious little.

The only link I had to the outside world was a creaking satellite phone. On that Sunday afternoon, the day we arrived, we set up in the garden of the hospital alongside our colleagues from the BBC. Our advantage was a line to the outside world—to feed our 'on the spot' reports from the hospital, and to have the duty staff on the foreign desk read back the news-wire reports from elsewhere in Thailand.

In the world of 24/7 mass communications, the truth is that head office always knows far more than reporters on the ground, and all too often the producers at home are feeding us lines of information that we, in turn, gush back authoritatively, as if we had uncovered these important facts all by ourselves. It is a necessary ruse, especially after the curtain goes up on a disaster with so many fronts. Behind every great reporter there is an even greater editorial life support system.

The stress caused by this communications blackout had to be ignored in order to get on with the job. The next morning I was a one-man reporting team tied to a sat-phone filing voice reports. I was blinded by our inability to reach by phone anyone else on the island, and left stranded by the superstitious refusal of drivers to take us a few kilometres away to the apparent heart of the story. The obvious need was for reinforcements but, in the heat of the moment, it didn't occur to me to stop and ask for help.

No one at head office offered it. In fact, the information vacuum was blinding them too; although the Sydney-based producers could get a sense of where there was trouble, they knew very little in detail. There were sketchy reports of deaths, injuries and damage to scores of hotels all along the Andaman seaside—on Phi Phi Island, north to the up-market resorts at Khao Lak and elsewhere. No one knew quite where to begin when alarms were flashing all over the place.

Clues as to what the Thai government knew about the scale of the tragedy took many hours to emerge. An official from the prime minister's office began saying publicly after twenty-four hours what the forensic scientist Porntip had said to us at the airport: they were preparing 1000 body bags. Maybe more.

On the other side of the island, in the Phuket town centre, I found chaotic scenes at the main disaster reception area, where volunteers were trying to reunite families separated during the tsunami. The weary and walking wounded filed in from the tsunami-battered outlying island of Phi Phi. They recounted scenes of devastation, confirming reports that hundreds of people had died or were missing and were presumed dead.

Damien Kloot, from the Queensland Gold Coast, approached me, holding up the passport of his Japanese wife who had been swept away. 'We were right in the pier where the boats were coming in,' he said. 'The water, the boats started going crazy on the pier. Within five seconds the water just came rushing in. I was ten metres away from my wife. I got pushed one way. I have no idea where my wife is.' Kloot said the middle of Phi Phi had been wiped out. 'There's nothing left.'

• • • • •

LOCATED, AS WE WERE, at the emergency operations centre, the assessment of the human impact was alarming but also frustratingly uncomfirmable. It was only when we recruited a young driver named Apple, who was willing to explore the coast, that we had a chance to find out for ourselves. It was Tuesday when we set out, two days after the disaster. We drove north, taking the bridge crossing over the small causeway that separates Phuket Island from the mainland. Until that day Phuket was largely all we talked about in dispatches. This was about to end.

Apple slowed down as we arrived at the first mainland tourist hamlet on the Khao Lak coast. Cliched as this may sound, it is true to say that the village had been smashed to pieces. Hotels that had stood two and three storeys high were stripped naked, with only their skeletal structures remaining. The debris of these broken buildings lay like long-neglected litter, carpeting a pristine sandscape with rotting and twisted piles of salty garbage.

The gentle breeze from the ocean carried a stench of death and decay, both human and animal. Volunteer recovery teams—the legendary body-snatcher brigades—were dragnetting stagnant pools of deep, brackish water for cadavers. Their haul so far—a dozen or so corpses—had been neatly wrapped in sheets of plastic and tied with rope. The shock of the scene came to me in waves. The scale of the disaster was unambiguously apparent, and so was our belatedness. Two days had passed before we'd found the story we were looking for.

What had we in the media been doing? Obsessing about the latest home video of the moment the tsunami hit, without finding out where it had been filmed and travelling to the scene ourselves? Fed by the endless supply of video by the news agencies Reuters and Associated Press, the electronic media elected to stay in Phuket covering the known disaster—with its convenient backdrop of Patong Beach—and only hinting at the existence of a greater tragedy.

Addicted to 'known news', we were slow to set out from base camp to see what more could be told. We played safe in order to feed the beast of hourly deadlines. But there are times when the broadcasting beast holds us back from doing our job—it is moments like this when you realise that the more we report, the less we are reporting.

Organisations that don't send enough reporters leave themselves exposed to situations like this. And those that are averse to taking 'risks'—such as missing the occasional bulletin that our direct competitor might file for—collectively allow themselves to be satisfied all too easily. Playing safe short-changes the audience and leaves us coming up short in our obligations to them. Here was a calamity that could be managed from the comfort of the Patong Beach Novotel. So, for a time, we did just that.

• • • • •

'JESUS FUCKING CHRIST!' It was Michael McAuliffe as we finally arrived at Khao Lak and for the first time took in its horrific vista. He was sitting to my right. David had his head down, seeing the panorama through the viewfinder of his camera. I was sitting open-mouthed, sensing the fast-tempo beat of my heart. My lips were parting, but no words were coming out. With my sense of sight and smell under assault, I was momentarily robbed of the ability to utter a sound.

As we ventured further north, we caught up with a small team of body-snatcher volunteers as they drove around the ruin of another resort hotel searching for human remains. They were dressed in overalls, like motor mechanics. On their backs was the name of the Chinese-Thai charity to which they belonged. In a country with virtually no formal emergency services and two million car accidents a year, Thailand's body-snatchers take on the role filled by ambulance workers elsewhere—they rescue the trapped and recover the dead. Volunteers believe it is good for their soul, that it builds karma—to protect them in this life and accumulate credit for their next incarnation. It is gruesome work, but somebody has to do it. The tsunami was made for people like this.

We left Apple and our van behind and joined the body-snatchers. Michael climbed onto the back of a dusty old utility truck and began recording a piece to tape for CBC radio, describing the grizzly scene. David and I climbed in alongside him. The ute was towing a trailer piled high with bodies wrapped in plastic and cotton. The body-snatcher on board, securing the bodies with rope, was smiling broadly. Watching him work demonstrated a very different cultural attitude to death. To a Buddhist, the body is a mere vessel—upon death, it is a shell from which the soul has departed. If you didn't know that, you would have thought he was just a sick bastard.

What transpired next was never to be broadcast, but it remained as one of my most persistent memories. The young Thai in charge of the bodies insisted on stopping the convoy so David could get some close-ups. The body-snatchers had no lack of enthusiasm for their work, but they weren't great shakes at tying knots. Bloated hands and faces and limbs kept slipping into view as the volunteer riffled through the remains, muttering, 'Farang! Farang in here!'

Like a proud assistant to Grim Death himself, the volunteer wanted to show us how many foreigners' bodies they had recovered so far. In Thai, David thanked him and insisted that he stop searching for the prized westerners on our behalf. We took him at his word that he had found so many foreigners and sent the body-snatchers on their way.

A few hours after we'd encountered the body-snatchers, we arrived at the Khao Lak Temple, where volunteers were depositing bodies. The temple is about the size of a football pitch and by Wednesday 29 December it was covered in corpses, neatly stacked in long gruesome rows. Those bodies that were wrapped in cotton were soaking through with blood and the juices of decomposition.

As David went to work filming the scene, I stood back and watched. It was early morning; the roosters and the hens who usually found refuge at the temple were now trying to reclaim their territory. It had to happen—eventually a rooster found a source of food in the remains of a body, pecking and clawing at what I assumed was the face. I turned and vomited.

In television reporting we choose our words very carefully. We don't have much time, and the words we use have to count. I am not normally lost for words, but the scene at the temple on this morning rendered me speechless.

The catastrophic loss of life in Thailand was all too evident after we discovered the makeshift mortuary system being established at the temple. There were three other temples nearby serving a similar function, according to the abbot, who estimated the number of dead Europeans at more than 2000.

As we spoke, body-snatcher trucks laden with an average of a dozen bodies each were arriving at the rate of one every five minutes. After a few moments of silence, the abbot turned to face me. Reaching for my hand, he said, 'I think I may have underestimated the number of souls we have lost.'

TEN
Seventy days to live

IT HAD BEEN A STEAMING hot summer's day in October 2007 and I had a really bad feeling about Benazir Bhutto. It was dusk and, against my better judgement, Wayne and I were still on the streets of Karachi, one of the world's meanest cities. A few hours earlier, the former prime minister had touched down in Pakistan's sprawling southern metropolis. It was the end of eight years of self-imposed exile, and the beginning of a campaign to win the prime ministership for a third time.

Clad in a conspicuous Koran-green tunic with a white headscarf, Benazir was ahead of us in a motorcade inching its way from the airport to the city centre, amid a thick crowd of 200 000 party workers and supporters. The security forces had dispatched 20 000 police and troops to guard the route. They'd been warning that militant suicide squads were gunning for her. Think Dallas, November 1963.

Vaingloriously, Benazir stubbornly insisted on turning her home-coming into a bread-and-circus spectacle, to extract maximum pub-licity. She was determined to use saturation media coverage to telegraph a message to the dictator, Pervez Musharraf, in his palace in Islamabad: *I'm back and I can still pull a crowd*. And she was willing to risk her life, and the lives of others, for it.

It was a security nightmare entirely of her own making. An offer of a military helicopter lift from the airport to the city had been turned down. 'This is the beginning of a journey for a better future for all of the people of Pakistan,' the high-born Benazir declared, modestly coupling voters, whom she openly referred to as 'the masses', with her personal ambitions.

As I walked in the wake of this parade, I mulled over the question of what soundtrack Benazir Bhutto might select for this momentous day in her life. It was no stretch to imagine a feminist anthem from the Harvard days in 1972, Helen Reddy's 'I Am Woman'. Up ahead, I could hear Bhutto roaring into a microphone, bellowing soaring rhetoric about restoring democracy. She was behind the bulletproof glass of a podium set on top of a purpose-built bombproof container box, loaded onto the back of a truck. If something went wrong, she'd be all right.

• • • • •

FOR THE BEST PART of a year, Benazir Bhutto had been packaging herself to the British Foreign Office and the US State Department as a one-woman Pakistan rescue mission. General Pervez Musharraf was unpopular with Congress and the Bush administration, and Bhutto was promoting herself as Plan B on the South Asia front of George W. Bush's War on Terror—a diva of democracy and a potentially sure-footed deputy sheriff.

The Bush administration must have been suffering from collective amnesia when they accepted such a ludicrous proposition from this suspected kleptocrat. During her first term in office—during the twenty months from November 1988—the incompetent Bhutto failed to pass a single law in parliament. Her economic record as a two-time prime minister was unimpressive.

Amnesty International said her human rights record was worse than that of the regime she'd succeeded. In her time there were more extra-judicial killings, more cases of torture and more deaths in custody. Worse, perhaps, was the allegation that Bhutto smuggled nuclear secrets to North Korea to help them build the bomb that now terrorises North Asia. Corruption was the watchword of the Bhutto years. Transparency International rated her governments amongst the most corrupt on the planet.

Benazir Bhutto was the mediocre daughter of martyred former prime minister Zulfikar Ali Bhutto, executed by military dictator General Zia. She possessed a famous name, but little else in the way of leadership credentials. But in her favour was the fact that Pakistan was an effective totalitarian state with a veneer of elective feudalism. She was born lucky, into Pakistan's elite ruling class. There are twenty or so of these rich families who, along with the army, have always run Pakistan like a personal fiefdom—exploiting land and mineral resources, dominating commercial and business life and, of course, massively cheating the taxman.

Benazir Bhutto only agreed to return to Pakistan after a complex power-sharing deal with the regime of President Pervez Musharraf, which involved her agreeing not to challenge Musharraf's re-election as president in early October 2007 in return for the government announcing an amnesty for all politicians accused of corruption between 1986 and 1999. Those politicians set to benefit included Bhutto and her husband Asif Ali Zardari, who had already spent seven years in prison on corruption charges.

The homecoming deal cleared the way for the Bhuttos to reclaim hundreds of millions of dollars in frozen Swiss bank accounts, a fortune largely amassed from corrupt kickbacks on contracts during Benazir's two terms as prime minister.

After the homecoming parade had passed by I noticed that the teeming crowd, which had been initially giddy and excited, was experiencing a come-down and getting bored. Young men, their eyes glazed and red, were soon turning their attention to us.

In South Asia most man-to-man conversation commonly begins with the invitation to surrender your name: 'What is your good name, sir?' But on this day in Karachi the friendly preliminaries were warm-ups for uncomfortable and pointed personal questions about our transport arrangements, or the dollar value of the television equipment Wayne was carrying. A pickpocket had already tried to lift my wallet—I'd seen him off with a swift kick up the rear and a short imperative to travel elsewhere.

'Let's go back to the hotel,' I said to Wayne. 'We've got enough footage. Reuters and Associated Press can body-watch Bhutto for the rest of the parade.'

Part of me wanted to stay and get close to Bhutto and film more footage for another longer story profiling her return. But it had been a long day and I could see Wayne needed a break.

There was another reason to hesitate. I thought I could smell marijuana, and the look on some young men's faces suggested they were high on something other than enthusiasm. If Wayne and I got separated, it would be a long and problematical walk back through the crowd to the rendezvous point with our mini-van transport.

Part of the preparation for our lives as foreign correspondents includes training, conducted by retired special forces soldiers, in how to survive in a dangerous environment. I'd done two courses, focusing on security and weapons awareness and basic battlefield medicine. If you dwelt too much on the range of possibilities of what could go wrong, you'd never get out of bed—and certainly not to go to Karachi.

Even before Benazir's homecoming stunt, Karachi was the kind of town that set off all my security-conscious alarm bells. Known to locals as the 'City of Lights', this sprawling city is Pakistan's financial and commercial capital. Until the establishment of Islamabad in 1960, it was the national capital too.

By population, it is the world's twentieth largest city. It is dangerous, congested with traffic and dirty. Full of poor and desperate people, it is renowned for random and not-so-random acts of political and criminal violence. It figured prominently in international news in 2002 when the *Wall Street Journal* journalist Daniel Pearl was kidnapped, tortured and beheaded here by al-Qaeda terrorists.

After that incident, I vowed not to travel to Karachi—putting Wayne and our local fixer, Irshad Rao, at risk—without a very good reason. But the return of Benazir Bhutto, so flawed and fascinating and newsworthy, could not be ignored.

• • • • •

I HAD JUST GONE to bed that night when the telephone rang. 'Peter, I think you will have to re-file your stories on Bhutto,' said the overnight producer at the radio news desk. 'There's been an explosion at the parade.'

I switched on the television. Pakistan's English language cable news service, Dawn TV, was broadcasting live pictures of the motorcade when the explosion happened.

It was the midnight hour, but the Bhutto motorcade was still being mobbed by thousands of supporters. Then there was a bright white-and-orange flash of light, followed by a low booming sound. It was the unmistakeable signature of the much-feared attack on Bhutto, and most of the crowd that had been trying to keep up with her vehicle turned and ran the other way in blind panic.

Around 700 bystanders were cut down when the lone suicide bomber detonated an estimated fifteen-kilogram explosive device. The carnage was made many times worse by the bomber's cruel decision to pack thousands of ball bearings into the bomb-carrying device disguised under his tunic.

The mutilation was horrific. Limbs and dismembered bodies were strewn over the parade ground. More than 130 people died immediately, while wounded and panicked victims tried to crawl away, perhaps fearing another bomb blast. In one unforgettable image, a bloodied man, with one leg missing, tries to hop to safety.

The leader of the Pakistan People's Party had just climbed down into the compartment of her truck. Benazir had been revising a speech on the theme of tolerance when the explosion happened. Her close protection team scrambled to remove her from the scene, dragging her down from the truck and shoving her roughly into an armour-plated four-wheel drive. As she was driven to the safety of a family compound in the city, hundreds of blast victims were rushed to local hospitals.

It was the most deadly terror attack so far in Pakistan's violent history, and all I could think was, *This is going to be like Bali.*

• • • • •

WHEN THE BOMBING happened, it was a few minutes before six in the morning in eastern Australia, making the atrocity the lead breaking news story in the always frenetic and demanding hours of breakfast news. For the first few hours I remained in my hotel room and filed updates for radio news every thirty minutes. On top of that, there were live crosses into two editions of the *AM* current affairs program, to Radio National *Breakfast*, to Radio Australia's current affairs programs and to Australia Television, the ABC's international television network.

In between I fielded planning and co-ordination calls from producers and reporters from half a dozen more radio and television programs. I felt like an air traffic controller, calmly guiding aircraft in to land during a typhoon. Every time I put the phone down, I'd take a deep breath, light up a cigarette (surely a sign of a man under stress) and wonder where the next hit was coming from. It took only a few seconds for the phone to start ringing again.

At moments like this, adrenalin charges around your body. Some reporters fear being overwhelmed and reduced to a blubbering mess by the demands of breaking news. I thrive on it. I discovered at the Bali bombings that disaster focuses my mind. Under ridiculous pressure, I manage to organise, prioritise and respond to these work-crazy demands with, mostly, good humour.

Management picked up on this trait too, and harnessed me to act as a sort of United Nations peacekeeper at times when colleagues were tired, testy and a little too confrontational. But I'm no angel—I confess I have snapped a few times, and done it with volcanic force. But most of the time I try to be graceful and good-humoured, and to get on with the job at hand.

• • • • •

IN KARACHI, the job demanded a particular ritual of the news business during disasters: Go To The Hospital. As at Bali, hospitals are full of chaos and human drama. The camera loves them both.

Wayne and I arrived late—too late to witness the drama of the living. But a young doctor intercepted us and offered to guide us to the mortuary. Puzzled by this urgent and unusual offer, I asked why he was so enthusiastic about visiting the mortuary.

'You will see soon enough,' he said mysteriously. 'I want the world to see what these maniacs have done.'

In a courtyard of the hospital, behind the main building, we passed a number of small ambulances belonging to a local medical charity. Like seamen sluicing the deck of a boat, volunteers were hosing and wiping gore and blood from the vinyl seats that had ferried the dead and dying.

In a small, unmarked annexe, we were ushered into a white tiled room where the dead far outnumbered the living. 'The mortuary,' the doctor declared, unnecessarily.

Weeping men were searching limbs and torsos for missing relatives and friends. Attendants tried to maintain order, urging bereaved civilians to take care to identify a body correctly before removing it. In accordance with strict Muslim tradition, they all wanted their dead to be buried before sunset.

Nobody mentioned DNA samples and international forensics procedures. This was not Bali, and no foreigners were among the dead. In Pakistan, trying to stop someone reclaiming a body for burial might have caused a riot and more bloodshed.

The white floor was wet and slippery, and I lost my footing. I still cannot recall who steadied me, whether it was Wayne or the doctor, but they saved me from falling face first into a row of mangled bodies.

Even more traumatic scenes awaited us outside, where we were confronted by a man hysterical with grief and fury. He had been standing next to his two brothers and three friends, and had seen them blown apart. Remarkably, he had barely a scratch on him. 'Who did this? Who did this?' he demanded, before insisting on showing us the bodies.

· · · · ·

I FOUND ONE OF THE youngest survivors of the bombing in the intensive care ward. His name was Sajjad, and a ball bearing had lodged in his spine. The neurosurgeon looking after the fifteen-year-old boy held an x-ray up to the light, clearly showing the marble-sized hunk of metal lodged in the spinal canal between the third and fourth cervical vertebrae.

'Will he walk again?' I asked, hopefully.

'He is quadriplegic,' said Dr Haroon Ur Rasheed. 'He's not even having movement of the hands.' The doctor looked down at the floor, and back at me. "There are worse,' he said, pointing at a man in another bed, his head heavily bandaged. Dr Haroon explained that flying debris had shattered the man's skull.

'What are the chances of him surviving?'

The medico paused again before responding. 'In the long term, if he survives, he will remain in a vegetative state. Like, just opening his eyes and moving his limbs. *If* he survives, God bless him, *if* he survives.'

• • • • •

THAT DAY, Benazir Bhutto didn't go to hospital to offer her sympathy to the maimed, or express condolences to the families of the dead. Instead, this remote aristocratic woman bunkered down behind the walls of a heavily guarded compound, creating the impression that she was frightened or indifferent. It was an opportunity to demonstrate courage under fire, to show the 'masses' what Benazir Bhutto was made of. And, in a way, she did.

In anticipation that Bhutto would make an appearance before the media, Wayne and I joined several hundred reporters and camera crews in a long, tense wait outside her Karachi compound. We sweated it out for hours, standing in a tight cordon in the street, exposed to any follow-up attack.

Tensions were running high after local reporters relayed police alerts that the bombers might strike again, having missed their intended target during the night. 'We could all be killed,' said a news anchor from Pakistan's Dawn TV service, who demanded Bhutto's security team open the door to her compound.

When, some fifteen hours after the blast, the goons protecting her finally relented, Benazir Bhutto put on a disgraceful performance. She conceded that she had been told that four suicide bomb cells were in Karachi and planning to mount an attack. Police had urged her to scrap the street parade and take a lower-profile journey from the airport, but she'd insisted it go ahead.

'Well,' she complained, 'I know that some people will think it was naive, but I think it was the right decision. Because, as I said, if you fight for something you believe in—a cause you believe in—you have to be ready to pay the price.'

When Bhutto attempted to sound a note of sympathy, she blew it by reading from a prepared statement that seemed to confuse grassroots civilian political supporters with soldiers. 'Our thoughts, prayers and sympathies are with those who laid down their lives,' she said. 'They made the ultimate sacrifice for democracy.'

Then came one of the strangest, most insensitive moments I witnessed in Pakistan, when Benazir Bhutto thought it appropriate to explain that she had descended the stairs to the safety of her bombproof box because the strap on her shoes was too tight, and it was making her ankles feel sore.

'Oh, you poor love!' said a scornful woman reporter from the BBC, standing nearby.

•••••

SEVENTY DAYS LATER, on 27 December 2007, an assassin finally succeeded in murdering Benazir Bhutto. It happened at a political rally in the garrison city of Rawalpindi, close to the capital. Bhutto was campaigning for her party ahead of parliamentary elections scheduled for January. After climbing into an armour-plated four-wheel drive, she made the fateful decision to open an escape hatch built into the roof of the vehicle, to stand and wave to supporters. A gunman standing to the left rear of the car fired several shots in Bhutto's direction moments before an explosion.

There was a great deal of conjecture about the exact cause of Benazir Bhutto's death—did she die from a gunshot, the blast or, more prosaically, from hitting her head on the handle of the escape hatch? A Scotland Yard report concluded it was the latter—that the force of the explosion had forced her head to collide violently against the side of the escape hatch. The British police noted that their work was hampered by their inability to carry out an autopsy on Bhutto's body, an instruction given to the hospital by her widower, Zardari.

I thought Benazir Bhutto too cavalier about safety. I wondered whether she had developed a recklessness, born of fatalism from so much family tragedy. Whatever the psychology, I was angry that her quest for political and personal redemption put so many people at risk.

Seeking a return to power as prime minister seemed like a vanity project for an entitled woman too used to getting her own way. It was not as though her past political career portended the dawn of a grand new age for Pakistan. Nothing could have been further from the truth. Benazir represented a return to the worst kind of business as usual— old wine, old bottle.

Some journalists gave Bhutto a benefit of doubt that she did not deserve, given her dismal record as prime minister. But they needed access, especially those at 24-hour news networks. For them, the price of access was a kind of servility. I have acquaintances from those channels who've admitted that they treated her like a princess in order to stay on her good side.

Bhutto tended to talk only to networks that had global reach, believing that those were the broadcasters watched in the State Department and White House. They were her true constituency, not 'the masses' of a country she had chosen not to live in for eight years.

The sometimes too flattering and sympathetic media coverage drew frustration from the regime in Islamabad. At a media conference I attended in November, President Musharraf openly challenged a BBC reporter who had preambled a question by stating that Bhutto was popular. 'Who says she is popular?' asked the exasperated dictator. 'You?' He had a point. At that time, Bhutto had not faced the voters.

• • • • •

SO IT WAS MORE than passing strange that the day Benazir Bhutto died I cried. Sitting in the forward cabin of an aircraft en route to my bureau in New Delhi, after having had my holidays cancelled, I sat with a copy of the newspaper reporting her death in my lap. Above the fold was a huge and flatteringly beautiful photograph of the woman who had so fascinated and frustrated me. For two hours I sat and cried. And once I started weeping I could not stop.

Finally, as the plane descended to land, the man sitting next to me turned and asked, 'Are you all right?'

I turned to face him and began telling a lie that I maintained for months afterwards. 'Yes,' I said, 'I am all right.'

But I was not all right. I was crying over a death I believed was entirely unnecessary and preventable. *For heaven's sake, how incompetent can security guards be when they let the woman stick her head through an escape hatch?* I had seen that car many times and I knew that the opening in its top was not a sun roof. I knew that Benazir Bhutto had made a basic and stupid mistake, and paid for it with her life.

I was crying because two children from a seemingly cursed family had just lost their mother. I was crying because Pakistan, a country I had fallen in love with, was edging closer to an abyss.

At a personal level, I was crying out for help from an accumulation of stress—from too much pent-up fear and worry and danger. I was crying also because I knew that, to keep covering these stories, I would have to put myself back in harm's way once more. The truth was that, at this moment, at the very end of 2007—having travelled twice to Pakistan and then been involved in a long and frustrating embed with the Australian military in the dangerous south of Afghanistan—I was physically exhausted.

I desperately needed rest. I needed to get away from the relentless demands of being a one-man South Asia foreign correspondent office in a network whose appetite for news content was only growing.

But instead, I stayed quiet. I sucked in the grief and stress, and I bottled it up again.

And then I went back to work.

ELEVEN

The fugitive

MY FALL FROM DAYLIGHT into post-traumatic stress darkness began a few days into the New Year of 2008. For a while, there was only one nightmare—reliving that moment in the Karachi mortuary when I had nearly slipped into the pile of dismembered bodies. But soon there were more—haunting nightly reveries of the Bali bombings and my conversations with the dead man, Ben, and then the tsunami and the soundtrack of Ivana, the grieving mother.

I would jackknife awake—sometimes yelling, often sweating and panting for breath. In the case of the Karachi dream my legs would be spinning, as if I were the Road Runner escaping from a trap set by Wile E. Coyote.

The acknowledgment that these nightmares existed and the insights into them that I now possess began to emerge much later in the year, after my life unravelled in Singapore and I entered trauma therapy. Until then I kept these demons from myself—and other people. Until then I was a fugitive, a man in flight from his own past.

I had been banishing these nightmares to my subconsciousness—to the psychological equivalent of the 'safe house', far from the gaze of my waking self. During these months, it was not that I would get out of bed each morning and think, *That was the same bad dream, again—I must seek urgent help*. What happened was that I simply woke up feeling unusually tired and sad, and yet unable to pinpoint a reason for it. I would arrive at work late, and explain my lateness as an inability to sleep caused by a 'bad mattress'.

Of course, it was a grand act of self-deception. Karen, my therapist, was to later explain to me that it was rooted in the innate human need to protect ourselves from things that might threaten our survival. That makes a lot of sense because, at the beginning of 2008, I was already convinced that I was a dying man.

I'd had no sick days during all my time living in Bangkok, between 2002 and 2006. Tropical life and Thai food generally agreed with me. I did pretty well too at first when I moved to India in June 2006. But then I began experiencing alarming and persistent stabbing stomach pain. Having seen the inside of India's malnourished public hospitals during a few stories, I made a beeline for a private hospital near the ABC office in South Delhi that was part of a parallel health system that caters to the 'rich', or those who can scrape up the cash to pay service fees.

The first test carried out by the doctor was for my blood and liver function—to screen out the hepatitises, A, B and C. Once that was clear the doctor shook his head, gave me some general antibiotics and sent me on my way. 'It will probably clear up by itself,' he predicted confidently.

A week later, after the antibiotic course had finished, the pain was just as bad and had spread to my left flank. I was waking up at night doubled over in pain. Sleeplessness is not something that I cope well with—I get cranky, and I start to obsess about minutiae as I lose sight of the bigger picture.

That was when I turned to Google. Doctors tell patients not to do this, for very good reason. People without medical degrees make extremely neurotic and dramatic diagnosticians. I came up with stomach cancer, stomach ulcers and pregnancy.

Going gay in 2006 had been a pretty big game-changer, but I was pretty sure that I was not up the duff and fairly certain that I could rule out 'immaculate conception', a fiction confected by blokes who could not cope with the idea that mothers have sex.

When I went back to the doctor with my discoveries he looked down his glasses at me and said, 'Mister Peter, I think one doctor in this room is quite sufficient.'

'Okay. I will stop Googling. But you have to do more testing.'

The doctor flicked his head to the left and right, the way Indians do when they accede to a request without feeling the need to expend energy verbalising.

Picking up the nuance, I stepped in. 'What test then?'

'Let's do the big one. A chest CT.'

A day later I was back in the doctor's office to learn the dramatic news that the CT scan confirmed I have a chest cavity holding an inventory of: one heart, two lungs, two kidneys and a stomach. All of them were the right shape and size and the correct colour. This, said the doctor, proved that I was in robust health.

'And yet I have pain in my stomach?' I replied, testily.

Pausing for some time, the doctor finally steadied himself in his chair and said, 'Mister Peter, there is nothing wrong with you physically, as far as I can tell. Maybe you have picked up something like hepatitis E, and it is just working its way through your system.' And then he sent me home.

· · · · ·

A WEEK AFTER THE doctor made me feel like the most needlessly anxious person in New Delhi, I was heading back to Pakistan to cover the parliamentary elections that had been delayed by the assassination of Benazir Bhutto. I should have stayed home, and gone to bed for a fortnight.

But I felt as though the cost-conscious bosses were counting on me; if I pulled out, they would have had to spend money unnecessarily on a fly-in, fly-out reporter who does not know the story as thoroughly as a full-time correspondent.

Pakistan had become a complex and intriguing story by February. With Benazir dead and her Pakistan People's Party in the ascendency in the wake of an enormous wave of sympathy, the seven-year rule of Pervez Musharraf was looking shakier. But Pakistan had now become a far more dangerous country for us to visit—the election season emboldened militants to ramp up the number of suicide and other bomb attacks around the country. For the first time we were carrying helmets and flak jackets to visit Pakistan. It was meant to be an election story, but to me it felt more like an assignment to a war zone.

For a few days I went on the road and followed the campaign of Benazir Bhutto's nemesis, Nawaz Sharif. During the decade after 1988 Bhutto and Sharif had taken turns as prime minister, like a game of political ping-pong. Each had corruptly manipulated incumbency to try to ruin the other's family businesses and political dynasties. They had used the tax authorities like attack dogs. Their visceral hatred for each other was legendary, based more on feudal-style family rivalries than any established points of philosophical difference. It was a Muslim Romeo and Juliet, the Montagues and Capulets without the romance.

By the time I caught up with him, Sharif had plundered the now dead Bhutto's anti-regime rhetoric and learned valuable lessons from her murder. We joined a campaign rally outside Lahore, the seat of his vast feudal land holdings. The candidate had just arrived in an armour-plated Land Cruiser identical to the one that had carried Bhutto around. The small escape hatch on the roof was tightly shut, and Sharif remained inside the vehicle's protective cocoon until an all-clear from the security detail.

When Sharif invited the media corps to join him on the stage, I could see how the Bhutto assassination had changed the look and feel of politics. A noisy crowd of grassroots supporters had been corralled like livestock behind a low white wall. Armed and menacing security guards were stationed at every few feet, hurling orders at them to stay back. Then there was a deep gap, a dry medieval moat, separating the assembled masses from their feudal lord and master.

'This distance,' he told me angrily, 'has been created by the dictator Musharraf. The government is not taking any adequate steps to protect the leaders of this country.' It was a cheap shot. There was no evidence linking Musharraf to the Bhutto assassination. Indeed the available evidence pointed to the militant Taliban leader Baitullah Mehsud, later to be assassinated himself by the Americans in one of the CIA's many Predator air strikes carried out on Pakistani soil. And since when did Nawaz Sharif rely on the state for security and protection? All of his muscle was of the hired-gun variety, paid by Sharif and loyal only to the man who wrote the cheque.

Sharif, however, was right about one thing. The effect of the 27 December killing was to end Pakistan's long tradition of rowdy, face-to-face campaigning. High-profile candidates like him were forced into undignified and unprecedented levels of skullduggery, turning these politicians into hit-and-run speechmakers. The venue and timing of Sharif's appearances was kept a secret until the eleventh hour, to keep militants in the dark as much as possible.

Wayne and I were worried about our safety too, so on this day in Lahore we shot as much tape as we needed from the Sharif podium and made a quick getaway. I had already made a decision not to linger around candidates for longer than necessary, and to stay off the streets as much as possible. The surge in suicide bombings around the country was giving me sleepless nights, and I spent many hours strategising how to minimise our public exposure while still getting the footage needed to prepare our reports.

I probably seemed lazy and uninterested, but I no longer felt confident that we were safe from random acts of violence. Had I been more demanding about filming additional material of Benazir, back in October, Wayne and I could have been casualties, blown apart on the street at the Karachi bombing. We'd had more of a narrow escape from that tragedy than I was prepared to admit to anybody.

I was obsessing about narrow escapes for another reason. In neighbouring Afghanistan, the plush Serena Hotel in Kabul had just come under attack. It was the hotel we had chosen for its security measures. Wayne and I both tended to use the hotel gym in the early evening, which was the precise time that the Taliban mounted their suicide bomb and gun attack targeting foreigners working out. Six guests and hotel workers were killed, including a Filipino woman whom I remembered as one of the foreign guest workers at the gym. But for a different schedule, the dead could easily have included either Wayne or me.

When the Taliban started killing people in places where I spent time, in places that I thought were safe, I realised that luck was all that really separated us from the dead. Luck, as any gambler will tell you, eventually runs out.

Back in the Serena's sister hotel in the Pakistani capital, I began drawing closed the heavy curtains and switching on all the lights. I was obsessed with the idea that a bomb would go off at any moment outside the hotel, sending shards of glass and debris flying into the building. I slept on the side of the bed away from the window, ready to roll onto the floor and cover my body with a duvet. I rehearsed the move a few times. At breakfast I would drink four or five double espressos. On the road I would chain smoke. And at night I would drink, heavily, before falling into another uneasy sleep.

On the day of the election we filmed our story at a polling booth at Rawalpindi, the bustling garrison city just outside Islamabad. The capital—with its wide thoroughfares and roundabouts modelled on Canberra—was bleak and devoid of ordinary-looking Pakistanis. For reasons of theatre, not substance, we needed to travel elsewhere. Rawalpindi looked like Pakistan—teeming and noisy.

The booth we chose was at a government school a few blocks from the park where Bhutto had been killed. I was on edge and remained on the street for only as long as it took to film a piece to camera in one take: 'This polling station is in Rawalpindi,' I began, 'where Benazir Bhutto was assassinated last December. The city has also seen numerous bombings and suicide attacks throughout the campaign. So these people came here today with a real sense of fear and trepidation about how safe it is to come and vote.'

My script said far more about my preoccupations than those of the locals. 'In a country where the car bomb is the weapon of choice, it seemed extraordinary that vehicle traffic was allowed to get so close to crowds of would-be voters,' I intoned, before following up with sound bites of locals expressing the same outrage.

Anti-Musharraf parties won the election. Benazir Bhutto's Pakistan People's Party formed government shortly afterwards. Six months later Pervez Musharraf finally quit the presidency. And a month after Bhutto's widower, Zardari, the Dick Dastardly of Pakistan, a former prisoner convicted of plundering the state, became the nation's thirteenth president.

TWELVE
Darkness to daylight

IT'S AMAZING WHAT prescription medication can do for your state of mind. A day ago I was drowning in melancholy. Then the 'happy' pills kicked in, restoring my black sense of humour. I wrote an email to a friend describing the disadvantages of certain methods of suicide: 'I'm not one for heights,' I said, 'so I have had to rule out leaping from a tall building. I can't stand knives, so the Rome option is out.'

Today's newspaper reported that my accuser, Saini bin Saidi, was sentenced to ten months in jail for possession of ice. I don't know why but his sentencing made me feel better, like there is an end of sorts in sight. I told my friend that too: 'I'm not going to let this kill me. I'm going to come out of this a stronger me. You know it. I know it.'

Pass the pills—they're terrific mood enhancers.

• • • • •

IT HAD TO HAPPEN. Today I received a bill from the lawyers. It's the first instalment and there will be much more to pay before this case is over.

I don't have any qualms about paying for legal advice. I'm just shocked when the numbers are there on paper in expensive 'look at me, look at me' black and white. I have a lot of affection for Jeeming because I believe he is a sincere man who is also trying to save my neck. I think the world of Haq. He's a wily operator who, I'll wager, is doing most of the heavy lifting in this case.

Still, there is a passage from Paul Theroux's *Ghost Train to the Eastern Star* that comes to mind whenever I encounter a lawyer. It goes like this: 'Time is everything to a prostitute. As clock-watchers they are keener than lawyers, though the term "solicitor" applies to both, and they share the concept of billable hours, every minute needing to be accounted for in these foot-tapping, finger-drumming professions. The prostitute also shares the lawyer's fake sympathy, the apparent concern for your welfare, the initial buttonholing how-can-I-help-you? clucking, the pretence of help that is a way of ensnaring you and making you pay. In both cases, as long as you go on paying you have their full attention, but they are always in charge.'

• • • • •

I RECEIVED AN EMAIL from a former ABC foreign correspondent. His comments, about his own struggle with stress, reminded me of me: 'I couldn't cope well with the terrible events I'd find other people in,' he said. 'The direct threats to my life became insignificant. I was angry, frustrated, became quite arrogant and was terrible to live with.'

This is my reply: 'It's hard to see the daylight from the darkness at the moment. Being aware of being "mad" is worse than just being me and keeping secrets.'

• • • • •

I'M ON MY WAY to see a therapist, again, but I'm not looking forward to this session at all. I think I have therapy-fatigue. *Is there a therapist for that?* I'm thinking.

I've been seeing Dr Ang every week. I like Dr Ang—he gives me prescriptions for happy pills. I catch the train up to Karen's place for a chat every week, sometimes twice if she can fit me in. But there is a third wheel. Dr Ang has me seeing another psychologist called James, at the Mount Elizabeth Hospital. James is making me feel very bad. I've been to see him twice now, and each session ends with me walking out believing that I am a fake who needs to surrender to the authorities and plead guilty to all charges.

I'm with James now, sitting in a small, cold room overlooking the vertical air-conditioning vent for the main hospital building. There is a stepladder next to the shaft, to allow maintenance crews to reach the rooftop. I'm thinking about how many steps it takes to reach the rooftop when James's voice interrupts my concentration: 'Peter, I didn't see that many bodies in your stories.'

His tone is mocking. I am convinced that James thinks I've been making this up. I've been telling James about the number of bodies at the Bali bombings, so he asked to see a videotape of my stories. His reaction is suspicious and strange—I feel like I have to educate this bloke about television, as well as get his help. *Why am I paying $150 an hour for this?* I think.

'Of course you didn't.' I'm really irritated. 'What we witness is not what we show. We cannot show that much gore—we self-censor. Maybe ten per cent of the things we actually see end up on tape, and even less in the final cut of the story that is broadcast. The audience would go nuts if we showed them unvarnished reality.'

'I see.' James is nodding, but I can tell that he doesn't see at all. I feel like I have to justify everything to this guy. And I keep catching him stifling yawns and gazing up at the clock—as though he can't wait for this session to finish.

I'm clutching a cushion against my chest, a barrier between him and me. 'James, if you don't believe me, why are we here?'

'You think I don't believe you?'

'That's what you're saying, isn't it?'

He ignores my question. 'Peter, tell me more about your feelings about journalism.'

'My feelings?'

'Yes.'

'I hate journalism. I'm a liar. I don't help people. I hurt them.'

'Why do you say that?'

'I caused the Bali bombings.'

'You did?'

'Yes—well, not directly. But, you know, I wish for big stories to break. That means I'm to blame. That's bad, right?'

'But you didn't set off the bomb.'

'No. But we get a professional boost from someone else's misery. That's . . . that's evil, right?'

'No, it isn't.'

'It isn't?'

'No. Listen, Peter. There is no other way to say this—you're not that good. You are not God. You are not that powerful. You don't have that much influence. The Bali bombings happened—regardless of whether journalists got some sort of professional advantage out of the experience.'

I'm counting steps again. The rooftop is close. I wonder if you reach those stairs by the same elevator that I used today.

'Peter?'

'Yes.'

'What are you thinking about?'

'Death.'

'Whose?'

'Mine.'

• • • • •

A DAY LATER, I'M SITTING on another psychologist's settee. Clutching another psychologist's throw cushion.

'Do you get these at graduation?' I joke. They look like the cushions in James's office.

'What?' Karen has no idea what I'm talking about.

'Never mind,' I mutter. 'It was just a thought.'

'You were telling me your concerns about seeing too many experts?'

'Yes. I have to break it off with James.'

'It sounds like a bad romance.'

'Well, I'm not feeling the love, I can tell you.'

'Why not? If that's not too personal a question about another therapist.'

'He doesn't believe me, or at least I feel like he doesn't believe me. I know there is a difference.'

'Very perceptive.'

'Well, the thing is—I was telling him about how I felt that I was responsible for the Bali bombings.'

'And?'

'I know I'm not—now. But when that dream started, with the guy in the mortuary, I felt kind of responsible. Like me not helping him was some sort of metaphor about guilt.'

'Guilt about what?'

'Reporter guilt. The old story. You know—for us to have a good day, someone else has to have a bad one.'

'You feel that?'

'Sure I do.'

'But you don't think you "caused" the bombings?'

'No. Now, sitting in this room, I know that is nonsense. I know that really is nuts. But a few weeks ago—before all of this started unravelling—that was how I felt every time I had that dream.'

'Do you want to talk about that dream?'

'Not really.'

'That's okay.'

'I'm not sure that going back to that moment is going to help me right now. I'm afraid of that dream. I haven't had it for a few weeks, and I like it that way. I want to bury that dream.'

'Do you have the other nightmares?'

'Yes. Less so than before. Less now that I am on medication. Happy pills do wonders for this condition.'

'Yes, they do, don't they?'

'You see, Karen, the thing is that I feel trapped by this condition. I'm in this mental prison and I want to get out—that's what's occupying my thoughts right now. It's funny—the charges . . . I just feel like they belong in the future. I feel like they will work themselves out somehow.'

Karen is silent for a while. We've been going through a number of psychiatric conditions lately, comparing my situation to the textbook definitions of illnesses other than post-traumatic stress disorder, or PTSD. It's not that Karen has been trying to pathologise me. I've just been interested in some of these conditions, so we've talked about them in a roundabout way. I'm a bit concerned by some of the conditions we're touching upon. They're a bit more serious than PTSD. We've talked about schizoid personality disorder (we've decided that I haven't got that) and attention deficit disorder (the jury is out on that one).

I went home after our last session and Googled schizoid. This is what it said: 'Schizoid personality disorder [SPD] is a personality disorder characterised by a lack of interest in social relationships, a tendency towards a solitary lifestyle, secretiveness, and emotional coldness.' The condition is extremely rare, with a prevalence estimated at less than one per cent of the general population.

One of the characteristics of people with SPD is they have trouble expressing anger, according to the main diagnostic manual of the American Psychiatric Association. Now that made me laugh out loud. Anger is an emotion I can do comfortably, even now. (Laughter is another emotion not often displayed by those with SPD, so I'm guessing that I am off the hook again.)

• • • • •

IT'S THREE DAYS AFTER my session with Karen. Today I'm back in the gloomy wood-panelled Subordinate Court for the first time since the media mugged me on the front steps. After I got out of the taxi, I was followed by a single television camera and a single press photographer—just one from each medium.

That means I'm officially demoted to 'pool coverage', where each network pays a share for a single freelance cameraman to cover the event. It's a sign that the editorial interest in my case has diminished to the point where all that matters now is the verdict. That's how it works with court cases—one minute you're all over the front page, and the next you're a sidebar item on page five next to the advert for the weekly grocery specials.

'Good morning, Peter.' It's Haq, all dressed up in a black suit. 'Just take a seat and wait for me. I'm going into the judge's private chambers to meet with him and the DPP.'

There are several reporters sitting behind me in the public gallery. They must not have covered the case from the start, or they don't recognise me from the photos. Or they don't care.

'So, how is this case going to pan out?' says one voice.

'Beats me. He's Aussie. Maybe they'll do a diplomatic deal,' says a woman with a high-pitched Chinese accent. She's a local.

'No chance.' That's a self-assured American voice. Maybe it's the guy from Associated Press. 'Look at Corby. No one's coming to rescue her.'

I take a peek and see a policeman sitting in the back row. I remember him from the prison hospital—I think he escorted me to Changi prison on the Friday night. He's Malay. Seemed like a nice guy, for a cop.

Haq is back, and he's got a poker face. He's scanning the gallery with suspicion, like there are ears peeled to overhear this conversation. 'Come with me.'

We're stepping outside, shadowed by several reporters with note-books in hand. They're ready to pounce, but they're giving us space.

'Here's the deal,' says Haq. 'The police are prepared to hand over the first information report and your statements. But you have to pay up first.'

'I have to actually buy my own statements?'

'Yes. They wanted to know if you were still in hospital—I told them you were in court.'

'Okay.'

'We have two weeks to make representations—to give them something on paper in response to the charges. Then, two weeks after that, we're back here on the twenty-fifth of September.'

'Okay, so we have two weeks to get a report together—to cobble together a report from Dr Ang, and from you, to make a case, for what exactly?'

'The most important thing—the only thing right now—is getting them to withdraw this trafficking charge. If we can get them to under-stand that this guy is lying—that you didn't sell him drugs—then that would be a major victory.'

'And the other stuff?'

'Peter, listen—the other charges, they aren't going away. You know that. You were caught with the stuff and it was in your system. You've already indicated to the police that you're going to plead guilty. That stuff is small beer. Trafficking, Peter, you have to get them to withdraw trafficking. That's what we're going to go hell for leather on.'

I'm putting on my most impenetrable expression, trying not to react to what I'm hearing. The reporters are in the background, taking notes, assessing my composure again. It's the same game as before, when I was first in court. Observation is the key to reporting in a case bereft of information—how does the accused react after a consultation with their lawyer? If they react badly, you can be pretty certain that the case is not going as they'd planned. I'm not prepared to give the game away—not here, not now.

'Let's get out of here.' Haq is leading me to the lift. Reporters, summoning up the courage to ask him questions while we are trapped with them in the lift, are following us. That's a smart move—the kind I'd pull.

'How is the case going, Mr Haq?'

'Fine.'

'Any indications of a trial date?'

'None at all, we're just in the process of exchanging information. It's quite early days yet.'

'How about you, Peter?' It's the Chinese woman. Her halitosis is not endearing me to this close-quarters chitchat.

'I'm not talking today, but thanks.'

Gasping for clean air, Haq and I make for a taxi, ignoring the camera crew chasing us down the steps. 'Peter . . .' He's got something to tell me. 'This trafficking charge. It's five years minimum, right? There are no deals. The judges have to give people the full five years. You understand? That's why knocking this trafficking thing off is the most critical step right now.'

'I understand.'

'Okay. Because, on top of the mandatory minimum, there are five strokes to contend with too. I've seen the after-effects of caning of prisoners. It's bad news, man. You don't want to have to go through that.'

• • • • •

THE TAXI IS DROPPING me at the Paragon Medical Centre off Orchard Road. I'm on my way to see Dr Ang. I can't get the thought of caning out of my mind. It's brutal. Until recently I thought that caning in Singapore was like being caned at school, copping 'six of the best'. But what I'm learning is quite different, and quite frightening.

We have the British to thank for Singapore's practice of judicial caning—they introduced it into British Malaya during colonial times. Lee Kuan Yew wastes no time reminding westerners of this fact whenever Amnesty or some other human rights group makes a complaint about the cruelty of this form of punishment. What old Harry Lee, as the British called him, neglects to mention is that, under his regime, the use of the cane has been expanded dramatically. Since Singapore won independence, the number of crimes that can be punished with caning has increased from a handful to more than thirty, as has the minimum number of strokes a prisoner can receive in one session. It is now twenty-four.

'Come in, Peter.' I'm back in Dr Ang's office. It feels familiar to me now—the books lining his wall, the trinkets of oriental art and philosophy, and the gigantic computer monitor, on which Dr Ang brings up reports and photographs.

'Is this mega-screen some sort of shock therapy?' I ask.

'Huh?'

'Never mind. I'm feeling a lot better, now that I'm on the happy pills. They seem to be keeping me from feeling as desperate as I was a few weeks back.'

'That's good. And how is it going with Karen?'

'Okay, I guess. I'm not sure how you measure progress, though. We've been exploring some of the experiences I have had, but we're not really dealing with the nightmares directly. I'm not ready for that.'

'That's understandable.'

'So we're talking about . . . I don't know—my life, I guess. I talk a lot about all sorts of things that don't really seem to narrow in on dealing with my nightmares. But afterwards I feel better, you know?'

'How are you sleeping?'

'Better. To be honest, I sleep better when Mazlee is there. When he is away, I don't know—it just gets away from me. I wake up a lot in the first hour—sometimes my legs are spinning, like I'm running. It's the mortuary dream. Then I can go for days and have no problems.

I'm pretty sure that the frequency of nightmares is less since I began taking medication. That helps a lot.'

'Good. How are you feeling within yourself? Do you still think about suicide ideas?'

'No.'

'That's good.'

'But I'm struggling with this "awareness". You know, it's painful to know that you are mentally ill, or at least are having problems. You know what I mean?'

'I do.'

'You see, before I was blissfully ignorant. Not knowing, ignorant, and I was able to function. Or at least I could try to function. But now that we're talking about PTSD—giving it a name, saying it out loud—it has become powerful. I'm not sure I feel better to be diagnosed. Being ignorant, and sick, was easier. I mean, it was something that I could— that I did—ignore. Right? And isn't that how I got into this mess in the first place, eh?'

'Yes it is.' He's sitting forward. 'But Peter, you have to give it time. A diagnosis is nothing more than a guide for us to help you—to usher you in the right direction. You are basically a strong person—you have it in you to find your own way out of this.'

'I do?'

'Yes, you do.'

'But, Dr Ang, the thing is this: I can deal with the legal stuff. That's away in the future. Right now I'm in a mental prison. That's what I need to get out of, fast. I'm not happy here.' I'm tapping my forehead.

'Then that's what we will work on. At the same time as we explain to the police that what happened—that what you did—was not "you" but a mentally ill person. There is a difference, and I believe that my report on you will show them that difference.'

'I hope you're right.'

THIRTEEN

Grand Prix week

THE MEDIA HYPE SURROUNDING the first-ever night-time Formula One Grand Prix race, which is to be staged in Singapore, is at fever pitch. The king of morning radio, seemingly anointed as spruiker-in-chief, goes by the absurd nickname the 'Flying Dutchman'. His real name is Mark van Cuylenburg. 'FD', as he likes to be called, glories in an on-air persona that is pure caveman. It is raw-meat sexism of the type that makes the hair on your arms stand on end.

FD borders on open misogyny. But to go that far would, presumably, risk alienating half the available audience. FD's jokes about 'the weaker sex' and 'hommer-sexuals' are bada-bing hilarious! FD has an explosively forced laugh, something between a cat hacking up fur balls and someone trying to make the loudest 'look at me' noise at a party.

This guy has been oozing golly-gee factoids and statistics about motor racing all week. One wonders if FD is paid extra for every F1 reference as the program is nothing more than a life support system for F1 tedium. For the public relations operatives down at F1 headquarters, boosterism like this is surely the stuff of wet dreams. I can't stand it—listening to the Flying Dutchman hector and bully and blow hard makes me feel the need to take a long shower.

'Jesus Christ, is there someone else we can listen to?'

Mazlee looks up, surprised at the vehemence of my fury. 'Why?'

'Don't you find this guy totally offensive?'

Mazlee shrugs his shoulders. 'I like the music.'

'So do I, when this idiot shuts up.'

I go up and down the dial searching for relief, but I only find more broadcasters—women who sound like Californian Valley Girls—singing the advantages of staging 'the world's first night-time race'. Disadvantages must exist, but they never rate a mention on state-controlled media. Intelligent and lively debate is not allowed lest people get dangerous ideas about thinking for themselves all of a sudden.

'The way these chicks purr, everything sounds like soft porn.' I'm laughing and flicking the dial. 'Maz, can you tune this thing into rebel radio, or something? I want to hear what the "free thinkers" in Singapore say about Formula One.'

'Oh, puhlease. Just ignore it.'

'Oh, I forgot—the free thinkers are in jail, or exile. Or dead.'

'Peter. Just ignore the radio.'

He's not keen on my jokes about political freedom in Singapore. Except they aren't jokes. I'm thinking, *I am suffocating in Singapore. What did Richard Burton say about islands? 'Small islands are all large prisons.' Yeah, too right they are.*

It's as if the whole Singapore radio spectrum has been reading from the same set of talking points issued by the Ministry of Propaganda. Which is possible in Singapore. Two players dominate the media scene: Singapore Press Holdings, which has close links to the ruling party, has a virtual monopoly of the newspaper industry; and MediaCorp, owned by a state investment agency, operates eight television channels and thirteen radio stations. The hive mind is at work—the Singapore media has a collective consciousness. That's the beauty of a pocket-sized, authoritarian state—it's that much easier to keep the mob under control when the few radio and TV outlets are all, by hook or crook, party-controlled.

When he was a struggling opposition politician, Lee Kuan Yew thought differently about media freedom. 'If you believe that men should be free, then, they should have the right of free association, of free speech, of free publication,' he said in April 1955, adding, 'no law should permit those democratic processes to be set at nought'. This is one of the many contradictions of Lee, a man whose talent for soaring rhetoric seemed to dry up over the years. I can see why people of a certain generation find Lee an inspiration. I can also see why he inspires contempt, especially with his self-serving U-turns like: 'Freedom of the press . . . must be subordinated . . . to the primary purpose of an elected government.'

'Why are we so politically correct indoors?' I ask. 'No one can hear us.'

Mazlee is fearful in Singapore, worrying about little things from spiders to spies. Last week we had a row after I walked naked near the balcony window. 'Put on some clothes,' he yelled. 'If the neighbours see you, they will call the police.'

'Really? So a person who is minding their own business, parading in the privacy of their own home, as God intended—they can get charged? But the pervert peeping Tom gawking at you—they get a pat on the back for being a good citizen?'

'Yes. It's the law. You must respect it.'

'That's fucked up, Mazlee!' I had proceeded to range from room to room, bloated on fury. 'That's George-Orwell-fucked-up!'

Here we are a week later, and we're doing it again. We tiptoe around this apartment, paying obeisance to a cloak of invisible oppression, the kind that seeps into your mind and seizes control. The kind that makes people fear thoughts and second-guess actions. In Singapore, be careful what you think—before you know it, those thoughts will be on your lips. And then everyone will know you're a rebel.

I'm surrendering. 'I'm going to have a shower.'

Mazlee has put the radio back onto Class 95 FM. I can hear the Flying Dutchman laughing again. Resistance is futile.

• • • • •

I'M DUE IN COURT in a few days. This is the email Jeeming received from the court officials, addressed to me: 'I have been directed to inform you that the Pre Trial Conference date on 25 September 2008 at 9am in Court 2 is to remain. Defence Counsel is requested to inform your client and his bailor accordingly.' In other words: be there. No excuses.

We expect that the prosecution will respond to a defence submission by Jeeming, seeking the withdrawal of all charges with the exception of the single possession charge. It's a big ask; but even withdrawing all other charges and maintaining the possession offence still guarantees the accused jail-time in Singapore—there is no bargaining your way out of trouble in this place. Jail sentences for drug possession have become mandatory.

In his submission Jeeming drew heavily on a report prepared by Dr Ang, which states in part:

> Peter has been having symptoms of mild Post-Traumatic Stress Disorder (PTSD) for the last few years but they were largely undetected, undiagnosed and untreated . . . Like many media workers covering traumatic events and disasters, he was exposed to the brutal killing, sight and smell of the dead, cries for help and the suffering of the wounded, wailing relatives identifying dead bodies at the mortuary, relatives grieving over their dead ones. These traumatic events would elicit intermittent episodes of flashbacks, nightmares and dreams in Peter but it was only from Jan 2008 onwards that he noticed that such episodes were getting more intense, more frequent and unbearable. He was also feeling more anxious than usual and his mood was low most of the time. He could not concentrate well and his productivity at work deteriorated.
>
> Owing to the increased frequency of his nightmares and bizarre dreams, he was getting either not enough sleep or disturbed sleep. As a result of poor sleep or insomnia, he found himself unable to concentrate well the next day.
>
> Paradoxically, although he wished to sleep well or for longer periods, he was also afraid of going to sleep because of the dreams and nightmares. Hence, each night was a struggle for him.
>
> He also discovered that from the beginning of 2008 onwards, he would lapse into periods of feeling dazed and detached and then could not recollect what happened afterwards (so-called 'dissociative states'). He was feeling tense and restless throughout most of the day as he just could not feel relaxed or rested.
>
> He tried to cope on his own by exercising and relaxing but he continued to feel anxious and irritable most of the time. He said there

was an occasion in Feb 2008 when he took ice (Methamphetamine) in Bangkok 'just to be stimulated and to keep myself awake so that I don't have to face the consequences of having nightmares and dreams'. It was purely consumed out of curiosity and a desperate attempt at self-medication to control or avoid the nightmares.

After he discovered that ice could make him feel less anxious and also avoid the nightmares, he decided to get some more. On 9 July 2008, whilst in Singapore, he managed to meet up with Kim to get some ice . . .

He was neither a chronic drug abuser nor someone who was selling ice for profit. I hope the authorities concerned will seriously consider the chronic and complex nature of his Post-Traumatic Stress Disorder in deliberating the case.

I picked up a few mistakes after Dr Ang's report went to the DPP. I tried ice for the first time in Singapore, not Bangkok. I was in the city for a family reunion visit with Kirsty and my son, Tom. The night before they arrived I went to a party organised by some friends of friends. A few people were sitting on lounges, arranged around a coffee table. They were bent forward, fascinated by something on the table. I wandered over to see what was so interesting.

There was a guest cutting lines of white powder. I assumed it was coke, and said as much. The guy with the busy credit card didn't look up. 'No, it's ice. I've crushed it up to make lines, to share.' He laughed. 'Looks like coke, feels better.'

They were the magic words. 'Better how?' I asked.

'Happier.'

'I'm up for *happier.*'

I was offered the last line, after two or three others had hoovered up the rest. It hurt, as though someone was stabbing the inside of my nose with a thousand knives. I held my fingers against my nose, in case of unsightly bleeding—that would be very uncool.

The 'Kim' referred to in Ang's report was the guest at the party cutting up lines with the credit card. My accuser, Saini bin Saidi, was at that party too. It was Saini who provided me with Kim's number months later, in July, in Singapore. That's how I came to meet Kim again, on the street, in Wheelock Place, a few days before my arrest. I had suspected, correctly, that Kim might be able to supply ice.

I can only assume that Saini was another happy customer, although Saini never told me that. I told the police that Saini was protecting someone else by implicating me. I now believe that person was Kim. I don't know what happened to Kim. After I was arrested the police seized my telephone and sent him text messages. Entrapment begets entrapment, I suppose. Jeff Lee made a veiled remark to me a few weeks ago about how Kim was 'in big trouble'. When I asked what he meant, Lee said, 'This is not his first case.'

People have asked me whether I was a regular drug user. I think I could have become one had I lived among the temptations of the developed world, but I then lived in the Indian capital, New Delhi, which is not in the developed world. India is a planet in a galaxy far, far away from the decadent west.

In two years in India the only drug I encountered was a stinky block of hashish—and the perfume alone made me want to throw up. Years earlier I had tried hard to inhale at university in Australia, but only managed to embarrass myself be going a vile shade of green and disappearing into the bathroom to heave my guts. The glorious isolation of planet India probably did me a huge favour. What happened in Singapore was a perfect storm of circumstances: I was here on an unscheduled visit and unwell. I acted unwisely. I made a huge mistake.

Jeeming's submission to the DPP emphasised the absurdity of Saini's allegation that someone with a full-time professional career would be motivated to sell a drug in such a minuscule quantity that it would fill no more than the nail of an adult's pinkie finger, for the grand sum of seventy-five Singapore dollars. At that rate, it would have taken me a millennium to become Pablo Escobar, and I do not have that kind of patience.

• • • • •

'IT'S LIKE A TRAIN WRECK, eh?' It's my Canadian friend, Michael McAuliffe. He is in full conversational flight. As he talks both hands are up and out, waving and wobbling like penguin arms. 'And what you have to do, okay, is pick up all of the tiny little pieces of the train wreck and put them back together. Right?' He's sucking back on a cigarette with vacuum force. Through the plume: 'But you do it one by one. It takes time.'

Michael is holding forth on the subject of PTSD and recovery. He arrived today from Bangkok for a morale-boosting two-day visit. He's been going through PTSD counselling after a number of years of tough and confronting assignments with his media company, the Canadian Broadcasting Corporation, CBC.

Michael and I worked closely together at the tsunami, so he's seen firsthand the events that primed my condition and his own. But when I began living in India, Michael and I started to lose touch. What I hadn't quite understood, until now, is how profoundly PTSD had affected him, and how he had been confronting that private hell in the months that we were drifting away from each other.

'PTSD robs your confidence—you don't any have faith in yourself,' Michael explains. So when someone says, "Hey, you have PTSD," you stop and say: "No, I don't. I'm just a fuck-up." It takes time to accept your anger or whatever behaviour you adopt in reaction to the pressures of the work we do.'

'I did. I do,' I say. 'I'm still not quite there. I still can't quite bring myself to say, "Hello, I'm Peter Lloyd, and I have post-traumatic stress disorder."'

'That's right. But you will.'

We're at the courtyard bar of Raffles Hotel in Singapore. Michael loves the good life—the wine, the food and the bon vivant conversation. When I lived in Bangkok we had several dinners where the end of the evening is a booze-addled mystery. One minute I'd be sitting at a restaurant as Michael ordered a fourth bottle of expensive French red wine, and the next I'd be in bed, violently hung-over and uncertain as to how I reached home. I fear today could end like that.

'It sounds like the five stages of grief: denial, anger, bargaining, depression and acceptance,' I say.

'Yeah. Except with PTSD the order is different.'

'I'll drink to that!'

There is something validating in speaking to somebody who has experienced PTSD. There are certain common experiences—such as being aware that something is not right in your life, but being unable to identify it—that sufferers relate to. It is comforting to meet someone with similar anxieties, fears and phobias. Misery, I suppose, loves company.

Yet at the same time, I'm aware of how judgemental I've been. I had assumed Michael's long silences in communicating with me by phone or email were a snub of some kind. I had not stopped to consider that something was going desperately wrong with his life, that he was deliberately isolating himself as the condition enveloped him and that this might be a sign that Michael needed his friends. Here I am, propped up on a bar stool, telling my tale.

'So he's sitting there, staring at me like he's seen something really hideous, like a massive pimple.' I'm telling Michael about my therapist, James. 'And I can see his jaw flexing as he stifles a yawn. Can you believe it? I'm paying $150 an hour to a guy that *I'm* boring to death.'

'Ditch him.'

'I did.'

'You have to talk to someone that you have a connection to—and you have to stop talking to so many people.'

'I know. I have.'

'Who do you see?'

'My main—my only—therapist is Karen Gosling. She's Australian, and spent years doing trauma counselling in hospital emergency rooms.'

'Yuk!'

'Precisely. And I'm seeing Dr Ang every week to check in with him, and keep up the prescription meds. He's supervising the work with Karen—they're in touch with each other. You know, talking about me behind my back.'

'How are things with Mazlee?'

'Difficult.'

'Why?'

'We're not talking about "it". We talk about everything that is rosy and happy, but nothing of substance. Nothing that is tough, like, *Why did you buy drugs and drag my good name into this?*'

'I see.'

'Yeah. So, you know how it is. He pretends that he's not really mad at me and I pretend that I don't notice how mad he isn't being.'

'Give him time. Maybe he needs to join you at Karen's and talk about how this has affected him.'

'I've invited him. He won't respond. He nods, so I know he can hear me. But when I have an appointment, so does he—across town.'

FOURTEEN

Deal or no deal?

I'M BACK AT KAREN'S for another session of therapy.

'It's coffee for me today,' I say cheerfully as I bound down the steps.

'Good to hear,' says Karen. 'And the gingernut biscuits are inside.'

I'm directed into the bunker of Karen's house, where she holds counselling sessions. It's hot and the air-conditioning is not working. She's explaining, before I even make a comment. 'We will have to work with the door open today, I'm afraid. The power is off because the electricity company is doing some work.'

'Why's that?'

'Our bills have skyrocketed lately and they're trying to figure out why. We think someone has been tapping into our service illegally. They're doing a trace down the lines as we speak. It's all very mysterious.'

'Indeed.'

'Now, what about the mystery of Peter Lloyd—how is he today?'

'How is he today? He is doing okay, he thinks.'

Karen is laughing. 'Sounds to me like the "Two Peters" are here in the room together.'

'Could be.'

The 'Two Peters' is Karen's description of episodes of dissociation, periods where I was hovering next to, or outside of, my body and observing with the detachment of another person.

Last week Karen pulled out some notes that said: 'Dissociation is an escape from overwhelming trauma, an escape from consciousness

. . . Trauma is the loss of faith that there is order and continuity to life that occurs when one loses the sense of having a safe place to deal with frightening emotions or experiences. Dissociation is a first-line defence to trauma of all kinds and a long-term basic coping strategy for ongoing or re-occurring trauma. It is an alteration of consciousness because the pain of consciousness/reality is too much to bear. In other words, it helps the person to contain the pain of trauma . . . Dissociation is an escape when there is no escape—an escape which serves important adaptive functions, but does so at great cost, a fragmentation or splitting of the personality that is usually integrated and coping.'

'Karen, I need to tell you about the night that I arrived here in Singapore,' I say to her now.

'All right.'

'The doctor in Jakarta had wound me up—he had said that my eye looked so infected that it looked like there was permanent damage. He was wrong, of course. It was just a fug of infection, but I didn't know that at the time. I was off my head with anxiety. The idea of losing my eyesight was like a metaphor for everything that felt wrong in my life. Like I was losing control from the moment Benazir died.'

'Go on.'

'So I remember getting on the plane in Jakarta, and sinking back into the seat. After take-off they dimmed the lights. I felt like I was floating away from myself. I looked out the windows and saw stars. And I had this overwhelming desire to fall backwards, out of the aircraft.'

'You wanted to die?'

'I wanted to *disappear*.'

'And not come back?'

'Yes. If the plane had exploded in mid-air at that moment in time, I would have surrendered to my fate. It would have been a relief. It would have been a release.'

'You sound like you were in an altered state, before you've even landed.'

'I was numb. I can remember the taxi ride to the city. But after that, it's a blur.'

'The other day, you said you don't remember buying drugs.'

'That's right. I'm not saying I didn't. The police have arrested the guy I bought the drugs from. I'm not saying that it isn't true. I'm saying that *I* don't remember the transaction. I called a mate to get the dealer's number. After that—I don't know.'

'Have you told the police this?'

'Yes.'

'What did they say?'

'Nothing. It doesn't matter—Karen, I did it. I'm just blocking it out.'

'I don't know that "blocking it out" is quite the way I'd put it.'

'How would you put it then?'

' "Peter" has morals and values—correct?'

'Yes, sure.'

' "Pete"—this dissociative persona—is carefree and reckless. "Pete" did what he had to do to get through this trauma. "Pete" is a traumatised part of you.'

'I don't like "Pete" very much.'

'Is he here?'

'No—I told him to fuck off.'

Karen's laughing. 'Well, let's hope he stays that way.'

'I think that I'm being kept steady by the anti-depressants. Happy pills are keeping "Pete" at bay.'

'They work miracles.'

'You can say that again. I tried going off them a few days back and got into bother straight away.'

'How?'

'I got up one Saturday morning and decided that I didn't need medication, that I was going to do this on my own.'

'Trying to be a hero, eh?'

'Kind of. So I was due in town to meet someone—it was Kirsty. She'd come up to see me for a few days.'

'What happened?'

'I got on the bus at Upper Thomson Road all happy and content. And then I just started to shrink.'

'How do you mean *shrink*?'

'I could feel myself sort of splitting into two—the smaller me was sitting next to the larger me, who was staring out the window. I felt cold and numb. By the time I got off the bus in Orchard Road I was a mess. I could feel the pressure of adrenalin coursing through my chest; I felt sick, and my hands were all clammy.'

'What happened next?'

'I'm not sure. I sat with Kirsty and she could tell that I wasn't okay.'

'Where were you?'

'At Starbucks. So I had a strong coffee.'

'Did that help?'

'Not really. I just had to settle down and think about my breathing, and get my thoughts together. Then a few minutes after that I felt the episode end, like I had drifted back inside myself and felt a "whole" person again.'

'Sounds like classic dissociation.'

'Something else happened that morning.'

'What?'

'Mazlee says he called me, and had a conversation with me while I was on the bus.'

'And?'

'I don't remember any of it.'

'The phone call?'

'Yeah. None of it. As far as I remember, it didn't happen—although Mazlee says it did. That really scared me, Karen.'

'It is scary. Are you back on the meds?'

'Yes. But I can't live like this. I need to get out of mental prison before they send me to a real one.'

When Karen and I began working together we spent a few sessions on the anatomy of the brain. I learned a lot about how the things we see with our eyes are received by the brain and stored away. It was a bit like taking apart a laptop and seeing the hard drive's connections to the electrical panels and keyboard. In particular I learned about the amygdala, which is a nut-sized part of the brain that processes and holds emotional memory and memories of emotional events. Memories of this kind can elicit a fear response—rapid heartbeat, increased respiration and the release of the stress hormone, adrenalin, which has been unleashed into my system in massive doses over the last few years, to the point where I now feel a visceral sense of being overdosed by my own body.

It would be nice to think that you could switch off the amygdala when you go on a tough assignment, as a way of blocking the mind from remembering all of the terrible things that you're about to witness. But that's not such a good idea, as science has shown. Early research in the nineteenth century on rhesus monkeys who had the little nut cut out of their brains showed alarming behavioural effects—they became hypersexual, lost all sense of fear and began shoving inappropriate objects into their mouths.

Sitting on the lounge watching Karen at the whiteboard helped me understand my world. It was like grabbing a torch and heading down to the basement, to examine the foundations of the house. Everything upstairs makes perfect sense when you see what's holding up the building. We talked about the nature of dreams too. My favourite dream trivia was this pearl of wisdom: when we snore, we're not dreaming.

· · · · ·

'I DON'T KNOW WHAT TO do about Mazlee!' I'm talking on the telephone to Kirsty, in Canberra. 'He's so passive-aggressive at times. I got off the phone with my lawyers the other day, and it is obviously bad news. And he just shimmy-shammies around the apartment like he's heard nothing. It's obvious that I'm upset. And you know what he says?'

'What?'

'He says, "Hurry up and have a shower. We're due at dinner at seven." But I don't want another dinner—I want an exit stamp and the first flight out of this freak show.'

'Calm down.'

We're quiet for a few seconds. 'Kirsty, he's killing me with the silences. He won't talk to me about what happened. It's like it never did. He is capable of existing in a little fantasy world, where everything is perfect and lovely and the flowers are all arranged just so. If we all just hold our noses we can pretend that a dirty great elephant hasn't taken a giant shit on the living-room carpet.'

'Peter, steady on.'

'He is. He never gets angry. He won't acknowledge that he is really pissed off with me at all. He just sits there and looks at me with that look of profound and solemn disappointment. Like a disappointed daddy. It kills me. He won't express himself. He won't engage me. Not the way we did.'

'He's not like us—but that doesn't make him wrong.'

'Oh, great. The wife is defending my boyfriend for being the iceman!'

'Nice phrase.'

'You know what I mean.'

'I do.'

'Jesus, you're enjoying this!'

'I am.'

'Fuck you too!'

'Fuck you three!'

I'm pouring a glass of Shaw & Smith sauvignon blanc. I've been drinking a bottle a day lately. When Mazlee is away I drink a bottle and a half and fall onto the bed in a white wine haze. I don't seem to be having many nightmares with that much booze in me, along with the doctor's magic happy pills.

I know this is no way to live, not in the long term. Yet, by taking my self-medication to this level, I have become a more acceptable and mainstream fuck-up, doping on legal pills and booze instead of dabbling in the shadows of illicit drugs. I'm acting out the lifestyle of the broken-down celebrity, or the bored, lonely and sad middle-class housewife.

'So. What do I do with this guy?' I ask Kirsty.

'Peter—he's just processing.'

'Processing? What kind of namby-pamby crap is that?'

'The kind you need to think about. Have you tried talking to him?'

'Yes.'

'Confronting him?'

'Ha!'

'Why?'

'Mazlee doesn't do confrontation. I'm talking to a passive-aggressive gay man who swans around the apartment talking about the really big issues of life, like, "Isn't it a nice sunset." Fuck me. Fuck the sunset.'

'Oh dear. That is so gay.' Kirsty is gulping wine too. I can hear it. 'Listen, Pete, he's coping in the only way he knows.'

'His "coping" is killing me.'

'Don't be a drama queen.'

'Don't pretend you'd tolerate the silent treatment.'

'Touché, my friend. Touché!' She's pouring herself another glass. 'Hang in there. Things will sort themselves out. And take a word of advice, eh? Don't be too tough on Mazlee. He loves you. If he didn't, you wouldn't be out of jail and he wouldn't have you living there in his apartment.'

'You're right. You're right. I know you're right,' I say, pausing for the effect of those words on Kirsty.

'You're quoting *When Harry Met Sally* at me?' She's up for a trivia challenge.

'Carrie Fisher,' I respond. 'But where and when?'

'When she's talking to Sally in the bookstore,' Kirsty confirms, adding softly, 'And still your favourite movie, eh? Even though you're a fag?'

'Of all time.'

'I love you.'

'Love you too. Goodnight!'

• • • • •

WE'RE OUT TO DINNER, at this new Thai restaurant called Kha. It's just had the grand opening and the reviews in the newspaper are fulsome. Kha is part of a phrase in the traditional female Thai greeting—*Sawadee kha*. Boys say *Sawadee krap* but, amusingly, when most foreigners are learning Thai they get it mixed up, so half the time we men come off as little girlies. Since I'm in Singapore and my Thai accent is horrible, I'm sticking to English tonight.

I'm sitting opposite Sophie, Mazlee's downstairs neighbour. She's a banker from France who has been living in Singapore for a few years now. Mazlee and Sophie are very good friends. I like Sophie, but I can tell that she's a bit sick of my long face.

Sophie is—fortunately for her—naive about matters criminal. The other day she asked me whether I would have access to email in jail. I had to break it to her that not only would I be temporarily offline, but also that there were no TV sets in the cell in Singapore.

'I'm heading for hard labour,' I explained.

'Oh my God!' she said, in a remarkably exaggerated *'Allo 'Allo!* accent. 'That's terrible. Can they do that?'

Mazlee is sitting next to Sophie, across the table. He's sending daggers my way. 'What the fuck?' I mouth, raising my hands to demonstrate confusion.

I'm sitting next to Natalie Haldermann. She's Swiss. Natalie came to hospital to visit me during the lost week of psychiatric treatment and we've struck up a good friendship. Every now and then I catch sight of her looking at me longingly, like I am a disappointment for switching sides. Either that or she's just feeling pity at my stupidity. Who can tell with girls? They're hard to read. Not like boys. And not like Mazlee. His moody silence is coming across the table loud and clear.

'Oh, is that an iPhone?' He's gushing over people at the end of the table.

Another couple, Peter Holbein and his wife Caroline, occupy those seats. They are also from Switzerland. They've gotten to know me through Natalie. They are a lot of fun, and I'm sure the notoriety of knowing me is going to provide them with dinner party talking points for some time to come. They're getting the 'Oh, what a fascinating new phone' bullshit from Mazlee.

Okay, I think, *two can play that game*. I'm the only diner who has lived in Thailand, so I've been elected to order the food. I'm going to get as many dishes that Mazlee dislikes onto this table if it's the last thing I do.

'Okay.' I've summoned the waiter. 'Tod poh phia—*song*. Kai hor bai toey—*sam*. And tod man poo—*song*.'

I'm feeling pretty good about my pronunciation, but the waiter is staring at me like I had just asked him to undress and rub soy sauce all over his body. 'Sorry, lah—I'm Chinese.'

I can hear sniggers, but I'm not rising to the bait. 'Okay. We will have two orders of spring rolls and crab cakes, and three chicken in pandan leaf.'

'And for main course?'

'Thai beef salad, red duck curry, soft-shell crab, and spicy pomelo salad.' *Now*, I think, *for a dish best served cold.* 'How about wok-fried vegetables.' Mazlee's eyebrow just arches slightly, but he doesn't blink. 'Two serves!'

Still nothing—he's holding his nerve. He can't possibly complain publicly about an innocuous vegetable order. But I know I will hear about it later. He's not fond of vegetable plates—he calls it cow food. He's not impressed by my latent vegetarianism and rolls his eyes when I order vege dishes, like daddy seeing his child through a precocious adolescent phase from which I need to recover.

'I can't stand the way they do that here.' It's the other Peter complaining about something in Singapore. My ears have pricked up, like a dog that has just heard a whistle.

'Yes, I agree,' I say, and lean in for the kill.

• • • • •

THE NEXT MORNING, there are three of us in the apartment: me and Mazlee and the heavy silence that followed us home from dinner. I feel like there is an intruder in the house, and someone needs to call for help.

'Why didn't you sit next to me last night?' Maz asks.

'Is that what this is all about?'

'No.'

'So what gives?'

'You're so negative.'

'How?'

'This is my country. Why do you have to say what you think all the time?'

'Because it's what I think!'

'I don't like it.'

'Mazlee, I didn't start the conversation about Singapore last night—Peter did. And Natalie.'

'But you joined in.'

'Sure I did—it's called "conversation". People exchange opinions and views, and they test each other. It's not set in stone. It's just talking.'

'I don't like being the only Singaporean sitting at a table and hearing all these foreigners criticise. It's too much.'

'Mazlee, we were also critical of our own countries. As I recall, there was a pretty robust conversation about Australians and racism. Do you hear me complaining about that?'

'No. But that's you. I'm not comfortable with these criticisms.'

'Mazlee, criticism is a normal, healthy function of a free mind. Singapore is out of step, not the rest of us. You guys have so many no-go topics that it's impossible to have a discussion about politics or government. Jesus Christ, just saying the words "Lee Kuan Yew" around Singaporeans makes you freeze and look for the nearest exit. It is stupid.'

'So am I stupid too?'

'What?'

'If Singapore is such a stupid place, then I must be stupid too. I must be no good.'

'Maz, that is not what I meant. Come on. Please—I'm sorry if I hurt your feelings.'

He's left the room. But the silence is still here.

$$\bullet\ \bullet\ \bullet\ \bullet\ \bullet$$

'GOOD GRIEF. Some of these people are so uninformed about the world.' Ed Roy has arrived from Sydney, bringing a refreshing level of scepticism about the inhabitants of the Republic of Singapore. 'I've been talking to people about Burma, and you know what? They haven't got a clue what kind of country Burma is. They pretend there is no repression, no dictatorship. Hey, it's all hunky-dory over there.'

Ed is a talented chef who happens to earn a living as a broadcast journalist at the ABC. Indian-born but in some senses more Australian than the kangaroo or emu on the coat of arms, Ed tells me that both animals have one trait in common: neither can go backwards. Trust a man who delights in cooking all kinds of animal species to know such outback trivia.

'Tell me about it, brother.' I'm warming to one of my themes. 'This is where the butchers of Burma bank their loot and go for the annual poke in their prostate.'

'Exactly. Lee's regime turns a blind eye to the fact that Burma is a narco-state—Harry doesn't mind having them to a state dinner—and then he hangs the poor buggers who get caught trafficking Burma's only export commodity.'

'It's a little contradictory, eh?' I chuckle.

We're walking to the Subordinate Court. It's the twenty-fifth of September. Two days before the Grand Prix blows a hole in the ozone layer, and ten minutes before the DPP announces whether they will accept all or part of Jeeming's lengthy submission on the charges.

Mazlee has not come to court again. He is afraid of being photographed or filmed. Ed wanted to come along for moral support. He doesn't ask after the whereabouts of the missing partner.

Haq meets us inside Courtroom Number 2. 'Okay, sit tight,' he says. 'I'm going to see them now.'

Ed leans in. 'Who is that guy?'

'My lawyer. Hamidul Haq. He's solid.'

'Hope so.'

'Singapore-born, but his people are from Silet in northern Bangladesh.'

'Is that right?'

For decades, Silet's main export commodity has been humans. Most of the Indian restaurants in London are owned and operated by Bangladeshis from Silet. They're everywhere. It's my good fortune that Haq's family came to Singapore instead, where their son took up the study of law.

'Before he joined a private firm, Haq was a deputy senior state counsel and deputy public prosecutor.'

'Yeah?'

'He helped put Nick Leeson away.'

'The guy who broke the bank?'

'Yes.'

'Wow.'

Nick Leeson's name has drifted off the radar for most people, but Singaporeans still remember him as something of a legend, albeit of the notorious kind. Leeson's unauthorised trading on the Singapore Monetary Exchange caused the collapse of Britain's oldest and stuffiest investment bank, Barings, and Singapore threw the book at him. He had committed the most grievous crime: causing Singapore to lose face in the international financial community. The Chinese in Singapore have a word for that—*kiasu*. Kiasuism means the desire to win, and to win all the time. The corollary is that not winning is a monumental loss of face. Leeson's carry-on made Singapore's ruling elite look like they had their eyes off the ball while a foreigner played them for fools. He was lucky they didn't have the death penalty for white-collar crimes.

After Haq's team prosecuted Leeson, the judge gave him six and a half years, but he was out in three after being diagnosed with colon cancer. Leeson's life after prison seems remarkably successful. He got better and wrote a book, *Rogue Trader*, that was trashed by reviewers and made into a movie starring Ewan McGregor. These days he runs an Irish football club and appears on the after-dinner speaking circuit, presumably not giving investment advice. A few years ago he released a second book, *Back from the Brink: Coping with Stress*. I might have a look at that.

Haq is back, and his face is grim. 'No deal.'

'On what?'

'Any of it. They are determined to stick with all five charges.'

FIFTEEN
The October surprise

YOU DON'T KNOW QUITE how far you've fallen until you hit the bottom, and it is only then you can start climbing back to the surface. I landed with a thud last week when the DPP said they were going ahead with all five charges. Ed Roy and I did what anybody does after receiving news like that: we got drunk. Ed and I made our way to Chinatown to a food stall where we drank copious bottles of Tiger beer and fresh-cooked seafood. It was a lubricant for the unthinkable: a possible conviction on all five charges and the near certainty of a sentence lasting between six and seven years, along with five scarifying strokes of the rattan cane.

Media reports have been exaggerating the prospective sentencing outcome, suggesting that the worst result is up to twenty years in prison. It is fortunate for me that I am a journalist and speak fluent journalese, and can identify copy that is geared for maxiumum sensation. That sort of punishment is never meted out to a first-time offender and has never been mentioned by the police or the DPP.

The tiny amount of drugs, too, is a mitigating factor that nobody has paid attention to. The media has instead been reading Singapore law too literally, or with too much *schadenfreude*, and failing to appreciate the nuances of the legal system. The High Court benchmark for first-time traffickers is five years—and it would take significantly aggravating circumstances for a judge to push the punishment further up the scales of justice without having to answer for it at appeal.

Jeeming says that two of the three sentences can be served concurrently. So, if I were to be sentenced for trafficking, a further sentence of a year each for possession and consumption could be concurrent. The remaining charges relating to implements are, legally speaking, small beer—likely attracting a month or two for each conviction.

'For once in our lives we are giving thanks for the mathematical certainty of life in predictable little Singapore,' I declared.

'I'll drink to that!' Ed wasn't even trying to put a brave face on the gloom. He knows me too well. *Pollyanna* was never on my Boy's Own bookshelf. And I've lived my life telling other people to face facts and be realistic. It's my turn to face facts—and the music.

'They can have my body.' I was a bit pissed. 'But they are never going to get this.' Tapping my temple. 'I won't give them the satisfaction.'

• • • • •

I'M AT PILATES.

'Jesus Christ, I'm going to snap in two.' I am prostrating myself on a long, rectangular bench frame that looks a little like a single bed without a mattress. In place of the mattress is a leather-covered board that you mount, and then you slide up and down it. Medieval-looking straps and springs are attached around the perimeter.

Later I am on my haunches, bent forward in a lather of perspiration. Jayanthi, the instructor, is trying hard not to laugh at me as I grimace at the personal improvement torture regime that I am submitting to.

'Do you think prison will be like this?' I ask her.

'Take it easy now, Peter. Remember the breathing, and control your core muscles.'

Appropriately, perhaps, this piece of equipment is called the Reformer. The long list of aberrant behaviours this Reformer sets out to reform is left to one's imagination. My future jailors, with their penchant for Confucian punishment values and its insistence on a period of reflection on the corruption of the soul, would, perhaps, applaud my submission. This contraption must have been inspired by some period in history of epic human cruelty—somewhere between

Spanish Inquisition and Reformation—because the Reformer has fundamentalist nut-job written all over it.

In view of the diabolic state of my life, I've made a few resolutions lately. The first is to start compiling a library of books that I can read in jail. My wish list is long—a healthy balance between have-you-read worthies, ripping classics and roughage of the Dan Brown variety. I have decided to tackle *Ulysses*. If Joyce and I are ever going to come to terms with each other it will only happen in the solitude of a prison cell, where I am denied every possible distraction or excuse to run screaming from what, so far, I have regarded as the nonsensical drivel of his 'brilliance'. I'm all for literary books, but the man could have done with a seriously good edit. Someone ought to have taken him aside and said, 'Listen here, what *are* you on about?'

The second resolution is to take control of my body. I'm learning Pilates because it is a form of exercise that can be practised in confined spaces without the resistance equipment in this room. This seems like a handy routine for a future convict.

So here I am, preparing to go to jail. I'm getting my body fit and ready for surrender. 'Let's try this now,' says Jayanthi, leading me across the room to another relic from a torture chamber. 'This one is commonly referred to as the Rack, but its correct name is the Cadillac.'

I'm laughing too hard to try to mount this piece of machinery. 'A rack, Jayanthi? They really call it that?'

'Yes.' Jayanthi is ignoring the bait. 'The Cadillac was devised by Joseph Pilates to help rehabilitate bedridden patients in a hospital in Germany during the war.'

'I see. So it's a rack invented by a Nazi, and now I'm paying for the torture privilege?'

'It was World War One. He was an orderly, not a Nazi. Now, as you can see, it is a raised horizontal table top with a series of straps and springs and levers. You won't believe me, but on this baby you can do eight different exercises. It has all the bells and whistles—just like a Cadillac. That's why he called it the Cadillac.'

'I'll be delighted if I survive just one of them.'

'Hop on board and we'll see how you go.'

This is the pointy end of resolutions—actually carrying through on the plan. Buying books for a personal library is going to be much more fun.

I'm mounting the Cadillac, following instructions, but my mind is elsewhere today. Jeeming and Haq are at their wits' end. They put in a hefty legal submission and had it knocked back entirely. My options are narrowing in this fight. Soon the DPP is going to want an answer to the big, hard-to-answer question: am I going to run up the white flag, or demand a trial and fight?

Fighting at a trial in Singapore is a risky and expensive business. Most people lose. There are no jury trials—Lee Kuan Yew got rid of them decades ago. Apparently jurors are too prone to feel sympathy for an accused and are difficult for the state to control.

The only glimmer on the horizon is a note that my lawyers received today from the DPP. It said: 'We are still investigating into various issues in the representations that were sent to us, in order to *consider an offer* to the accused.' The DPP underlined the phrase 'consider an offer' and that ignited fresh optimism in my camp. The next pre-trial conference is happening in three days' time. I'd better start paying more attention to Jayanthi.

'Now we're going to do something called "imprinting". This is one of the most basic Pilates exercises. It helps lengthen and relax the spine.'

'Really? *Longer?*'

'Yes, trust me.'

'I trust you.' But I'm thinking, *Do I really trust you? Pilates might be the exercise world's equivalent to Scientology—a cash-for-faith proposition for losers. Am I being sucked in? Is Jayanthi going to start talking about Thetans?*

'Okay,' she says. 'Now relax your shoulders.' She's behind me, making me relax my shoulders. 'Relax your shoulders and ribcage. Let the sternum drop and the back ribs move to the floor. Can you feel that happening?'

'Sort of.'

'Can you, or can you not?'

'Not.' I'm laughing. 'Do I have lazy ribs?'

'Lazy ribs? No such thing.' Now I'm being scolded. 'Just concentrate. Relax your abdominal muscles. When that happens, you can feel the abs settling toward the spine.'

'Okay. Done.'

'Right, now relax your spine. Let it feel the floor.'

'I'm feeling it. I'm feeling it.' I'm thinking, *I'm really feeling it. Praise be to the Thetans!*

'Good. Now, relax and try to visualise your spine lengthening and sinking down to the mat. See it, and feel it. Then you can breathe into those spaces.'

'Okay.'

'You feel it now?'

'Yes. I do.'

'That, my friend, is imprinting. You've learned one of the most important lessons.'

I've been learning a lot of those lately.

• • • • •

I'M AT HOME, PUTTING the finishing touches to a roast dinner of imported Australian lamb. Making meals from animals that moo or baa is an extravagance in Singapore, as meat and livestock goods at the supermarket are high-priced imports. But lamb roast aroma is pure magic—a heady fragrance of tender meat and garlic and vegetables baking in their own juices. Smell is the sense that summons up rich memories, more so than sight and hearing.

I grew up in the era of the ritual of the Sunday roast, a culinary symbol of the traditional family—a world inhabited by mums and dads, brothers and sisters, idyllic weather and undemanding friends. Its aroma is that of safety and security and childlike innocence.

The scent of the roast is putting me in a sentimental frame of mind. Tonight I'm feeling more than sentimental—I am also feeling regretful. I've been mocking and insensitive and wilful and self-pitying, yet Mazlee patiently carries me along like a weighty burden in a burlap sack. He's bit his lip as I've been firing rockets from mine.

In moments of fury I command my vocabulary like a ruthless,

marauding warlord—slaughtering the innocent, razing crops, laying waste to villages. I spare no one, because I can. I have an unfair advantage—I'm working in my mother tongue, and he is battling for space in his second. While he has total fluency, he does not have my shelf full of vernacular, nor a cultural willingness to use it. By rights he should stop speaking to me in English and see how I fair in Malay, or German, or Spanish, his other languages. That would turn the tables. That would put me in my place. That might just shut me up.

I'm now overcome by the urge to make amends, turning over a new leaf by preparing this splendid dinner.

'Let's have a drink on the balcony,' says Mazlee.

It's the sunset hour. Mazlee's apartment faces due west, overlooking a spectacular canopy of lush jungle. It is dress circle seating for the wonderful spectacle of a tropical sunset. We often sit here in meditative silence, marvelling at the flaming orange ripples that shoot across the sky as the sun sinks over the horizon. Mazlee's not one for talking at these moments and tonight, for once, I'm resisting the temptation to slip into incessant babble. In the spirit of having something nice to think about, I offer a toast to Singapore for being a verdant city.

This is easily the prettiest little dictatorship going around. With his usual modesty Lee Kuan Yew takes full credit, as he does for any halfway decent achievement in a twenty-five kilometre radius of the Istana Palace. The Spruce Up Singapore effort began in earnest in the seventies under Lee's close personal supervision. There is an urban myth that the anally retentive Lee instructed work crews to collect leaves as soon as they fell, lest the city be perceived as untidy. Hearing that story had me wondering: did the toddler Harry Lee suffer from some awful potty-training incident that left him traumatised for life? Singapore must be the only country in the world where the chief gardener reports directly to the prime minister's office.

● ● ● ● ●

'DINNER IS SERVED!'

I'm both cook and waiter tonight. Our guests, Natalie and another friend, Daryl, are sitting expectantly at the dinner table. Mazlee was charging their glasses with shiraz before he disappeared into the kitchen.

I'm laying out the last tray, one laden with sliced and steaming roast lamb, when Natalie speaks up: 'Where did Mazlee go?'

I return to the kitchen to find Mazlee hovering over the sink, scrubbing pots and scowling my way.

'Washing up?'

'Yes.' He's terse. I can feel ripples of fury, and for once they are barely suppressed.

'Now, Mazlee?' I'm exasperated, but talking in a hushed tone. 'Now? When the guests are sitting at the dinner table waiting for you to come out?'

'Yes, now. Look at this place—you're making a mess!'

'It's called cooking.'

'I can't have it—my galley would never look like this.'

'Your galley?'

'Yes.'

'Mazlee, this is a house—not a jumbo jet.'

'It doesn't matter. This place is a pig sty. You should be more careful—look at all these scraps.' He is pointing at two strips of carrot skin. 'Clean as you go—that's what you need to do.'

'Fine.' I'm holding my tongue, and my vocabulary—this is a Be Nice Night. 'Go ahead, but I'm going back out there to join our guests.'

I'm back at the table, raising my shoulders, as if to say, 'You figure it out.'

'Dig in!' I command.

Natalie and Daryl look at each other, then towards the kitchen, and back to me. Their eyes are pleading for an explanation.

'Who knows?' I shrug. 'But he'll be out once the galley is shipshape.'

Daryl's known Mazlee long enough to decode what that crack is about.

'Mazlee!' Natalie is calling out. 'Come and eat! Do that later!'

'Almost done,' comes the disembodied voice. 'You start!'

And to my relief, they do.

About five minutes later Mazlee joins us, sighing heavily as he sits down next to me. I know that sigh—it's the sound of disapproval. I'm thinking, *Let it go. Be nice. He's a having a Tidy Town moment, and at least he's not inspecting the potted plants for falling leaves.*

Later. The roast goes down well, but this is turning out to be a dinner with multiple personalities. An hour ago I was being scolded for committing a gross violation of the Singapore code of conduct—untidiness. Now the glacial ice has melted and Mazlee is sobbing on Natalie's shoulder. 'I can't do this,' he is saying. 'I don't know what I will do if he goes to jail for five years.'

Then, looking at me, he says, 'I'm drunk, and you're going to jail. You're not going to be here.'

'Yes, Maz, that's right—I am going to jail. And I won't be here to mess up the galley.'

Ouch. Those words came out too hard and too fast, and with unintended matter-of-fact force. I'm seeing the shock at my harsh tone registering—Natalie and Daryl are sitting back in their chairs, like a foul odour has just descended.

I sound like a condemned man hurrying to his own execution. Mazlee is weeping. I just landed a cruel and cold blow. *I don't mean to be like this,* I'm thinking. *Why am I such an arsehole?*

I'm trying to turn this bombastic supertanker around. 'Hey, baby, it's not a done deal yet,' I'm pleading, and cajoling. 'Who knows what will happen at the next hearing, eh? Jeeming and Haq are doing their best. Maz—please. Look at me. It isn't over. I promise.'

Now I'm gilding the lily. It *is* over. I'm done with the stages of bargaining and anger—it's time to accept that I'm going to go to jail. I have to accept this, for my own sake. Mazlee isn't in the same place as me, not yet. Maybe he never will be. I don't know. I'm lost. What do I do? Hold him up, to stop myself from falling down?

To Natalie: 'Hey! Let's not waste this night being sad. We have to live in the now.'

'He's right.' Daryl is coming to the rescue. I like Daryl—he's a dad, and a gay man. We've got a lot in common. 'Mazlee,' he says. 'Peter is here. You are here. Don't lose sight of the here and now. Tomorrow? Who knows what tomorrow will bring.'

Daryl is looking at me, eyes wide. His folksong philosophy doesn't fool me—or him, I suspect—but he is trying to bring Mazlee back from the shadows.

I'm gazing at my partner, who looks desperate and disconsolate, and then a penny drops: *What is the worst thing to have happened in Mazlee's life? Me*, I think.

This is not melodrama. I have to end this relationship, soon. For Mazlee's sake.

• • • • •

I'M WITH KAREN, coffee and cookies in hand. I'm wondering if she's noticed a confident step in my stride. She's sitting in her chair opposite, expectantly, like someone preparing to receive a gift.

'So, Peter Lloyd. What gives?'

'What do you mean?' I'm being coy.

'You're—I don't know . . . *different.*'

'Karen—it's time.'

'For?'

'To. Harden. The. Fuck. Up.'

'Oh, really?'

'Listen!' I'm leaning forward, in my typical listen-to-me pose. 'I'm going to jail soon. Let's get real! It is time for me to take back control of me. I've had enough of this self-pity and oh-woe-is-me crap. Peter is back in charge. I'm not going to be a victim. This stuff—this PTSD—is not going to beat me. I'm going to knock it out of the park. We're going to do this, Karen, okay? Because I have to get ready for reality— they're going to put me in jail soon. Okay?'

Karen is slightly taken aback. I've come in here with some-thing to say, and she's reeling from this blast of Peter Lloyd self-assuredness. I'm not sure Karen has seen me like this before. Until now, I've been the broken crockery. Today, I'm teflon—and nothing is going to stick.

'Right. That's good.' She's going with it.

'Too right!' I declare. 'I'm over it. *Sick* is for someone else. I'm not going to let this stuff take me down. It's bad—all right. But the world is full of challenges. We rise to them, or we kneel down. I'm not kneeling down and letting trauma take me down too. I won't go, Karen. I won't.'

I'm adamant. I really mean this. Something has happened since the DPP turned down my pleas. They've hit me with hardball, and I'm going to stand up and take it. I got myself into this mess and I'm going to deal with it. I'm not going to roll up in a ball and surrender my dignity. Fuck them. Fuck the world.

Out loud: 'Karen, I'm going down with my head up.'

'That's the spirit.'

'So, let's talk about what we're not talking about.'

Arching an eyebrow, Karen says, 'You want to go there?'

'Shoot.'

'Okay. Let's explore these nightmares.'

· · · · ·

I'M CLIMBING THE STAIRS at the front of the Subordinate Court. It is a cloudy Thursday morning, just like every other day. In the cab on the ride here, the radio announcer reading the 9am news said it was already '29 degrees and 84 per cent humidity' with a kind of stagey enthusiasm that suggested such information was somehow interesting and newsworthy. I'm thinking, *So what, buddy! It's 29 degrees and 84 per cent humidity here all the time.* In this sovereign gilded cage, even the weather is unceasingly safe and predictable. Still, the driver thought it was exciting stuff: 'Hah, 29 lah,' he guffawed. 'Twenty-nine already, lah! Very hot, lah!'

Singaporeans have gone soft. They're too used to living in the cosy, refrigerated world that Lee Kuan Yew created for them. They go from air-conditioned homes to air-conditioned cars and buses and trains, and scurry across air-conditioned malls to air-conditioned offices. At lunchtime they scurry back out to air-conditioned hawker centres and frigid shopping malls to scoff food that's cheap and cheerful, chosen more for value than quality. Then they scurry right back to work again until it is time to brave the heat and head back home to the safety and security of 24/7 air-conditioning. If you time your arrivals and departures just right, it is almost possible to avoid the natural equatorial climate of Singapore altogether.

'Yes, uncle, very hot,' I reply. *Who am I to rain on his parade?* I think.

Up in Courtroom Number 2 I'm greeted by my nemesis, Police Investigator Jeff Lee, minus reflective sunglasses. Lee's demeanour seems different, slightly less formal than before. 'You will be getting good news today.'

'What do you mean?'

'Let your DC find out.' Lee nods over my shoulder and walks away.

Hamidul Haq has just arrived. 'What does he want?' my counsel asks.

'Says you're about to get good news, for me.'

'Really? I'm going to go and see the judge with the DPP. Wait here.'

If Haq has any inkling of a change in the prosecution plan, he is not betraying it to me. I've brought a copy of the *Economist* to read while I wait in the public gallery. I have learned from past experience that a pre-trial conference for an accused person in Singapore requires no involvement by the accused, bar sitting at the back of the court waiting for the lawyers to return from their closed-door conference with the judge.

A few reporters are sitting in the gallery with me. The Chinese reporter with the halitosis condition is sitting to the right, loudly complaining about the slow pace of my case to another reporter. *Does Miss Sensitivity know I'm sitting here?*

Lee takes the seat next to me. 'So good news, lah. The trafficking charge has been investigated—and the DPP has decided not to proceed.'

'For sure?'

'Yes. This is a big break for you.'

I'm in a state of happy shock. I'm conscious that the media is monitoring Lee and me, so I'm trying to contain any joyful reactions.

'That's, that's . . . terrific news, Jeff.'

'But Peter, the other charges—you can't win those. You were caught.'

'I know. That's always been the case, hasn't it?'

'Yes. You are very unfortunate with your medical condition. I am sorry this happened to you—the law here is strict. They won't make many allowances for you.'

'How long will I get?'

'Well, given the circumstances, probably a few months. They won't push for that much.'

'When will they sentence me?'

'Not up to me, but probably in a few weeks. You need to make arrangements.'

Haq is coming back from the judge's chambers. Lee takes his cue and shifts to another bench. Haq is signalling for me to follow him outside the court.

'Okay, this is very, very good Peter. The DPP is withdrawing the trafficking charge.'

'That's official?'

'Yes. It is gone. I don't know why—I don't care why. This is huge, Peter. A huge win.' Haq leans in, conspiratorially. 'Now listen, the media are here. I don't think we should say anything. I don't want to appear triumphal. I don't want to inflame the other side, okay? Do you follow?'

'Sure,' I say. 'Don't say a word.'

'They want us back here on November fourth, to discuss whether we are claiming trial or not. After today, there is no point. I will talk to you and Jeeming about this, of course, but I would recommend we come back in November and tell them that we're going to go straight to a sentencing hearing on the other charges. A trial at this point would be very difficult to win. You understand that, right?'

'Yes.'

Anywhere else in the world I would fight these charges, pleading for mercy and commonsense. But with no jury to plead to and a conveyor-belt, one-size-fits-all legal system, winning is impossible. Haq and Jeeming have already explained to me that Singapore's criminal judges work off a printed sentencing schedule handed down by the higher courts. On paper there is no minimum sentence for possession, but in practice the High Court has set a twelve-month sentence benchmark and instructed the three lower courts to follow. Dutifully they do, without exception. Even in cases like mine, it is impossible for a lower court judge to circumvent this system of predetermined sentences and exercise independent-minded judgement.

Like everyone else in Singapore, judges follow rules handed down from above. And those above are largely connected, via a web of familial, scholastic and fraternal tentacles, to the ruling People's Action Party. Singapore is what happens when a lawyer with a narcissistic need for absolute control invents a country.

$$\bullet \ \bullet \ \bullet \ \bullet \ \bullet$$

'THAT LITTLE TOE-RAG bastard!' I'm throwing the *Straits Times* newspaper onto the floor of the apartment. I am alone, but talking out loud as I often do in one-way conversation when something agitates me. Usually it is what's on the television, but today it is the handiwork of a local hack trying to land a blow on my credibility by sneaking in a low-life editorial comment.

The journalist, Sujin Thomas, has written: 'Australian journalist Peter Gerard Lloyd, 41, was a figure of confidence, smiling and waving at reporters outside the subordinate courts on Thursday morning after his court appearance on drugs charges.'

This is why politicians don't argue with billionaires who buy ink by the barrel. Thomas's opening paragraph is a massive fib, and he knows it. The exaggeration is a dog whistle that says: 'Decadent foreigner continues to disrespect rule of law in Singapore.' To which the recep-tive, tut-tut, finger-waving, moralistic mob will no doubt respond, in unison, 'Lock him up!'

If Thomas were honest, he would have written that I had said hello and raised my hand in greeting to a single *Straits Times* photographer with whom I am familiar—he is, after all, one of the people who have been photographing me for weeks. It was an act of public courtesy, not contempt, on display. Thomas is displaying all the signs of the anti-foreigner, Singaporean hive mind at work. 'Another regime poodle,' I say to the wall.

Thomas is probably motivated partly by frustration. He was smart enough to pick up that there had been a development in the case, but not sufficiently clever to extract the information after Haq dangled a carrot by telling Thomas that 'he is hopeful of a resolution in the coming weeks, although nothing is firm now'.

Mazlee is in Europe, and I rang him last night with the good news. He cried with relief. I never imagined that we'd be excited by the idea that I'd be jailed for 'only a year'. But that's how life is—you have to accept the cards you are dealt, and find a way to accommodate them.

My mother, when I called her, thought that it was a genuine miracle— like a cure for cancer after a visit to Lourdes. I'm not a believer but I believe my mother believes, and it is more than enough for me that she's getting a break from worry and stress. Apart from Mazlee and my family, the decision to drop the trafficking charge is a secret.

SIXTEEN
The long goodbye

AS A REPORTER, I always knew a case was getting to the serious stage when a hapless defendant suddenly turned up to court in an ill-fitting suit, the kind you wore to your first job interview. It is an indication of self-consciousness in the face of impending judgement as well as an outward nod of deference to the authority figure of the judge. Today is the fourth of November. This is my penultimate court hearing and I am, for the first time, wearing a beige, single-breasted Italian wool/cotton blend. I've elected to go without a tie, as much a nod to the climate as a coded up-yours to the authority figure of the regime's judges.

As I head up the Subordinate Court steps with the latest *Economist* tucked under my arm (masthead conspicuously showing), I am wondering if the Singapore hacks will take heed of the symbolism of the style change that is to accompany today's pending revelations about progress in the case. Grey flannel seemed too obvious. Black is simply too bleak. Beige seemed to strike the right sartorial note—somewhere between stylish and legally indifferent, it's a fashion statement that declares, as did Gloria Gaynor, 'I will survive.'

'Nice suit.' It's Hamidul Haq, as usual a man in black, drily commenting on my sudden escalation up the sartorial ladder. 'Take a seat, and I'll go see the DPP and judge.' Courtroom Number 2 seems underutilised, as usual. I've been here three times now, and I still haven't laid eyes on a judge or a public trial of any kind. It is like going to a circus on the performers' day off. The Subordinate Court complex has the superficial look and feel of a western-style court complex, but with none of the spectacle and excitement of actual public trials. Like everything else in Singapore, the real show—the exercise of real power—goes on behind closed doors, away from the public glare.

At moments like this, my imagination runs riot. For all I know, the judge hearing my matter is sitting in a smoke-filled room out the back knocking back beers and losing his wife's fortune gambling over a mahjong table. For all I know, the judge is an old bloke getting a happy-ending massage from a lithe young transsexual Thai woman in a tight-fitting sarong, or is strapped to a giant cartwheel being whipped by a leather-clad dominatrix—a kind of cat-woman from Chinatown on a charge-by-the-hour Mission to Thrill. For all I know, the judge is not even real—instead, it's a voiceless computer program, some kind of a law-and-order dispensing matrix created by the Singaporean Almighty, Lee Kuan Yew.

I'm thinking, *I need to stop thinking.*

The usual suspects are present here on the public benches at the back of the court, including the woman with the invisible toxic halo of halitosis and a Malay-language reporter who has engaged me twice as Lloyd Peter, and twice as Peter Lloyd, having a bet each way on which is the correct form of address. He's a pudgy man who dresses for comfort—more taxi driver than reporter. I have yet to identify Sujin Thomas—I had been under the mistaken impression that Sujin was a woman, but Mazlee insists he is a man. Why doesn't he act like one, and come up and talk to me then? I was still steamed up over his 'objective' reporting.

The lawyers are in with the judge now. I'm flicking through the *Economist* but I'm thinking about my own affairs, not those of the world. After the dropping of the trafficking charge, I decided not to claim trial on the remaining four charges. The lawyers reckoned there were better ways to skin this cat. Under Singaporean law, it is possible for a charge to be effectively dropped but still remain officially on the books. This is a category called 'Taken Into Consideration', or TIC. The TIC is another way of getting the DPP to reduce the number of charges being considered at the sentencing hearing. Haq's proposal was that the DPP proceed to sentencing on only consumption and possession, and TIC the rest. Both lawyers thought it best to ask for the other charges to be 'Taken Into Consideration'; they believed the more potentially face-losing avenue of having them formally withdrawn might be asking too much, too soon, after the climb-down on trafficking.

Well it was. Yesterday the DPP wrote back. 'Having carefully reviewed the facts of the case,' he said, 'I write to inform you that the prosecution is unable to accede to your request.' The final DPP position is this: to proceed to sentencing on three of the remaining charges, but to take into consideration the fourth charge, relating to utensils. It is a small concession that means sentencing will be for three of the original five charges. Haq is in with the judge now, confirming my agreement to this arrangement and trying to negotiate a few more weeks before the sentencing hearing.

I'm only halfway through the introduction to Pilates, and my book-buying bonanza is still but a dream. I have been procrastinating on buying books, because it makes jailing seem that much more real—not some fuzzy, notional moment far off in the future. I am staring intently at this magazine in my hands, but I haven't read a single word.

'Let's get out of here.' Haq looks tense. Leading me across the lobby, my lawyer continues, 'They've gone as far as they are going to go.' He is pausing now, looking at me intently. 'Peter, you will be sentenced at the next hearing.'

Outside, on the steps of the Subordinate Court, cameras and journalists and photographers are coming at Haq and me. *Where did they all come from? There weren't this many reporters inside the court.* Just short of the taxi, Haq pauses. He has never done this before, and the hacks take their cue to ask for developments in the case. A moment ago we had agreed that it was time to reveal the dropping of the trafficking charge, and confirm that the next hearing would be the last. Now Haq is explaining. 'The Attorney-General considered all the circumstances and, after due process, they decided to withdraw the trafficking charge against Peter.'

'So the charge was dropped?'

'That's right. He does not face any trafficking charge now.'

'What about the remaining charges?'

'Peter has expressed his remorse to the court and will plead guilty to some of the lesser charges.'

'When?'

'The next hearing, December second.'

It is over in seconds. Haq is motioning for me to get into the cab. I'm climbing in after him as the follow-up questions come hurling my way. I'm under strict instructions not to speak. My lawyers believe that I have nothing to gain, and everything to lose, by saying anything that might upset the authorities.

•••••

I'M WITH KAREN GOSLING, my psychologist. It's a few hours after the hearing. I've explained what has happened with the case, but there is another, more urgent, problem weighing on my mind.

'Mazlee wasn't in court?' she asks.

'I told him not to come.'

'Why is that?'

'I know how difficult it is for him, coming and going from the building with the media there.'

'Do you want him there, to support you?'

'Of course I do.'

'Have you told him that?'

'No.'

'Why not?'

'Because I shouldn't have to ask—it should just happen.'

'What do you mean?'

'If you have to ask a partner to support you, what sort of partner do you have?' Karen is silent, so I continue. 'Remember what Dean Martin said about Frank Sinatra?'

'No.'

'He said, "It's Frank's world, we just live in it." Well, this is Singapore. This is Mazlee's world—I just happen to be visiting it.'

'Meaning?'

'Meaning, I won't die from disappointment that he doesn't come to court. And I can see his point of view, when I think about it.

He doesn't want to have his picture splashed in the papers every time I make an appearance in court. He has to live here, after I'm gone. He's a minority in an intolerant, deeply conservative, Chinese community. The people who run this place have a long memory, and they are good haters. Sure, I want him by my side, but I also have an instinct to protect him. I just have to live with him not coming to court with me.'

'Does he support you, in private?'

'On his terms, yes.'

'What do you mean?'

'I mean that he gets annoyed if I have an appointment with you, or Pilates, when he is on a day off from flying. He thinks that I should schedule my stuff around his free time.'

'How does that make you feel?'

'Angry. I mean—as if that were possible. It's as if the whole world revolves around Mazlee and his days off. No, I won't do it.'

'Does that cause tension?'

'Sure it does. We finally had a fight—I mean a real fight.'

'What happened?'

'We were out, and drunk. He was seething with anger, because I did something really stupid.'

'What?'

'I went to the bar and ordered the most expensive bottle of champagne on the menu.'

'Why?'

'Because I'm going to jail, I suppose.'

'How did he react?'

'He was not impressed—thought it was a waste. So I started drinking the champagne like it was water. Just throwing it back.'

'Classy.'

'Oh yes. It was. I bugged him until he drank it too. Then we had a fight and he stormed off. I followed him home, and when I walked in he just started up at what an idiot I was.'

'And you replied?'

'Oh yes. I'm not sure who started throwing punches first, but we smacked each other in the face a few times. And then I picked up this potted plant with small stones packed around the surface, and threw it at his head.'

'Oh no!'

'Oh yes. I missed. But it hit the bed and smashed into a million pieces.' After a pause: 'Karen, I think Mazlee and I are broken too.'

'This is a lot of stress to put on any relationship, and yours is not that old.'

'That's right. I think he's sick of me. I don't blame him—I'm sick of me.'

'Maybe he is. Maybe he is just waiting for the sentencing, and that's the end.'

'I think so.'

• • • • •

TENSION PEAKS WHEN I encroach on Mazlee's space and time, like a poacher trespassing on prime land or an intruder asking for extra time to ransack your belongings. During those weeks when my appointments with lawyers and doctors and Pilates instructors clash with his days off, we fight. Or more often than not we don't fight, but he simmers. I suppose that these events infringe on Mazlee's legitimate desire for normalcy. They are painful reminders that we are living on borrowed time.

The most painful incident happened the day that I said goodbye to my seven-year-old son, Tom, not knowing how long it would be before I'd see him again. I'm telling Karen this story now: 'It was about a month ago. Kirsty brought Tom to Singapore to see me for a few days. We all stayed together.'

'Where was Mazlee?'

'He was away, in Europe or America. It was better that way.'

'How was Tom?'

'Normal. We were all so normal together—it was like a holiday.'

Prior to the visit Karen and I had focused on child psychology, covering such issues as how to explain these events in Singapore to a seven-year-old, how to respond to questions and how much reality one should share with a youngster. It was good preparation, because Tom is a child who asks a lot of pointed questions.

163

'Did he want to know what was happening to you?' Karen asks.

'Oh yes. He wanted to know where I would be staying and would it be safe—would the people there be nice to me.'

'And the drugs?'

'I told him that I had made a mistake, and taken medicine that I should not have taken. He didn't probe, so I didn't volunteer any further information.'

'That's good. With children, the golden rule is never lie. But limit yourself to answering their direct questions—you don't need to elaborate. Very often that would only lead to confusion and worry for them.'

'The end was tough.'

'What happened?'

'We were saying goodbye at the hotel. He said, "I love you, Daddy—but when are you coming home?" And I had tell him the truth: "I don't know. But as soon as I know, you will know." Then he got into the taxi and they were gone. It was about six o'clock, and my phone kept buzzing with messages from Mazlee, saying, "Where are you? We have guests coming." '

'What was that about?'

'He had come back, and it was the Festival of Hari Raya and about a dozen of his friends were coming to the apartment to celebrate. He didn't ask me how it was with Tom, or if I was okay. He just told me to hurry up and get back to the apartment, like a poodle that had strayed too far.'

'What did you do?'

'I walked along Orchard Road for a while, in a daze. I could feel myself splitting into two people.'

'Dissociating?'

'Probably. I felt like I was floating above myself, looking down as I walked along in the crowd. I felt numb. I was too sad to cry. I didn't feel anything at all.'

'Do you remember where you went?'

'No.'

'How long before you got home?'

'I'm not sure. I arrived before the guests, but not by much. Mazlee was furious that I was "late home". He didn't ask me anything. He just kept telling me that I was late, and that guests were coming. Like I said, it's Mazlee's world, and I just live in it.'

• • • • •

A DAY LATER, I AM READING this in the newspaper at Starbucks: 'Lloyd came to the Court dressed in a crisp grey suit. He sat in the public gallery, engrossed in a news magazine, while his lawyer went into the chambers to discuss his case.' Engrossed? If only Sujin Thomas knew.

I'm doing the rounds of the major bookstores today, purchasing some more books for the personal prison library. In the past, anything over 500 pages has deterred me, but right now 500 pages seems like lightweight reading material. A few days ago I bought a cheesy-looking bio on Vice-President Dick Cheney, just because it was a big book. I don't particularly like Cheney's politics, and I doubt that a few anecdotes about how he enjoys fly-fishing and cares for butterflies is going to make me think the better of him. Still, the book is huge and a dissertation on 'Why Dick Isn't All Evil' will help me get through a few days in jail. And I will probably read Cheney before Joyce.

When I was browsing in the memoir section I came across the second volume of Lee Kuan Yew's memoir, *The Singapore Story: 1965–2000*. This modestly titled book runs to 777 pages. I bought it immediately. Lee fascinates me and, now that I am to be a guest of his state, it would be discourteous not to make the effort to read his memoir. I am not going to pretend that I will read this book with an objective mind—I have long since formed the view that Lee Kuan Yew is a tired old crank and a bully—but I'm curious to see how self-serving his book will be, especially in comparison to other critiques I have read.

I think I will take the Lee book to my sentencing hearing. It will be an amusing exercise to walk into prison with the memoirs of Singapore's Dear Leader tucked under my arm.

• • • • •

THERE IS A STORY about me in the newspaper today, but this one is different. This time I co-operated, by speaking to the reporter from the *Sydney Morning Herald*.

I've just read it online, where it ranks as the number-one story by page views. Jennifer Cooke's article begins, 'As an ABC foreign correspondent, Peter Lloyd saw more mass casualties in six years than the average soldier—and it took its toll.' It's a long story and she managed to interview others besides myself, including Kirsty ('Kirsty McIvor, a former ABC reporter, mother of his two young boys and, until his arrest, the United Nations spokeswoman in Jakarta'), who told her: 'We left Australia a happy family . . . and within a year or two Peter had covered some of the worst terrorist and natural disasters in decades. He did this alone with no psychological support or counselling. I know for a fact that it affected him and he changed.' Kimina Lyall, previously the Southeast Asia correspondent for the *Australian* during a period that overlapped with mine, has now left journalism after a PTSD diagnosis, but she recalls my successive twenty-hour days during the tsunami and wondered how people operate under such stress: 'Whereas I generally had one deadline a day, Peter would have three or four major ones and then be constantly taking calls from dozens of ABC local radio stations wanting to do "live crosses" with him.'

According to Professor Alexander McFarlane, a PTSD expert and the head of psychiatry at the University of Adelaide, people 'underestimate the stresses of journalists': 'These are the people who are having repeated exposure to horrific scenes and rather than getting used to them the evidence is that they do eat away at people and the occupational risks are to self-medicate with alcohol or other substances.' The *Herald* story mentions that the managing director of the DART Centre for Journalism and Trauma Australasia, Cait McMahon, has found that about 15 per cent of 115 journalists surveyed—85 per cent from the Asia-Pacific region—have suffered symptoms of probable PTSD while doing their job.

• • • • •

'YOU WERE IN THE PAPER.' It's Karen Gosling, settling into the chair opposite me for one of my last counselling sessions before the sentencing hearing.

'I'm running out of time to have my say, so I said it.'

'Well I'm glad to see you sounding so strong and confident. You've made a lot of gains here.'

'I sure have.'

'And, for my profession, anything on PTSD that gets into the newspaper is a good thing. So what's been happening with you?'

'Well, I had a gay version of *Guess Who's Coming to Dinner*.'

'How's that?'

'My mother met Mazlee for the first time. We went to dinner at the Mediterranean place, Esmirada, at Chijmes in the city.'

'What's her name? How did it go?'

'Pat. Pretty good, I think.'

'You think?'

'Well, the elephant was in the room—but we studiously ignored it. I was on my best behaviour. Mazlee was too. Mothers love him—he is neat and tidy, and terribly polite and well-mannered and all of that, so it's just impossible not to like him.'

'Did they get on?'

'Did they what! By the end of the meal, she was giving him a hug and a kiss and telling him how wonderful he was for looking after me.'

'Really?'

'Yeah. Cathy was there—my sister. She and I were practically vomiting.'

'What did you expect?'

'Who knows. But I did not expect this year to include my partner and my mother having an after-dinner "moment".'

In fact I hardly expected to see my mother at all. This trip to Singapore was her first outside of Australia since a 1975 family holiday across the Tasman to New Zealand. Never, in all the years that I have lived outside of Australia—and that's a lot since 1989—has my mother shown the slightest inclination to visit. She is just not the travelling type. But now, at the age of seventy-nine, she's come to Singapore because of the profoundly sad realisation that, if I am jailed for more than a year, we may never see each other again.

Of course, this is just one of the elephants that sits quietly in the room whenever we are together. Talking openly about difficult issues is not my mother's way. Pat Lloyd was born and raised in the Depression era, a time when emotional openness was as rationed as food.

Karen is looking down at some notes in her lap. I think a change of topic is coming.

'So,' she says, 'what am I going to tell the judge?'

Karen is preparing to submit a letter to the judge. I've been mulling a question in my mind—it's a question that has been bugging me for some months; I suspect it's a question that would occur to a judge too. 'Well,' I say, 'the question I think I have to answer in court is the one that has troubled me for ages, Karen: how is it that a supposedly rational person like me did not ask for help earlier?'

'I think you're being pretty hard on yourself if you are still troubled by that.'

'What do you mean?'

'Peter, a person with a mental illness doesn't diagnose themselves. You were sick long before you knew it. There is a difference between being consciously aware that something is wrong, and being unconsciously aware. Dissociating is what happens when you cannot cope.'

'How do you tell that to a judge?'

'Well, I don't—at least I don't have to say it alone. Dr Ang is going to say it. And you have a second opinion too.'

Karen is talking about a report that has just come in from a top doctor at the Singapore Government Institute for Mental Health, IMH. I was sent to see Dr Devan, the psychiatrist who usually writes reports for the prosecution. He wrote a report that included the following conclusion: 'I am of the opinion that the patient is suffering from PTSD from the beginning of 2008.' His report will be sent to the judge along with a final assessment from Dr Ang Yong Gong.

SEVENTEEN
The day of judgement

IT IS THE DAY BEFORE my sentencing. Mazlee is sleeping beside me. Some days when I wake up first, I lie here quietly observing him curling around a pillow—a picture of contentment and vulnerability. I can talk to him, coo and cluck, and unconsciously he responds. 'What are you dreaming about?' I tease. And he smiles and curls a little more, and mumbles that he is dreaming about us. I imagine us too—together and far away in the future, long after the case is settled and long after my time in jail. But it is just a fantasy. I am certain that I have killed this relationship.

Now he is stirring and sighing, like a vessel coming to the surface after a long, deep dive. The sun has yet to reveal itself, but there are hints of unfolding daylight in the brightening sky outside. I lie back, taking a final stock of my surroundings.

Since July, this high-rise apartment has been a sanctuary of sorts. Getting into the lift on the ground floor often feels like getting onboard a rocket ship that transports me to a safer place, away from all terra-firma drama. Some days, when the long silences between us have blanketed me in despondency and gloom, these rooms seem more of a gilded prison.

Mazlee used to call me 'Blabber', because I talk so much, but in truth that stream has been drying up. I have seen the pain and anxiety that my crime has inflicted. I have seen Mazlee wrap himself into a smaller and smaller target, into a ball of indifference, perhaps to avoid emotional contamination. And in my own way I have responded in kind.

The safe and happy world we were building stands condemned through an ugly turn in circumstance. We are behaving like our time together is connected to a giant illuminated countdown clock that arrives at zero in twenty-four hours. Neither of us is actually saying it is over, not in so many words. The thought is exiled to the room of sorrows—that dark corner of all relationships where we dispatch and store grievances too large and too ugly to be seen and spoken of.

• • • • •

I'M SHOWERING. I TOOK hot showers for granted until I was arrested. Now I count every bead of water as though it were my last. The scent of soap seems heightened today. It is as though my body is storing up memories in preparation for a long, hard period of sensory deprivation. Today I am free to shower; tomorrow I won't be. Showering will be deemed a privilege, not a right, and it will be a functional experience. There won't be any lingering in a wet cocoon just for the fun of it.

'Good morning, baby.' Mazlee is awake and forcing a chipper mood. I take my hat off to airline cabin crew—they fake cheerful like a whore fakes an orgasm. 'Are we still on for breakfast with Kirsty?'

I'm rubbing the water off the shower screen so I can see his face. 'Yes.'

'Okay,' he says, his voice trailing off. 'Afterwards I want to go shopping. I need an uplight.'

Kirsty has come back to Singapore, this time with her new partner, David, for moral support. She is coming to court for the hearing. Mazlee keeps asking if I want him there too. I have avoided a direct answer to this question for weeks, but last night I finally broke. I told him explicitly that I want him by my side. He hasn't said whether he is coming yet. Somehow I doubt it, but I send that negative thought off with the morning dispatch rider to the room of sorrows. I don't have any fight left.

We're in the PS Café, in the Paragon Centre on Orchard Road. It's just after 9.30 in the morning and we are the first customers of the day: Kirsty and David, Peter and Mazlee. A passer-by might have a hundred years at their disposal and still never guess the provenance of our foursome. Nothing in this tableau vivant of middle-class comfort and civility betrays the shock and anguish and crushing anxiety that brings us together on this day in early December. I've studied the menu three times and comprehended nothing. I'm going to order, simply because that's what is expected when you are sitting in a restaurant with a menu in your hands and a cheery waiter is hovering overhead.

'Fresh juice and Eggs Benny, thanks.'

Kirsty arches an eyebrow and fires off a sarcastic, 'Eggs *Benny* is it now?'

'That's what it says here.' I'm pointing at the menu card. I lean over, conspiratorial-style, and add, by way of explanation, 'Gay—but not that gay.'

'I hope not,' she says with a wink.

This is the first time I've met David face to face. Until now we've been exchanging pleasantries on Skype. He's rake thin and wiry, like a boxer twitching with pre-bout energy. He clutches Kirsty's hands, openly declaring a new Republic of David.

My phone is ringing. It's Haq. 'Peter. Stay by your phone. We may need to talk to you during the day. Okay?'

'Sure. Anything wrong?'

'No. I'm just negotiating a few last-minute matters with the prosecution, to make sure tomorrow goes smoothly. I'm hoping to get confirmation that the DPP will not be addressing the court on sentencing—you know, seeking a deterrent sentence to make an example of you.'

'Would they?'

'No reason to, but I want to make sure of it today. And we've already drawn up a notice of appeal should the sentence be massively disproportionate.'

'How much is too much?'

'Anything over fifteen months would, in my view, be grounds for an appeal. But that's not something that affects you yet. No matter what, start the sentence tomorrow. You can carry out an appeal from inside, and count the time against any reduction of sentence. There is no point remaining out on bail after tomorrow.'

'Okay.'

'I'll call back if there are any further queries we need to clear up.'

I hang up the phone and say nothing. Nobody else needs to hear this stuff. It will only put them off their Eggs Benny.

• • • • •

AN HOUR LATER I am across town, in the lighting shop. I can't quite believe that I am shopping for lighting accessories on my last day of freedom, but I suppose it's better than sitting around the apartment reading the same newspaper paragraph over and over.

'Which one do you think?' Mazlee is holding up two lights that look exactly the same to me.

'The white one.'

'Peter. They are both white.'

'The really, really white one then,' I say sarcastically before walking away to answer my telephone.

'Hi, it's Karen. I hope I'm not interrupting.'

Laughing: 'No, Karen. You just saved me from a big gay boys' dilemma: the white light, or the really, really white light.'

'What?'

'I'm in a lighting shop watching Mazlee, uptight, buy an uplight to shine on his potted plant.'

'That sounds like fun.'

'Not really. I once trailed behind him in the manchester department at Robinsons when he wanted to buy a sheet set. It took four hours. Four hours, Karen! I could furnish the whole house in that amount of time.'

'It's quite something.'

'Do you think they will make me watch people shop for hours in prison? That would be my idea of torture.'

'Glad to see you still have a sense of humour.'

'Yeah, well that's something, I suppose. To what do I owe the pleasure?'

'Well, I have just had an interesting phone call from a colleague at the Institute of Mental Health. He has been commissioned by the courts to do a study of all the reports on your case, and report back to the judge.'

'Really? So what does that mean?'

'Well, I guess it says that the courts are taking a very close look at your PTSD. That can't be a bad thing. My friend can't tell me what he will say, but he wanted me to know that the issue was being taken seriously.'

'Well, thanks for letting me know.'

'How are you doing today—apart from shopping?'

'I'm going to keep busy, and have a few drinks and fall into a drunken coma as late as possible.'

'Well, that sounds like an understandable plan. I will see you at court tomorrow at ten. Okay?'

'Thanks, Karen.'

I hang up and go back to the lighting department. Mazlee has already picked out a light. It is black.

· · · · ·

DINNER. FOR THIS NEXT tableau of improbable provenance, we have Sophie from downstairs and Sarah (my AFP friend), and Peter and Mazlee. The venue for this Last Supper of sorts is the Hard Rock Café, situated just off Orchard Road. It is busy for a Monday night—a series of separate office parties are underway in its dark corners. The Christmas décor adorning the walls and tables is heavy and obvious, like everything at the hard-sell, hard-to-hear Hard Rock Café. Subtlety has never been on the menu here.

I am uncomfortable in this setting, because it takes me back to the Bali bombings. After the terrorist attacks occurred in Bali, accommodation close to ground zero was scarce and the ABC's Jakarta bureau had to book my crew into the Kuta Beach Hard Rock Hotel, which features 418 tribute rooms and suites (individually 'adorned with images of rock history', as they proudly boast). I was in the John Lennon tribute room—a shrine, to be more exact, loaded up with all manner of kitschery. I monitored local TV coverage of the disaster on the John Lennon television. I channel-surfed the CNN and BBC disaster coverage using the John Lennon remote control. I slept fitfully under the John Lennon duvee, and showered off the juice of the corpses while standing in the John Lennon bathtub. When my appetite returned, I could order John Lennon french fries and club sandwiches from a John Lennon room service menu.

If a Mark David Chapman look-alike, packing heat, had delivered room service, I would not have been the least bit surprised. I liked John Lennon (after he ditched Paul), but the former Beatle, even at his most narcissistic, would have puked at the crass commercial abuse of his name and image by the Hard Rock hotel chain.

Ordering at a Hard Rock restaurant, whether in Singapore, Bali or Bangkok, is an uncomplicated business. The generic menu consists of a range of exotically named burgers that somehow become, at the moment of consumption, conspicuously identical to the tastebuds. Everything on the plate—the hunk of pure beef, the toasted bread, the limp leaf, the plasticised cheese, the oversized French fries—tastes exactly the same no matter what the order. It's a clever business that ensures nobody feels let down by the experience. By being all things to all people all the time, the Hard Rock food chain epitomises a culinary race to the bottom of the palate. Nobody escapes with the impression that they ordered badly because, by definition, everyone does badly, equally. It is the grilled-meat common-denominator opiate for the masses, and tonight I'm surrendering to the numbing blandness of it all.

With a self-satisfied grin I look to the waiter and declare, 'I will have the SOS burger.'

I love Sarah's big, wide Aussie smile, always the entrée to her verbal main. 'A rescue-themed meal,' she says approvingly. 'Good choice!'

Mazlee tries to laugh, but he's contained and close to tears with pent-up tension. Sophie stares across the table in wonderment, or possibly shock, at my black-humoured openness. I sometimes catch Sophie looking at me with undisguised curiosity that seems to say, *You're really fascinating, like an alien landed at my table.*

We've ordered garlic bread, but this appetiser seems beyond the usual blandness. And the red wine, decanted and shared, feels watered-down and robbed of bouquet and body. I wonder if I am alone in experiencing a desensitised palate.

My first experience of the Hard Rock Café was, curiously enough, here in Singapore. It was back in October 1993, and I was on my honeymoon with Kirsty. I may be imagining this, but I think we sat at, or near, this very same table. Back then—in another life, in another time—we ordered a bottle of Jacobs Creek and paid the then princely sum of forty dollars for a bottle that could have been purchased in Sydney for a quarter of that sum. As I recall, that '93 drop was vintage *chateau de crap*, but for very different reasons.

• • • • •

'PETER, WHAT ARE YOU thinking about today?' asks the reporter.

This is the first time I've spoken to reporters as I stride up the courtroom stairs. I reply, drily, 'I'm thinking it is about ten seconds between here and the front door.'

I'm on my way up to Courtroom Number 5. It is showtime at the Subordinate Court circus, and I am the main attraction. Kirsty and I came in the first taxi, and in the vehicle behind were the men in black—the lawyers, Jeeming and Haq.

The black team had drawn up a tight protocol for today's spectacle, which looked like a Special Event Running Order. It began with a 10am rendezvous, and a joint arrival at court. This is the legal equivalent of a show of unity—the kind of act politicians perform in public before they go behind closed doors to knife each other in the back.

The morning has sped by, so far. I left home in a big hurry—I didn't see any point in lingering in discomfort. I was up and dressed and ready to leave before Mazlee had uttered a word of goodbye and farewell. He might be in denial about what is happening to me today, but his frigid display was a cruel and final blow.

I went to meet Kirsty at Starbucks on Orchard Road, and drank a coffee and made smalltalk with her and David. Then, out of nowhere, Mazlee appeared. He sat in hollow silence, unable to summon up words to express whatever it is that he is feeling today. He shared the cab to the lawyers' office.

I was on the street when I put it to him. 'Are you coming to court?' I demanded.

'No,' he replied.

'Then this is goodbye, Mazlee.'

He hugged me awkwardly, turned and walked away.

• • • • •

I'M SITTING IN THE public gallery with Kirsty. She's keeping it together remarkably well for someone who is breaking into a million pieces inside. We have had this arrangement throughout our lives, that whenever one is fragile the other is strong. Today I'm the one playing the role of strength, in support of her agonies. That is the least that I can do for her.

'My God, you look so calm,' says Sarah as she hugs me warmly.

'I'm faking it,' I reply.

'Well, you keep on faking it. Don't give them the satisfaction.'

'I won't.'

In a sense, I'm not faking it—I really am standing on my own two feet now. I know that I am strong enough to contend with whatever sentence is handed down today. I am quietly optimistic that it will be measured in months, not years.

All of those difficult and confronting sessions of therapy since July with Karen Gosling and Dr Ang have paid off. The crisis phase of my PTSD condition has passed, and now I am well on the way to a full recovery. I feel the strength and confidence and optimism of my former self being restored every day. This is a moment of climax, and the judgement about to be delivered signals the commencement of the denouement—a long catharsis that will release the tension and anxiety and pave the way to my personal resolution. You don't have to give up entirely in order to let go of the past and look forward to the future.

'I'm going to own this sentence. It's not going to own me,' I told Ed Roy over those drinks after court. I was only half joking when about a month ago I started referring not to a prison sentence, but to my 'monastic sabbatical'. The people I told probably quietly rolled their eyes, but I really meant it—I have studied an exercise regime that is suitable for a prisoner and I have compiled a library of books that will form the basis of my study. To the extent that I can control my experience, I will.

My library is an odd patchwork. I have heavy tomes like *The Histories* of Herodotus, regarded as one of the seminal works in all of history, and the writings of Aristotle and other philosophers; some memoirs of the great and the good; travellers' tales from the likes of Theroux and Bryson; a range of studies on state power and public policy; the sheer roughage of Archer and Brown; the absurdness of Joe Queenan; plus the standard classics, Shakespeare, Austen and Dickens.

I have half an idea that guilty pleasures lie ahead. Joyce will be there too, but I have a funny feeling that ploughing through *Ulysses* will be about as much fun as colonic irrigation. I know that the literary crowd will wish me hanged for saying so—for failing to grasp the purity of the stream of consciousness form, the brilliance of the structure and the delight of Joyce's prose. They will excoriate me for ignoring the election of *Ulysses* as the best English-language novel of the twentieth century. But let's be frank: I'm a hack, and I'm going to jail. Who really cares what I think?

• • • • •

'LLOYD PETER GERARD.' It's a court official, motioning for me to come and stand in the dock. I'm crossing a threshold, from the public gallery to the criminal dock—to a parallel universe, where my name is mud and, if it is said at all, it is said backwards. I've brought a bag to court that contains three items: a pen, a notebook and a book to take with me to prison, Lee Kuan Yew's memoir.

'My client is not a drug abuser.' Haq is on his feet, pleading my case. 'The main reason he had endeavoured to have the drugs was to deal with a mental illness. It became a sort of self-medication for him. He was not taking drugs for recreational purposes.'

I'm sitting in the dock, observing the scene as calmly as possible. It is not so bad. I thought this would feel much worse. I am not even panicking. I now possess the sort of steady calm that earned me a reputation for coping with a crisis. I feel like I am passing some kind of pressure test.

To my right I can see the DPP, Natalie Morris, sitting at the bar table listening thoughtfully to Haq. She is a slightly built woman, clad in her finest legal-eagle black outfit. A few blue-uniformed police are assembled to the right, poised to snatch me if I try to make a break for it. I'm outnumbered—there are five of them. One has a pair of handcuffs in his hands; I imagine they are for me. Up ahead, I see the judge. She's a heavy-set Malay woman. She is looking sternly at Haq, a fixed expression on her face. She looks like a tiger set to pounce on him. Maybe she's bored by his presentation. Maybe she's read it all and wonders, like me, why on earth he has to read it aloud. *Who is the audience for this dissertation?* I'm thinking.

Over to my left, there is a table of reporters from the local media. *Local knowledge. They knew where to sit to get the best angle to watch me. Well, good luck. I'm not going to give you a moment of reporting joy.* I'm reaching into my bag. I want to remember what Haq says too, so I'm going to take notes. Old habits die hard. I can almost imagine that I'm not in the dock today, that I am still the reporter, and Haq's speech is of the utmost importance to my report.

'It's all very well for Mr Lloyd to say these things.' It's the DPP's turn. She is reading from notes, and doesn't sound very convinced by her own argument. 'It is apparent to us that the accused can still tell right from wrong, although he was taking such drugs as a coping mechanism.'

I'm glad I didn't waste money on a trial against this black-and-white mindset. It is impossible to argue against the self-satisfied moral certainty of authoritarian Singapore. Nothing is grey to these people; all life is black and white, right and wrong. It's a realm that feeds off clearly defined racially superior winners and racially inferior losers. If you understand the kiasuism of the Hokkien Chinese—their fear of death, their fear of losing, their unerring need to win at all costs and all the time—then you understand everything about the Chinese who run Singapore.

Months of carefully explained medical evidence about PTSD has been sifted by the DPP and now I'm hearing it torn down and declared to have no merit or, in the harsh black-and-white words of DPP Natalie Morris, 'it is not a justification, neither is it a good excuse'. *What would be a satisfactory excuse for you, Miss Morris? Would you like to walk in my shoes to a few bomb-blast mortuaries? Would you like to spend time, as I did, holding the hand of the weeping man who begs you to poison him and his family, so they can be relieved of the agonies of their lives in a refugee camp?* I am on the wrong end of the kiasu spirit today.

I'm hoping this curt dismissal of my pleading by the prosecution is not the shared view of the judge, who is summoning me to stand for sentencing. Her name is Hamidah Ibrahim.

'For the first charge, the sentence is eight months. For the second charge, an eight-month sentence. For possessing the paraphernalia of the case, two months.'

Bang! She strikes a gavel.

The reporters in front of me are racing from the room. I can't read their reaction, to know what has just happened. I heard the judge talking, but she was speaking so fast I don't understand the mathematical calculations she has just uttered. *Is that eight, plus eight?*

I'm looking down at Haq and Jeeming. They have their heads together at the bar table; they are comparing notes. Jeeming is coming over. 'Peter. That is a good result. Do you understand? That's ten months. With one-third off automatically for weekends and public holidays, you will serve just over six months. That is a very, very good result.'

Haq is on his feet again. I think he is confirming the sentencing with the judge. I can't hear him. All I can hear is Kirsty behind me, weeping. I turn back and give her the look that says, 'It's okay. I can do this. Don't worry.'

'Okay, Lloyd. Turn around!' I am being handcuffed. It is the beginning of my descent into the bowels of the Subordinate Courts, back to the catacombs. 'Let's go!'

I don't look back. I'm not going to feed the beast.

EIGHTEEN

Prisoner 12988

IT IS SOMETIMES EASY to forget the Republic of Singapore is a tropical jungle 137 kilometres north of the equator. The abundance of air-conditioned homes and condos and hotels, buses and cars and trains, shops and malls and offices lull inhabitants into believing they live in climate-Disneyland, where even the elements have submitted to authoritarian People's Action Party control.

That uniquely Singaporean delusion ends once you enter the criminal justice system, where a sharp dose of climate-reality smacks you hard in the face. Moments after my handcuffing, I am shunted down a series of descending staircases into the clammy subterranean basement of the Subordinate Court. As a metaphor for going down, journeying down so many staircases seems quite apt. The atmosphere in the prison underworld is feverish and thick and musky. My once crisp grey suit is wilting, and I sense rising damp in my armpits.

'Lloyd Peter Gerard,' commands the officer in charge of prisoner reception, 'you have been convicted and given a ten-month sentence, understand, lah?'

'Yes.'

'Now you must surrender the contents of your pockets. Remove your belt and place it in this bag with your personal items.' He is pushing a long manila envelope across the table. 'And give me that bag.'

He's referring to the knapsack I brought to court. It contains my notebook, a pen and the Lee Kuan Yew memoir.

'These items will be transported to the prison with you today,' he explains, 'and kept in custody until release. Understand, lah?'

'Yes.'

'Any complaints?'

I'm thinking, *Isn't it tempting fate to invite a person who has just been sentenced to jail to complain?* 'No,' I reply.

'Then sign here.'

I am signing my name for the last time. Prisoners in biometric Singapore confirm their identity by pressing the right thumbprint onto an electronic keypad. My official paperwork is affixed with something new: a number. I am prisoner 12988.

I'm led to a crowded holding cell, where there is a feral odour like a skunk is lurking somewhere in the shadows.

'Hey, brother, welcome home,' says a smirking prisoner of Tamil appearance.

I smile faintly: enough to acknowledge this stranger's gallows humour, but not enough to encourage him to utter more banalities. I walk to the back of the room and find a space against the wall, sinking slowly to my haunches. I fix my stare at the floor, as if it were the most absorbing slab of flooring concrete in all of Christendom. *The first part is the worst part. The first part is the worst part,* I'm thinking, mantra-style. *Just stay cool and roll with it,* I coach myself.

'What case?'

When I look up, I see the grinning Tamil again.

'What case?' he repeats.

'Drugs. Possession.' I'm editing, of course, for now seems like a good time to trust no one. *These guys are convicts,* I think, still in the process of adjusting my sense of identity to the fact that I am now one too.

'Ah. How long?'

'What do you mean?'

'Sentence. How long?'

'Ten.'

'Years?'

'Months.'

'Ah. This is good.'

'Good?'

'Yes. Others here get much longer sentences. But not me or my friends, over there.' He is pointing to a small group of Tamils. 'We are all being caned and deported soon.'

'What is your case?' I ask. I don't see any reason not to be just as nosy.

'Visa overstay.'

'Where from?'

'Sri Lanka.'

'How long have you been here?'

'Most of us, many years,' he explains. 'I was here for eight years. Them, eleven years each.'

'Eight years?' I'm genuinely surprised by the scale of this overstay. 'Wow, you really like to overstay your welcome, buddy.'

Laughing, he says, 'Yes, my friend. But it is better here than in Sri Lanka, no? They have a very bad economy, and it is very violent. We are Tamils. We came here with the correct visa, but we wanted to stay and keep working for our families. We did, for many years.'

'How did you get caught?' I'm intrigued, still functioning with the curious mind of the reporter-at-large.

'One of our friends was caught. The police said they would deport but not cane him if he helped catch any others. Bloody bastard. He betrays us. Now we get the cane and get deported. How will I support my family, eh? No job. No money. And my ass,' he is rubbing his buttocks, 'they are going to whip me, brother.'

This is shocking, but nonetheless a diverting distraction from my woes. Sitting forward now, I ask, 'What is your name?'

'Amar. It means long life.'

'Not if you keep overstaying your visa, Amar.'

He's laughing hard, like he wants to expel something. 'Yes, brother. Yes, you are right. Come. Come and meet my brothers.'

I'm escorted by Amar to meet the other visa busters. 'This is Maan,' he says, pointing one man out, 'and this is Selva and this Guna.' Then, turning back to me, 'What is your good name?'

'Peter,' I reply.

I'm surrounded, and they are all anxious to talk: 'What country?' 'What case?' 'Visa overstay?' 'For how long inside?'

I'm going to keep this simple, I think, so I give them a simple sentence reply. 'Australia, drugs, possession, ten months.'

'Cricket?'

I was wondering how long it would take before we got to this. I know from experience that any first-time conversation involving a man from the Subcontinent must involve a mandatory conversation about the Sport of the Commonwealth. I don't mind cricket when the game is compelling. But this criterion means I largely miss Test matches entirely—a fact I generally withhold from Indians, Sri Lankans and Pakistanis, because they are likely to receive such a confession as favourably as the suggestion that I want to have sexual relations with their favourite aunty.

Being a 'cricket-denier' leads to doubt about your manliness, since true believers adhere to the group thinkers' notion that no real man could possibly question the logic of the five-day Test match. I would absolutely prefer to watch paint dry, since drying paint is an activity with a one hundred per cent probability of an outcome. Cricket, as cricket-obsessives know only too well, offers no certainty—a point I like to illustrate by reminding them that in one infamous 1972 Test series, between New Zealand and the West Indies, all five matches were drawn.

'Ah yes, cricket . . .' I say. 'Ricky Ponting. Shane Warne.'

And with those two names, I am done.

I'm thinking, *Who else plays cricket? Oh, that's right—the guy with the bunny ears. What's the guy's name? Adam? It's Adam, yes. Adam Gilmore? No, that's not it.*

'Gilchrist!' I announce. Too vehemently perhaps, because the Tamils seem startled and are stepping back.

'Ah, Gilchrist veery good,' says one.

'Shin War, best ever, brother,' says another. 'Number one speen bolla.'

I've also gotten used to hearing men from the Subcontinent have great trouble pronouncing Shane Warne's name properly. If any bloke says 'Shin' in conversation I assume they are talking about the Aussie bowler with the infamous fetish for text messaging. I have often wondered if 'Shin' wished he were born in India or Pakistan, two countries where cricketers are worshipped with the respect and reverence of immortals. Nobody questions Indian and Pakistani stars about their peccadilloes or foul mouth or penchant for smoking a ciggie.

'So when will you be caned?' I ask the Tamil four.

Selva speaks first. 'No one tells us anything. We have to stay in jail for a few weeks, and then we will be sent back to Colombo.'

I am curious to know if they have any idea what is coming. 'Do you know what happens when they cane you?'

'Yes, brother. Very bad.' It's Amar again. He motions to the room. 'Some of them have been telling us what happens.' Now he is bending forward, demonstrating the caning position. 'It is like this,' he says.

Guna, the shortest, steps forward. He pauses for effect, like he has an important announcement. 'Everyone,' he is enunciating deliberately, 'scream for their mother!'

That grim prophecy silences us all. Given that I'd come close to having the caning experience myself, I am filled with sympathetic dread for these men in front of me. As far as I can tell they haven't hurt anyone, except, perhaps, the Singapore Inland Revenue Service. Amar says they cane everyone who stays ninety days beyond their visa.

'How many strokes?' I ask.

'Three strokes each,' answers Amar.

Another young man who has been listening to our conversation steps forward. 'I am Sri Lankan also,' he says. 'I am to be deported as well.'

The others eye with suspicion this new Sri Lankan. I don't think he is a Tamil. With his word-perfect English and lighter skin, I am guessing that he is Sinhalese, the mortal enemy of Tamils. I'm thinking, *Great, now I'm in the middle of a civil war feud.*

'What is your case?' I ask, trying to mend the invisible fence.

'I got drunk on Saturday,' he explains, 'when I was with my friends. I went to the 7-Eleven store to buy cigarettes. I don't know why, but I grabbed a bottle of wine and ran out of the shop. The police arrested me straight away.'

'And they deport you for that?' I ask, with a tone of unintended suspicion. It does not seem a 'hanging' offence to me.

'My visa was tied to my school enrolment. I am studying hospitality. *Was.* They cancelled my visa straight away. My school expelled me and won't give back my money for the rest of term. They will deport me in a few days.' The young man pauses as he fights to hold back tears. 'I can't believe it. One day I am a student. My parents are so proud of me. And now . . .' His voice is trailing off as he thrusts his hands into his pockets, as if searching for an explanation for his moment of poor judgement.

'It's tough, eh?' I offer. 'No second chances here, my friend.'

'None. I can't believe it. I have to go back to Colombo. I never thought I would have to go back. It is so unsafe, and there are no jobs. My country is a mess.' He is looking at the Tamil foursome. 'And we can't live with each other without trying to kill each other.'

His words strike a vein of empathy in the other men. I can see them soften towards this lost young man from their broken homeland. They step forward as one, surrounding him, rubbing his shoulders as he weeps into his chest.

I am the witness to a ceasefire.

• • • • •

WE'VE BOARDED THE six o'clock Subordinate Court Special, a Singapore Prison Service bus. This is the modern equivalent of galley slavery—we're stinking with sweat, shackled and shoved onto crowded benches with the rest of the captive oarsmen.

We have all been double-handcuffed around both ankles and hands, the latter held behind our backs to make escaping that much less feasible. We're jammed together on metallic bus benches, sitting cheek by jowl in a broiling heat. The only visible ventilation is a small square-shaped hatch in the roof, like that found on a commuter bus. It's propped open, and I can see a background of grey twilight against the whir of amber street lamps and passing tree branches.

This is an express service to the Queenstown Remand Prison, QRP to acronym-happy officials. QRP is a clearing house where convicted prisoners are billeted before assignment to a permanent address at one of Singapore's fourteen prisons and drug rehabilitation centres. Some of my fellow travellers are engaged in animated conversation, like fans heading to a footy match. *They must have taken this bus ride before.*

The bus seizes and jolts and wheezes while manoeuvring through the gates and security checkpoints at QRP. For each thrust and turn, the human livestock in the back are doing involuntary body slams on each other because our arms and legs are shackled and immobilised. *I will only eat free-range chicken, from now on.* Finally the bus comes to a halt.

'Out! Everybody, get out!' The disembodied and demanding voice seems agitated in the extreme. 'Out now, lah!' When the back door opens, I catch sight of a huge Tamil prison guard smacking the backside of the bus with a thick black truncheon. He is truly terrifying.

I follow a line of disembarking prisoner-passengers obediently hurrying off the bus. We're being ordered to assemble on a driveway, in two lines. To my left a soaring off-white wall, topped with a menacing coil of shiny barbed wire. In an open-air watchtower there is the shadow of a guard and a weapon muzzle, glinting in the dewy half-light. A gentle rain is falling, but I cannot feel the droplets on my greasy skin. My sensory awareness has dimmed to a single item of cognition: I am a prisoner of the state.

'Strip!' It is the menacing Tamil guard again. 'Take off everything! Leave your clothes in a pile!'

A few of us catch each other's eye, exchanging looks of shame and terror and bewilderment.

'I am going to walk in front of you,' the officer barks with his hands behind his back, camp commandant style. 'When I get to you, open your mouth for inspection. Raise your tongue,' he commands. He has holstered the truncheon and is using his hands to point to different parts of the body, the unnecessary illustration imperative.

'Then show me your cock and balls!' he yells. 'If you have any jewellery or cock rings or piercing, remove them! After you show me your balls, turn around—and hold your cheeks open!'

Did I just hear that right? I am commanded to expose myself to a prison officer? While I'm processing this crude instruction, the guard adds an ominous and, to my mind, quite unnecessary threat. 'If any of you is caught holding contraband,' he says, 'you will be charged and caned.'

None of my class of new arrivals responds or volunteers a comment. We submit in meek silence. To speak now would be to invite unwanted attention, probably amounting to a punishable offence. And what is there to say when such a humiliation is carried out in the open, without regard to modesty or dignity? This carry-on belongs in a concentration camp, not a supposedly 'civilised' penal system.

'Okay,' says the guard, with an air of conclusion. The inspection seems to be over. Now he is moving on to stage two of the induction. 'In that box,' he is pointing to a large cardboard crate, 'you will find shorts and T-shirts. Find your size, get dressed, and fall back in line.' The rain is falling harder, so we're naked and shivering and sheltering for cover under the awning of the jail's main entrance.

A frail Chinese man, whimpering and wiping tears from his eyes, searches the box. I lean in to help. 'What size?' I ask.

'Small,' he replies

'Let me help you.' I'm scrambling through the box, acting as his eyes.

'I'm not wearing my contacts today,' he explains. 'I can't read these labels.'

I can. I grab a large size for me and present the sight-challenged old man with the small-sized shorts and T-shirt from the box.

'Thank you, sir.' He presses his palms together and bows, a Thai-style *wai*—part greeting, part show of respect.

I grab his hands. 'Please. That is not necessary.' I'm suddenly conscious of our nakedness, and the shared shame and embarrassment.

He is staring at me. 'You are that Australian reporter.'

'Yes,' I reply.

'I am so sorry for you. My country is very hard. No one is allowed to make a mistake.'

We dress, and he becomes more talkative. 'I am here for six week for hiring a foreigner without the right paperwork,' he says, adding, 'Can you believe that! My staff made a stupid paperwork mistake and I end up in prison. I'm sixty-seven years old.'

Staring at me, examining my face, he says, 'How long did they give you?'

'Ten months.'

'With one-third off for remissions?'

'Yes.'

'So you will be out of prison . . .' He is calculating. 'End of June? The twenty-third, I think.'

'Yes. But how did you know that?'

Tapping his forehead, 'Accountant.'

'Hey! No talking!' It is another officer, tapping a truncheon against his leg. 'Inside now, sit on the floor and wait for your name to be called!'

Dressed in blue shorts and a white T-shirt, we new arrivals are now sitting in meditative silence on the reception centre floor, legs crossed like obedient schoolboys. Behind thick plate-glass panels is an office crowded with prison guards hunkered over computer terminals. The scene is reminiscent of a banking chamber.

'Prisoner Lloyd!' I hear my name hailed over a loudspeaker. 'Lloyd! Go to window three!'

I sit myself down at the window, like a job applicant.

'Name?' asks the young officer behind the glass. I'm thinking, *You called me, mister, don't you know that already?*

I reply, 'Lloyd, Peter Gerard,' saying my name backwards in another sign of surrender and submission. I daydream my way through the induction interview, giving rote answers to rote questions about my date of birth, nationality, age and other blah-blah-blah biographical data. I can feel the breeze of air-conditioning through the communication hole. And I can smell the pleasant odour of deodorant. If the officers smell that clean, I wonder, do prisoners smell unclean?

'Do you belong here?' The young officer has stopped tapping at the computer keyboard. He is eyeballing me, weighing my silence, and waiting for a clear response. My reverie on air and odours is interrupted.

'I'm sorry—did you just ask me if I belong here?'

'Yes.'

'Is that an existential question?'

'Again?' He leans forward, tilting his head to the glass.

'Never mind,' I say. Now is not the time to go on a *Hitchhiker's Guide to the Galaxy* tangent with this baby-faced officer, who probably has no clue who Douglas Adams is.

'What if I say no?'

'Then I have to classify you as a problem prisoner.'

'Me?'

'Yes.'

'I don't think I like the sound of that.'

'What answer do you think you should give, then?'

'I deserve to be here, unreservedly,' I declare, with a slap of my left hand on the counter.

'Good answer,' he replies drily. I think he is smiling. I can't be sure. The bulletproof glass needs a good once-over with a clean cloth.

After a short wait I am escorted up a series of staircases to a landing, where I am assigned to my first prison cell. I am in a room by myself. Standing in the middle of the room, I begin sizing up my environment. As I stretch my arms out, my fingers touch the walls on either side. Earlier, I stood at the back wall and took four long strides to reach the door. A real estate agent would describe this space as 'cosy'.

It is 9.30pm and the lights have just been switched off. 'Alone at last,' I say, stretching out on the thin, roll-up cane mat that is to be my substitute for a real mattress. Extreme tiredness, such as I feel now, is non-narcotic pain relief. Fatigue numbs the body naturally; it dims the mind and papers over the deep-down self-pity and misery and mortification. I am too tired to confront the shock and shame of being locked up in prison.

'The first day is the worst day,' I tell myself over and again, repeating the self-help mantra. I'm lying, of course, but this is the grand self-delusion that enables survival, a self-help benediction concocted to get me from one moment in time to the next without falling flat on my face.

As I'm lying here I begin thinking about the actor Morgan Freeman, and the voice-over in the movie *The Shawshank Redemption*: 'The first night's the toughest, no doubt about it. They march you in naked as the day you were born, skin burning and half blind from that delousing shit they throw on you, and when they put you in that cell, when those bars slam home, that's when you know it's for real.'

It's for real all right.

• • • • •

YOU MUST BE TIRED when you sleep through on your first night in prison.

The lights came on when it was still eerily quiet and gloomy outside. That much I know for certain, because there is a long ventilation window set into the bricks high up on the back wall of my cell. Captivity is akin to a form of blindness, brought on suddenly. Denied the ability to see beyond the narrow world of the prison cell, I am relying instead on what I can hear and smell and imagine. I am now lying on the bamboo mat with my newly issued white T-shirt draped over my eyes to simulate darkness, not wanting to surrender the oblivion of sleep yet. For those who lack the mad courage to attempt a breakout, sleep may be the next best form of escape.

I shut my eyes and concentrate and this is what I hear: sounds of cheap, Chinese-made plastic slippers, the footwear of all Singapore prison inmates, flip-flopping along the corridor outside. Low, murmuring voices and a sliding sound, like a heavy box being dragged from cell to cell. *Bring out your dead*, I think.

Outside, birds tweet and there's a low rumble of early-morning traffic. An aircraft climbing after take-off. These outside sounds are the din of the parallel universe, the free world, which is continuing without me for the next 200 days.

The voices of my present universe, strange and accented, have arrived at my door: 'Boss,' I hear.

When I remove my T-shirt from over my face, my eyes catch up with my ears. I can see a heavy-set man, Indian or Bangladeshi, and in his outstretched hand two sandwiches and a steaming mug. *A prison treat: breakfast in bed!*

'Peter—take your breakfast!' It's a tall, bald Malay guard looming at the prisoner's shoulder. 'Normally we do not open the door. Breakfast comes through the trapdoor,' he says, pointing to the small opening at the base of the door. 'But this is your first day,' he says with a warm smile. I know this face—it is Fahmy, the kind Malay guard who inducted me during my brief stay in this remand prison before I was bailed last July.

'Nice to see you again,' I say.

'How long is your sentence?'

'Ten months.'

'Not so bad. You can do this. Just accept and adapt. I know you can.'

'You bet,' I reply.

'I will come back for a chat later, okay?'

Prison food has much to be modest about. The bread is politically incorrect white. The filling is yellow goo, a cross between margarine and butter. I sniff it, like a household pet would inspect a bowl that it will devour regardless.

With my eyes shut, inhaling deeply, I put my sense of smell to the test of identifying the content of the mug. The memory library—the keeper of 10 000 smells—seems closed for business. 'What *is* this?' I mutter, as I take a hesitant sip. I cannot identify the smell, or taste. This is, for all intents and purposes, a steaming mug of brown.

• • • • •

I'M DOZING AGAIN, in a state of semi-consciousness, when the door swings open.

'Okay, Peter, come and have a haircut.' It is Fahmy, ushering me out of the cell to a chair parked in the corridor. 'Regulations require that all prisoners maintain a short haircut at all times.'

I should have seen this coming. Singapore is famous for the short hair fetish. It is one of the many oddities of Lee Kuan Yew that he regarded men with long hair in the sixties and seventies as a symbol of western decadence. Indeed, until the 1980s, men arriving in the city-state were inspected for hair length. Those who fell short of expectations were summarily shorn of their locks at border crossings.

'The cookie here will see to you,' says Fahmy, gesturing to the man who brought me the breakfast.

'What is a cookie?'

'That's the name we give to inmates who are workers. You will be a cookie too if you get work.'

Fahmy stands back while the cookie takes to my hair with all the sensitivity of an angry sheep shearer. Three runs of a number-two blade up the back of my head, two runs over each of the ears and three more across the top. It is over in less than sixty seconds. The cookie cum hairdresser hasn't uttered a single word.

'Wow, that's the quickest haircut I've ever had—can I see?'

'No, boss. No mirror,' says the cookie.

'Probably for the best.'

'Huh?'

'Never mind,' I say.

Queenstown Remand Prison is as old as me, having opened about a month before my birth in 1966. But it makes forty-something look pretty shabby. The pale lime-green walls and spotted concrete floors and gloomy lighting make the institution look old and tired and washed out. The authorities have done just enough to make it serviceable as a holding pen for prisoners, but little else. I have already noticed that nobody here, officers or prisoners, seems to smile. It is as though merely being inside QRP sucks the joy of life out of every single mortal being. Even the ants and cockroaches who share my cell seem to move with undue sluggishness. Perhaps they are veterans who understand that QRP food scraps are mean and undernourishing.

'Follow me!' Another guard is leading me up a staircase. The stairwell is covered with cyclone wire, preventing inmates from throwing themselves over. 'You've got yard time now for half an hour,' he says as we arrive at a carefully cyclone-fenced rooftop courtyard that is the size of half a basketball court. The sky is grey and cloudy, and the sounds of the parallel universe—commuting cars and traffic below, and jet aircraft soaring above—are closer. I can almost feel the vibrations. This is a strange sensation—to be so tantalisingly close, yet so far from all that is normal. When you are sent to jail you are uncoupled from society.

Yet dwelling on what I cannot be part of is no way to adapt. If I am to 'accept and adapt', I must tune out the white noise of the normal world and tune into the new sounds of captivity. I have to maintain focus on adapting to prison. The sounds of cars and planes and the hum of free life are no longer my main priority. What I must learn to accept is the rhythms of custodial life, and I have a sinking feeling that the flip-flop of slippers on concrete will be the soundtrack of that humble existence.

NINETEEN

Home away from home

I HAVE ARRIVED. My new 'home' is Tanah Merah Prison, on the far east of Singapore Island. The prison is just one hundred tantalising metres from one of the world's busiest runways at Changi International Airport, so close yet so far from a getaway. Perhaps the mandarins of Singapore Inc. do possess a sense of humour after all, however black. This deliberate act of geographic torture is simultaneously carrot and stick. *Wanna ride? Well tough luck, fella, you can't have it!* It is life on the edge of a runway where nobody is cleared for take-off. Tanah Merah is Hotel California, with avgas.

I reached TMP—that's the acronym used by the CISCO guards who delivered me—via a Prison Service mobile pigpen. I am sure that they have a far nicer name for it, but you get the picture. For the journey across from QRP to TMP I was obliged by the management to wear the salmon-pink jumpsuit and reprise my role as the human duck, trussed up again in cuffs around the wrists and ankles, joined together by heavy chain. I waddled into TMP, quackless and sacrificial and ready to be officially carved up.

Now I have switched back into the de rigueur uniform of white T-shirt and shorts, and find myself alone in the ground-floor reception hall of a long and airy prison wing which has the surprising and benign atmosphere of an all-boys high school.

My escort officer, humourless and efficient, instructed me to squat down against a wall and wait for an introduction to life in TMP by one of the worker cookies. Then he slammed the heavy blue door shut, cutting me off from the rest of the prison. That's how it works in Singapore. Inmates are marooned in closed-off subsections, corralled in small enough numbers to manage easily, preventing the threat of mass insurrection.

To my left, there are large industrial-sized urns mounted against the wall. This makes me think of tea ladies—those civil-service purveyors of snacks and donuts and chocolates, nowadays an all-but-extinct species of corporate life. In the near distance, voices of those I assume to be prisoners are competing in a game of what sounds like basketball. Conversations—oddly animated, jovial and happy—drift along the wide corridors. My surroundings are disquietingly mundane.

'New man, eh?' says a smiling inmate approaching with a transparent, rectangular storage box about the size of an apple crate from an orchard. This seems an appropriate comparison, given the name of the bearer of the box.

'I'm Mango.'

And I'm going to let that strange name go without remark. 'Peter,' I say, standing to greet him.

'Where you from?'

'Australia.'

'Wow! We don't have any of those here. Long way from home. What case?'

'Drugs.'

'How long is your sentence?'

'Ten months.'

'Okay, short sentence, lah.'

'You think?'

'Yes, brother. I am here for three years.'

'Ah,' I say, 'then I suppose I am here for a short time then.'

'And a good time too?' Mango is laughing at his own joke. 'Life here is not so bad—just follow the rules and stay out of trouble.' He hands over the box, like a solemn gift-presentation ceremony. 'This is your stuff,' he says.

I squat again, and open my new box. On inspection I see that it contains all my officially sanctioned possessions: two blankets, cup and spoon, roll of toilet paper, cake of soap, short plastic toothbrush and tube of green toothpaste. Inexplicably I see a Brillo pad.

'What's this for?' I ask, holding up the Brillo.

'Cleaning the cell floor,' answers Mango. 'No maids here. When you get to your room—we try not to say "cell"—there will be a plastic bucket.'

'What's that for?'

'Keep it filled up and use it for drinking water. There is a lid too, to keep it covered.' Pointing back at the rectangular box, he adds, 'Keep this full of water for your toilet business. The toilet is old-fashioned Asian—squat down. You know how to use one of them?'

'Yes.'

'Okay. Water is rationed. Shower works for twenty minutes at 7am and 11.30am, and again at 7pm. The rest of the time, all you have is the water stored in this box, so don't forget to keep it topped up. Understand?'

'Yes.'

'Now. Muster happens three times a day—at 7.30am, 12.30 and 6.45pm. When you hear the bell go announcing the start of muster, stand up in the middle of the room and wait for a guard to open the spy hole to confirm that you are present and accounted for.' Mango is pausing for the detail to sink in. 'You are not allowed to stay sitting or lying down. If they catch you doing that, you can be put on charge and sent to isolation.'

I'm nodding acknowledgment, but I am well past overload. Rationed water, standing to attention three times a day, Brillo pads. This sounds like boot camp and army life. Mango is asking me if I have any questions.

'No. None.' I'm a bit too stunned to think of any.

Then Mango stands up sharply, coming to a sudden and erect attention. He looks like he really is in some sort of prisoner army. I am amused and have not mimicked his reaction. Nor have I seen the officer standing behind my shoulder.

'You must always stand up when an officer is present,' the new arrival snaps.

To Mango: 'You can go.'

To me: 'Lloyd, follow me!'

I pick up my box and belongings and scurry behind the lanky officer. His nametag tells me that he is a superintendent.

'I know you,' he says.

'You do?' I am surprised, thinking where and how our paths might have crossed on the outside.

'Yes. You are the reporter from Australia.'

'Yes.'

'You helped the cameraman after he fell backwards filming you at the courthouse.'

'You know that?'

'Yes. They showed it on the news here.'

Up three flights of stairs, past two more heavy blue doors. After a stroll down another long corridor, with rooms on either side, I am instructed to pause before a door marked '30'.

'This is your room,' says the Super, as he produces a large key attached to a chain resting in his pocket. The door swings inwards, and he gestures for me to enter. 'Prisoners have time in the exercise yard every day, but you are new so you not entitled for two weeks.'

I am thinking, *Did he just tell me that I am in solitary confinement?* But before I can check, the door is slamming. A peephole in the middle of the door, about the size of a book, opens and the Superintendant's bulging eyeball peers into my room.

And then he is gone. I can hear him reinstating the key to his pocket as he lumbers away, heavy boots squeaking on the polished concrete floor.

•••••

TWO WEEKS LATER. Wild animals held captive in zoos and put on public display have my deepest sympathy. I've been stuck in this fishbowl of a room for a fortnight now. At the end of the first week one of the officers gave me the Lee Kuan Yew memoir, so I had something to read.

The other inmates on the landing, my new neighbours, have been stopping and staring through the officers' peephole, muttering and laughing and pointing as one would at a new and apparently hilarious exhibit: 'Hello! Mister Peter! Hello.' I can hear them saying, 'How are you today?' 'What are you reading?' Lee Kuan Yew, as it happens; but when I hold up the book cover, the inquirer inevitably reels back in shock or horror or possibly disgust.

Humans, like animals, are not meant to live in captivity. Opponents of zoos speak of the 'ecological minimum'—the space required to run and play and eat—robbed of animals in captivity. Animals denied natural space turn aggressive or strange, and sometimes the effect is permanent. Humans need space too and, once it is denied, go as stir-crazy as a safari-park monkey in a six-by-twelve cage. And that is precisely what this is. My 'cage' is exactly the same length and breadth as that in Queenstown Remand Prison. I can stand in the centre of the room and hold my arms out and touch the wall on either side; the journey from back wall to front door is about four good strides.

Being locked up might be okay for solitary types, but I am one of the more socially dependent of the species. I understood when I came to prison that the first layer of punishment is the denial of liberty, but the corollary, the denial of society, is a consequence that I had not fully appreciated until now. The apparent novelty of my arrival on this landing has not worn off, presumably because I am a foreigner with a celebrated case. All of the faces at the peephole are local: Chinese, Indian and Malays. Unsurprisingly in this unequal society, there are more of the latter than the former.

My new cell—or, as Mango urges me to say, 'room'—is newer and brighter than cells at Queenstown. The squat-down toilet and shower nozzle are located on the back wall, behind a two feet high 'modesty wall'. There is, however, no need for modesty in my cell since I am billeted alone.

I imagined that the walls of a prison cell would be daubed with obscene or subversive graffiti, messages of protest or gallows humour, but Room 30 is remarkably mute on the thoughts of past occupants. It is as if they had nothing at all to say.

Singaporeans have long since been intimidated out of the daring practice of graffiti by one of the political crackdowns mounted by Lee Kuan Yew. It was back in the mid 1960s when the regime passed an anti-vandalism act to curb the spread of communist graffiti. The same law was used in 1993 to punish the American teenager, Michael Fay, for spraying graffiti on cars in Singapore. The original sentence of six lashes of the cane was reduced to four after a howl of protest from the United States, led by President Clinton.

The only evidence of past occupancy in my cell is a faint silhouette on the wall next to where I sleep. Some days I lie here staring at the shadow—imagining the prisoner, penitent and lonely, sitting habitually in the same place for months, or perhaps years on end, in quiet contemplation of his crime. The Ghost of a Prisoner Past is the single most saddening feature of this room.

The Superintendent of the Prison, also known as SOP, interviews all new inmates after arrival in order to set them straight should they have any funny ideas about misbehaving. My induction conversation with SOP Matthew Wee went like this:

'You are here for a little over six months?'

'Yes.'

'Don't talk too much to the other prisoners. They are not your friends.'

'Okay.'

'You will find the accommodation here basic. I am afraid that is how Singapore prisons are. Do you have any needs?'

'Can I have an extra blanket?'

'We can do that,' says Wee, adding, 'Is there anything else?'

'I would like to write. Can I have access to a notepad?'

'I think so. But anything you write must be screened before you leave. We just need to be sure you are not writing about the security arrangements in here, like where the cameras are located.'

'I understand.'

'You have clearly got some skills that we don't see in prison very often. Are you willing to work?'

'Of course.'

'Okay. That is all for now. We can meet again in a few weeks to discuss ideas for how you can work. I would like to put your writing skills to use.'

'Sounds goods to me. Thank you.'

• • • • •

IT TOOK ONLY A FEW days to learn the rhythms of TMP. It's breakfast time and I am lying on my back, honing my sense of smell and hearing so as to figure out what is happening outside in the corridor. I have learned already that if I hear boots or shoes or the sound of keys jangling, an officer is on the landing. Officers try to sneak up to cells and carry out a spot check through the peephole by walking softly and holding their keys. But I have learned they are detectable through other means: most wear far too much deodorant and I can smell them coming from a distance. In general, the Malay officers wear more deodorant than the Chinese.

Amongst the inmates it is still hard to tell who is who in the zoo, but I am learning to identify the footsteps and cadence of three inmates who work as cookies. They deliver breakfast, lunch and dinner to the cell. There are no communal meals in prison in Singapore, where the basic rule of managing inmates is to divide and conquer.

'Good morning, Peter.' That's Pung. He is a cheerful Chinese guy who opens the small metal panel at the base of the door every morning, marking the start of the breakfast ritual. 'Do you have anything for laundry?'

'Yes,' I reply.

'Okay, then push it out here through the hole.' He is tapping the opening. 'We will collect it and send it to laundry. Laundry is back at lunchtime.'

'Thanks, Pung.'

'Don't thank me,' he laughs. 'Thank the nice judge.'

Pung makes the effort to talk directly to me in the mornings, giving advice on adherence to the routine. 'Don't forget to stand up at muster check,' he will say, or, 'You can have a newspaper every day, but don't get too excited because they censor a lot of the stories.'

'Cup.' That's my next visitor, Ismail—a Malay prisoner who is very hard to understand. He and I are communicating in single-word sentences.

'Cup?' I ask.

'Cup,' he repeats, echo-like.

I slide my cup out, and listen to the sound of another mug scooping liquid from a bucket that Ismail has been sliding up the corridor. My cup is returned full of the usual steamy brown liquid. Pung says cookies serve coffee or tea on alternate days, but it is still beyond my sense of smell and taste to detect which day is coffee and which day is tea.

I'm sniffing this morning's delivery when the third cookie arrives. 'You! Paper?' It is a Chinese called Goh. I know this because Pung told me his name, and warned me that he is the cookie who doesn't speak English. That much I did not need explained.

'What?' I say.

'Paper. You, paper?'

I may not understand Goh, but I do know when he is coming because his slippers flip-flop, flip-flop harder than anyone else. Goh also tends to make a lot of weird cat-meowing noises and laughs too hard, like a real maniac. He is Singaporean. Because he speaks almost no English, Pung usually comes to the tray hatch to translate. Here he comes:

'Peter.' It is Pung.

'Yes, Pung?'

'You want the paper, from today?'

'Yes, please. Is that what Goh was asking me just now?'

Laughing, 'Yes. Couldn't you tell?'

'Not exactly, no. Tell him I am sorry.'

'No need. He is an idiot.'

At night I hear a lot of the 'idiot'. Goh's cell is located about two doors down from mine. Like many Chinese, Goh is fond of karaoke. Every night during the first week of my confinement, between the evening muster check and lights out, Goh has been offering up his repertoire, starting with that insipid 1975 Morris Albert classic 'Feelings'. But being Chinese, Goh struggles with the 'l' sounds.

So awful is Goh's singing that each chorus earns him ovations of applause, wolf-whistles, calls for 'more, more, more' and, on several occasions, meowing sounds. I have no idea what crime Goh committed to get himself in jail, but his singing voice is capital punishment-bad and his sentimental song choices are worse. After the attack on 'Feelings', Goh gets on board the *Titanic* to murder Celine Dion's 'My Heart Will Go On'.

• • • • •

I HAVE A LIMITED arsenal against my creeping isolation mania. Sleep is the first frontier of escape. Lights out is at 9pm, and thankfully the singing is over by then.

I am getting used to the meagre sleeping arrangements. I have three blankets. One is rolled up to form a pillow. I sleep on the other two, a makeshift mattress. It is still very uncomfortable and I toss and turn a lot. Pung says that everyone gets used to it and after a while some inmates who grew up kampong-style believe that they sleep better on the floor than they did in a soft bed.

'What is kampong?'

'It's a Malay word for village. We use it in Malaysia.'

'Is that where you are from?'

'Yes.'

In the morning, when the lights come on at six, I wrap a T-shirt around my head like a bank robber's balaclava. Most of the time I can go back to sleep, but it depends on how much cat-meowing noise Goh wants to make. The man is seriously disturbed. After muster check and breakfast at 7.45am the lights are switched off, and I usually go back to sleep.

I am marvelling at the ease of this routine. If nobody makes any demands on me, I can sleep right up to lunchtime. That I could sleep this much does not surprise me. It is a form of escape. And I am at the back end of a year of sleep deprivation. My body needs to recover many lost hours from last January, when the nightmares started. At this current rate of slumber, I will serve half of my sentence unconscious.

Goh gave me a newspaper but I won't open it until after lunch.

I need to pace myself.

TWENTY
So this is Christmas

IT'S FRIDAY THE NINETEENTH of December and my two weeks of solitary confinement are finally coming to an end. It is not before time—I am going manic with sheer boredom.

I have examined and re-examined every contour of my cell, and committed the image to memory. I can close my eyes and mentally trace the outline of the walls, feeling for every crack and bubble, every pockmark and stain in the pale white concrete. I have slept away half of every single day with unerring dedication. I have quietly performed Pilates while keeping my ear cocked for a surprise inspection. I have read the *Straits Times* newspaper from front to back and back to front, classifieds included, every single afternoon. And lately I have taken to talking to ants.

Ants, like us humans, are social creatures, and I watch with fascination as they work as a team to seek and collect the food scraps that I have been deliberately leaving aside to attract their attention.

'Hello, mister ant,' I would say, solicitously. 'How are you today? Are you hungry? Where have you been?'

When they advance, I stir from my pillow and urge them to come closer. 'I have some crumbs for you. Come down from the wall, I can feed you.'

Smaller, orange-coloured worker ants come down the walls first, followed by bigger soldier ants with larger heads and longer mandibles. These soldiers seem to be giving orders, or the smaller ants simply fall into line like lower-caste servants. Ants communicate using a type of pheromone. I get a kick from imagining soldier ants farting orders. These lower-caste ants follow a familiar pattern of unquestioning social obedience, prompting this thought: *How did the People's Action Party get to them?*

When an ant identifies a new source of food it runs back up the wall, stopping here and there to mark a trail with its farty odour. Then other ants, seemingly heeding the signs, follow the original ant back down the wall to the food. When the crumb becomes too heavy I have seen two ants work as a team, jointly lifting the piece in the air and walking in two-step back up the wall. It's like watching a mighty Eastern European bloke perform a gold medal–winning snatch-and-grab manoeuvre at the Olympics.

I marvel at their gravity-defying antics. The crumb must weight several times an ant's bodyweight, yet they are steady and sure-footed as they make their way back to the colony, hidden inside my patchy white wall. Occasionally the soldier ant re-appears, prodding and nudging and cajoling like an impatient high-caste supervisor. I imagine a menacing pheromone message that says something like, 'The next ant I catch idling up the wall will be eaten.' It is way beyond time when I should be outside of this enclosed space, outside in the fresh air kicking a footy.

I hear heavy footsteps. I'm standing, my ear pressed to the door, listening for sound clues: keys turning, doors opening, prisoners shuffling to attention in the corridor.

My door is opening. I think, *Free at last! Free at last!*

A guard says, 'Put on your shirt and slippers, Peter. You have yard.'

I comply and slip into the corridor. It is cooler out here than in my room. The rest of the inmates are squatting down at their doorways, waiting for permission to move on. I mimic them, as if I have done this a hundred times before. The last thing I want is to be noticed.

'Okay—fall out to yard!' says the guard. 'And go quietly.'

• • • • •

THE EXERCISE YARD is a shadeless concrete space about half the size of a rugby field. There are water bubblers and outside loos at one end, and a basketball court at the other. Most importantly, I can see the sky. I can hear the airport, and I can feel a breeze of crisp, fresh air. Prisoners are assembling in two lines, squatting down before being officially received by another officer who supervises yard activities.

'Fall in!' he barks.

This is a new world of obedience and submission. Australians, unlike Singaporeans, are not required to participate in two years of national service. Being proud descendants of convicts and other equally anti-authoritarian shades, many Australians are genetically predisposed to rebel against efforts to inculcate obedience and discipline. This makes us the natural enemy of authoritarian states such as the Singapore regime, which specialises in the creation of genetically modified, fully compliant humans—humans version 1.2. Singapore is like an ant colony, populated by little red workers, slavish and obliging and loyal to the pheromonic, farting bully ant called LKY.

Another prisoner is by the officer's side, counting heads. 'Eighteen, sir,' he says. *What a crawler,* I think.

'Very well then.' And the officer puts both hands behind his back, like a commanding officer inspecting real troops. *He's an Asian Colonel Blimp, irascible and jingoistic and absurd from too much sun.*

'Yard—*Good afternoon, sir!*' prompts the helper-prisoner cum cheerleader.

And, in schoolboy unison, the prisoners around me reply, 'Good afternoon, sir!'

This is hilarious. I'm trapped in a Singapore production of *Dad's Army*.

As the men fall out, untidy and sullen to my mind, Colonel Blimp gives me a look; he's sniffed me out, identified a potential rebel in the ranks. 'Lloyd!' he commands. 'Follow me!'

Near the entrance to the courtyard is a caged viewing platform where the Blimp takes his seat. This is the raised area from which, magisterially, he will preside over all yard activities.

'Now,' he begins, 'this is your first day in the yard.'

'It is,' I add helpfully. His furrowing frown suggests my interruptions are not welcome.

'If you wish to participate in any of the sporting activities, you must not wear slippers. There are running shoes and socks provided. It is very hot outside, so you must drink a lot of water. Stay hydrated.' He pauses for me to acknowledge with a nod. 'If there are any fights between prisoners, you all lose yard privileges. Understood?'

'Yes.'

'Not just the culprits.'

'Yes.'

'Yes, sir.'

'Yes, sir.'

'That's better.'

'Yes, sir.'

Blimp pauses, re-examining my face for any sign of insurrection in that excessively obedient reply. I'm trying to stay poker-faced. Then I give him a gormless, Forrest Gump grin—the kind that only a mother could love.

'Dismissed!'

• • • • •

HALF AN HOUR LATER, I am under an unexpected cross-examination.

'Who is Pauline Hanson? And why does she hate us?'

The prisoners are standing around me in a semi-circle, curious to hear the answer. It is the second time I have been asked this question in the yard in recent minutes, to my surprise. I thought Pauline Hanson was about as newsworthy as yesterday's teabag and a distant memory. I assumed, wrongly, that prisoners are borderline illiterates with no consciousness of news and world affairs.

'She's a conservative politician,' I say to one inmate. 'And I don't think she does hate you,' I reply to the other.

'But she is anti-Asian!'

'Yes, she is. But she doesn't speak for me. In fact, I don't know anybody who she does speak for.' Actually that's not strictly true.

I know a few people who do agree with her views and some of them are relatives, but now is probably not the time to volunteer so much personal information. I am outnumbered.

Pauline Hanson, I explain to the mob, was a lightning rod for angry white voters. She was the anti-factor: anti-immigration, anti-political correctness, anti-elite and anti-intellectual. It took just one sentence in Hanson's maiden speech to parliament in September 1996 for Southeast Asians to identify Pauline Hanson as being at the vanguard of a much-feared return to a kind of White Australia policy: '*I believe we are in danger of being swamped by Asians.*'

Not unreasonably, that's about all Asians ever seemed to remember. And she lacked the capacity or concentration to debate constructively or develop and present meaningful public policy. Merely declaring 'I don't like it' was often the sum total of Hanson's contribution.

My potted history of Hanson-ism, such that it ever was an 'ism', seems to have disarmed the mob. My final gesture of peacemaking is to make a joke of the topic.

'Hanson hasn't been taken seriously for a long time,' I explain. 'The last time anyone saw her she was on *Dancing with the Stars.*'

• • • • •

CHRISTMAS EVE.

I have fallen into a pit of despondency and loneliness. The ABC dismissed me after my conviction. This did not come as a complete surprise but when the news came, via a message from my lawyer, it still hurt. Who wants to be sacked so publicly? I feel like an embarrassing member of a family, unwanted and abandoned. And yet I see the logic behind the dismissal. After two decades in journalism my instincts still force me to see the other point of view, however painful. I did the wrong thing by resorting to illegal drugs to self-medicate my condition. I broke the law. At this end of the argument, I'd have done the same thing to an errant employee. I'm punishing myself now by staying in this psychological 'hole' of my own making. If there is a way out, I cannot see it.

Last night they set up loudspeakers in the yard and blasted a concert of Christmas carols around the prison. In theory this was a morale-boosting nod to the season. In practice it was a gesture of unintended cruelty, emphasising the distance that separates my world from me.

The joyful host (I wished him struck dead by a lightning bolt) was cajoling the audience to get involved—'Come on, everybody, join in!' he would say. And on cue, everybody did. The crowd loved the saccharine sweetness of 'Jingle Bells', the wholesome Bing Crosby cheer of 'Deck the Halls' and the insipidly childish 'Frosty the Snowman'. And why wouldn't they?

I am throwing myself a party tonight: a pity party. I have been locked up for three weeks and all I have to show for it are cards and letters from complete strangers—nothing from family or friends. On one hand, I feel utterly estranged from my world. And on the other, the touching and unexpected compassion and encouragement of strangers makes me cry.

A viewer named Margaret writes, 'You have been through such a rotten time and it must seem a never ending cycle of sadness. But you did your job valiantly and anyone would break under the load you carried professionally. Take heart, you are a gifted, compassionate man and you will rebuild your life bigger, better, stronger.'

On a postcard featuring a rock wallaby another viewer, Jim, says, 'Hang in there. You did a lot of Aussies a great service with your reports. Thanks for that.'

These cards and letters are revealing. Until now I did not consider that I had a public persona. I am a private man with a public profession. For twenty years I have been filing reports for radio and television from all around the world without imagining that viewers and listeners have developed a sense of familiarity, to the point where some are prompted to put pen to paper. I began getting these positive messages before I was sentenced, but now they're arriving into the prison too.

'Just a quick note of support from an ABC viewer', begins another letter, from a man who felt 'quite distressed' about my situation. 'Lots of people in Oz are thinking of you, and wishing you well', he says.

And a woman who calls herself 'a fan' writes, 'Thank you for your wonderful reports. You will be missed by many others and me. The very best of luck as you regain perfect health,' she adds.

Broadcast journalism tends to attract a small number of characters that love the medium more than the message. They are addicted to the tally light that tells you the camera is rolling, or the 'on-air' light over a radio studio door. They love the sound of their own voice, and the sight of themselves on TV. They are the people who see a television story as nothing more than a life support system for their ten-second stand-up. At the ABC we have a saying for them: they are 'bitten by the snake'. I am not immune to vanity moments, but I pride myself on being a true believer in the importance of story over self and sticking to the rules of integrity and honesty in reporting. I've never stopped to imagine how the audience sees me, until this personal disaster. And as much as they are trying to lift my spirits, these correspondents remind me that I have let them down. I've notched up another failure. And the hole I am in seems that much darker tonight.

Even the ants, free to come and go, pause and inspect me. *Are they laughing at me?* I wonder. All I want for Christmas is to is go back to sleep, because that is the only safe place I know.

• • • • •

CHRISTMAS MORNING.

'Merry Christmas, Peter!' It is the ever-cheerful officer named Cedric opening the door. Cedric seems like a good guy. He looks like a pot-smoking surfer dude who got lost at the job office while collecting the dole. He's not nearly cruel and angry and bitter enough to be a career prison officer.

'You can come out of your cell,' says Cedric. 'You can enjoy some special privileges today.'

'Special privileges?' I reply, with undisguised cynicism.

'Yes, lah,' replies Cedric, with a fixed grin.

I feel like telling Cedric that I am a crazy man who talks to ants. I feel like telling Cedric that last night there was an act of murderous violence, right here in my room.

'Hello, soldier ant,' I had said.

Nothing.

'Hello, soldier!' I repeated.

Still nothing.

'You're a rude bugger, aren't you?'

Still nothing.

So I whacked the ant with my slipper, squashing the impertinent little bastard stone-cold dead.

'Next time, have some manners and speak when you are spoken to!' I had reprimanded the corpse, before flicking it across the room.

Now I am looking up, considering confessing. Cedric is grinning, like he really thinks this is a Merry Christmas kind of day.

No, I think, *I won't be bursting Cedric's bubble.*

· · · · ·

I'M UP AND DRESSING for Christmas in my Tanah Merah uniform of blue shorts and white T-shirt. I take my cup and eating spoon (another means of control: no prisoner can have a knife or fork) and shuffle down the landing with the other inmates who nominated Christmas Day as the religious holiday they wish to observe. Each prisoner is allotted one observance that entitles them to a day out of their cell and the promise of a splendid feast of 'special food'. Those with an active interest in more than one religious faith are forced to choose.

The Malays, being Muslims, couldn't pull off this claim to Christian piety and a free feed, but some of the Chinese did, and I know for a fact that they are atheists and Taoists.

'Good morning, Mr Fake Christian,' I whisper as I pass an inmate named Heng. He is the youngest person on the landing, possibly the best educated, and a self-described atheist. A few days earlier he had confessed, 'I hear the prison gives the best food to the Christians.'

Heng wasn't going to let me wreck his day: 'Shut the fuck up, or I will tell them you are Jewish,' he hisses back.

'Peace be with you too,' I reply.

The venue for our day of special privileges is the reception area of the third floor landing, where inmates watch communal television. We are sitting on the floor. Chairs are not provided in prison either, out of fear that they could be used as shields, or dismantled and used as weapons or missiles.

Pung is here, and Goh, along with a strange, far older man who looks like he forgot to leave prison when his sentence finished. He is skinny and wrinkled, with a face like a contour map. They call him Marlboro Man, because he is serving a sentence for trafficking illegal cigarettes. The one other inmate here is a Chinese I call Knuckles, because his hands are a mess, disrupted and shattered from fist fights. I'm curious, but I haven't asked too many questions yet.

'Okay, guys,' says Cedric, 'you have a special privileges DVD—a selection of movies for the day. And,' he is gesturing to takeaway boxes in the corner, 'some special food for breakfast. Enjoy!'

Everything is 'special' today, I think.

• • • • •

CHRISTMAS NIGHT.

I am more puzzled than despondent tonight. The day of 'special privileges' began with the strange excellence of the food. For breakfast, Tanah Merah's Christians and assorted impostors—I'm agnostic with a sweet tooth—enjoyed a selection of pumpkin soup, pizza slices and assorted chocolates and sweets. At lunch, we ate spaghetti bolognaise, washed down with no-name cola. And at the dinner hour, the kitchen produced an excellent combination of coconut rice and roasted chicken.

Pung was the first to say what was probably on everybody's mind: 'If they can make food this good today, why can't they do it every day?'

'Because we would never leave,' muttered Marlboro Man.

The 'special privileges' DVD was just as surprising—a compilation of the top half-dozen slash-and-horror genre films of the late twentieth century. There was *Friday the 13th*, a few *Halloweens* and a particularly bad Christian Slater film called *Mindhunters*. In ten hours of simulated murder and mayhem I witnessed beheadings, stabbing deaths, strangulations, electrocutions, death by drowning, death by frozen nitrogen (*vale* Christian Slater), and the most mundane crime of all: death by gunshot.

Halfway through this day-long gore-fest I piped up and said, 'I hope none of you is a serial killer.' Everyone laughed, including Goh, who isn't supposed to understand English—and he laughed a little too hard for my liking. I made a mental note to always keep him in plain sight.

As far as I can tell, the prisoners on my landing are small-time offenders: larrikins like the cigarette smuggler, petty thieves and opportunists, creative accountants and small-time drug users. In most western countries these men wouldn't be serving prison sentences; certainly none of the first offenders would be. But Singapore isn't most countries.

Still, I am left wondering what the prison hierarchy was thinking when it gave us this creepy DVD set to watch on Christmas Day. It is so dramatically at odds with the way officials carry on about other forms of media exposure. They happily censor newspapers on the dubious assertion that they are eliminating stories that will 'disturb' a prisoner's state of mind. But what could be more disturbing than a day of cinematic mad, bad and ugly?

• • • • •

TWO DAYS LATER.

It is the anniversary of Benazir Bhutto's death. I haven't thought about the murdered Pakistani political leader for months—not since I stopped having the dream about the Karachi bombing. And then, last night, I had the most vivid dream about Benazir. It wasn't a nightmare this time. It was a flashback of an event that happened a few weeks before she was killed, in November 2007.

Bhutto held a 'get to know you' cocktail party for diplomats in Islamabad. I was standing next to her during the meet-and-greet phase of the evening, and at one stage she turned to me with a big smile and said, 'Hello, I'm Benazir,' thinking that I was a diplomat queuing for an audience. So I replied, 'And I'm Peter Lloyd from the ABC. Definitely not a diplomat.' Benazir laughed.

That was the only face-to-face moment that Benazir Bhutto and I shared. The rest of our encounters were in frenzied media conferences, or in jostling scrums of cameras and microphones.

I wonder what Benazir would make of the business of politics here in Singapore. Today I'm reading in the newspaper about a local politician called Siew Kum Hong. He is urging Singaporeans to openly discuss and campaign for human rights. Siew is a subversive type, trying to coax reform of the Singapore political culture from within the parliament. He is not a member of the ruling party; rather, Siew is what is known in Singapore as a Nominated Member of Parliament, or NMP.

NMPs are chosen by the regime as the acceptable face of minorities and opposition points of view. They are MPs with strictly limited powers—for example, they cannot vote on supply bills. The NMP system is the Lee family's idea of controlled opposition. Liew does his best to make a fist of this absurd political window-dressing by making well-timed noises on legitimate issues that rock the conservative boat.

His best-known foray into the social reform agenda came during September 2007 when he tabled a petition in parliament for the repeal of Section 377A. This section of the Singapore penal code is the main piece of law that criminalises sex between mutually consenting adult men. The religious right, represented in parliament by another NMP, Thio Li-ann, went nuts. Thio responded to the petition by comparing gay sex to 'shoving a straw up your nose to drink'. She said homosexuality was a gender identity disorder. Thio, it must be said, is not a trained medical doctor—she's a lawyer who occasionally comes out with crackpot statements.

I am learning to love the *Straits Times* newspaper, especially the daily guessing game with the censors. The censorship process works like this: every day a senior officer reads the paper and puts a cross next to stories deemed unfit for prisoners to read. Then the paper is handed to a trio of prisoners from a non-English background.

I don't know whether it is deliberate or not, but some days they don't put enough paint on, and it is possible to read through the black and understand the copy. This slip-up is revealing. Stories being blacked out usually cover law and order issues, political reform, court cases, crimes of violence or big international news events like the Mumbai terror attacks.

It is apparent that the censor has no concept of the way the news cycle operates because, more often than not, a topic that is blacked out on the front page on one day is left uncensored a day or two later when follow-up reports, complete with full background, are published.

In this way, it is possible to miss almost nothing that happens in the news.

A week ago, I button-holed Colonel Blimp in the yard and quizzed him about this censorship: 'Why is the paper so full of black?'

'This is a tradition in Singapore jails that dates back to the British,' he replied.

Of course, I was thinking. *Blame it on the white guys, the stock standard alibis Singaporeans use to explain repressive activities. Race, like religion, is never far from the surface here.*

'The British left Singapore quite a while ago, didn't they?'

'Yes, but it is good practice. You see, we need to keep inmates calm,' he insisted. 'If they read stories in the newspaper that disturb them, that is very bad for their mind. We do it to take care of them.'

'But the papers are full of stories about unemployment and the global financial crisis, and all the prisoners talk about here are their fears for the future when they get out, and will they be able to find work. How come those stories are left to read?'

Blimp eyed me as if a worthy chess opponent has just declared 'check'. He licked his lips and surrendered. 'You may have a point.'

$$\cdot \ \cdot \ \cdot \ \cdot \ \cdot$$

THE CENSOR BOTCHED a paint-over job today, leaving me able to read about Singapore's most interesting contempt-of-court case in recent memory.

Three men who wore T-shirts depicting a kangaroo dressed in judge's robes were convicted and ordered to serve jail terms of between seven and fifteen days. According to the attorney-general's chambers, the trio 'scandalized the judiciary by publicly wearing identical white T-shirts, imprinted with a palm-size picture of a kangaroo dressed in a judge's gown, within and in the vicinity of the New Supreme court building'.

The political angle in the case wasn't hard to guess. The men had been attending a hearing in late May 2008 where a judge was assessing defamation damages against the leader of the Singapore Democratic Party, Chee Soon Juan, and his sister, Chee Siok Chin, after the pair had been found guilty of defaming Prime Minister Lee Hsien Loong and his father, Lee Kuan Yew, in his preposterous, self-appointed role of Minister Mentor. Where else in the world, apart from Singapore, does a cabinet of grown men, educated and experienced, require the enduring services of a political mentor? The implicit insult to their competence and trustworthiness is all too clear to the rational observer.

The contempt case cost the Singapore Democratic Party Assistant Secretary-General John Tan Liang Joo fifteen days of liberty. His co-accused—activists Mohamed Isa and Muhammed Shafi'ie Syahmi Sariman—were each ordered to be jailed for seven days. The sentences were probably less than the government wanted. The Deputy Solicitor-General, Jeffrey Chan, said the worst insult anyone could level at the Singapore judiciary was to call it a kangaroo court. Chan needs to get out more. I have heard much worse things said of the Singapore judiciary than that.

Accusations that the Singapore judiciary is openly crooked miss the point about what is really wrong. The problem of the judiciary in Singapore is structural: regime-appointed judicial officers and their political masters restrict lower court magistrates and judges to sentencing options that are far too narrow. By this method, the People's Action Party maintains tight control over the law-and-order outcomes in the courts. Freethinking magistrates and judges are held in restraint by the Singapore system. This was implicitly acknowledged by the regime itself in another poorly blacked-out story in the *Straits Times* on 12 December. The page-one report—under the headline 'More sentencing leeway for judges proposed'—said: 'The Law Ministry thinks judges should have a wider range of sentencing options, including ordering offenders to get psychiatric treatment, do community work or report to a designated centre daily.'

The report went on to say: 'The proposals are also a response to growing recognition that some crimes are a result of mental disorders.' Indeed they are. Whether the judiciary wins these reforms will be a test of the regime's frequent claims to be willing to loosen up and allow the community broader freedoms.

Another recommendation proposed by a review committee would lead to a genuine level playing field in criminal cases. At the moment, defence lawyers do not see what evidence the state has against the accused. This includes statements the accused made to police after arrest but before they have had the right to seek legal advice. As the *Straits Times* pointed out, 'all these surface only when the trial starts'. The editorial, unblemished by black paint, said: 'If the proposed changes become law, the prosecution will have to let the defense know, among other things, who it intends to present as witness, what evidence it will produce, and any statement made by the accused that the prosecution will use during trial.'

A prominent Singapore defence lawyer, unconnected to my prosecution, told me 'we fight cases here with one hand tied behind our back'. When I asked him for an explanation, he replied: 'I can explain it with one word. Kiasu. No Chinese wants to lose. The legal system is set up by kiasu-minded Chinese men who do not want to lose. There is no more kiasu-minded person in Singapore than Lee Kuan Yew. Being a defence counsel is a mug's game. But it pays well.'

• • • • •

NEW YEAR'S EVE.

The lights have just gone out and that means there are only three hours left of this personal annus horibilis of mine. The weather has been cool at night lately—cool enough for me to sacrifice the 'comfort' of having two blankets as a mattress. I need one of them as a blanket to cover my curling body. I have been pulling up a blanket for another reason. For a sense of security.

The last few nights, we have all been startled awake by the disembodied screaming of another prisoner somewhere else in TMP. It is a scream of pure terror, as if he has just awoken from a deep slumber and discovered himself in a cell filled with snakes and serpents. But it is more than that even. It is the primal scream of a real madman. Everyone is disturbed by it, even the night guards. I know this because nobody is mentioning it, as though acknowledgment makes madness contagious.

The nightmare of my waking world in here is already more than enough. I am marooned on an island of strangers. I am neither Malay, nor Chinese, nor Indian, just foreign. In the yard, the races seem to spontaneously divide. Chinese do not talk to Malays; Malays do not associate with Chinese. They are like oil and water, and they won't mix.

Mother tongue is the spoken language, always—even when I sit, like an interplanetary visitor, with one group or the other. Pung, being trilingual and Malaysian, is different and volunteers to speak in English. A few days ago he told me that the Singaporeans are convinced I am a government spy, because I am reading the memoir of Lee Kuan Yew.

'A spy?' I spluttered. 'You are kidding? Surely?'

'No. They hate Lee Kuan Yew. They won't even say his name. Then you turn up with the man's book—they think this is suspicious. They think you have been sent here to spy on their conversation. They think you speak Mandarin too, but are hiding it.'

'That's crazy.'

'I know.' Pung is laughing. 'But Peter, this is Singapore. Very strange people.'

Pung worked in Singapore before he was entrapped into selling an ecstasy pill to an undercover police officer. His mandatory five-year trafficking sentence ends a few months after my release in June. Then he will be sent back to Malaysia.

'Does everyone think that? What about the Malays?'

'They don't care—they already know their place in Singapore.'

'Where is that?'

'At the bottom.'

I know the feeling of being at the bottom. I thought that I had reached the lowest point of my life when the DPP was refusing to drop the charge of trafficking. That, it turns out, was merely a pit stop.

I thought that I had prepared myself for prison life—that learning Pilates exercises and compiling my own personal library of books would be my saviour, and that this would be my monastic sabbatical.

But I have been here for a month and still not received a family visitation, my books or a letter from anyone familiar. I am lost in the desert.

I had not considered the real depths of this melancholy. I had not considered how lonely one becomes in a crowd. Every day I feel flashes of panic, mania at the enduring isolation of prison. I feel a black dog companion here in my room. Every day I talk myself down from the psychological ledge. But dark thoughts and self-pity and negativity are my cellmates. They are like a stain that I cannot wash away no matter how hard I try.

TWENTY-ONE
Turn around

IT'S HALF PAST SEVEN in the morning and my sleep-through-the-sentence strategy is being rudely interrupted. My door is opening, and a harpy-voiced guard is calling me back from my dozy reverie.

'Peter, you must come out.' It is the officer ironically dubbed 'Mr Happy'. A scowling lump of a man, Mr Happy still wobbles with youthful puppy fat but has preternatural abilities in the exercise of crude, authoritarian power. Bossy and overbearing, charmless and rude, Mr Happy is one of Singapore's natural-born tyrants. When he swung the door inwards just now it narrowly missed striking my head, doubtless a disappointing outcome.

'What's happening?' I demand, mistaking myself for someone with rights.

'You are working, from today. Come join the cookies outside,' he replies, with that foot-tapping, don't-keep-me-waiting tone you often hear from bureaucrats with nowhere to be and nothing of importance to do.

This is news to me. 'Work? Doing what?' I am confused but pulling on my shirt, obligingly. Refusal is not an option in the face of this Gen Y crypto-fascist.

'Don't you know?' asks the sardonic Mr Happy, knowing full well that I do not know since I know only what I am told, and I have not been told this. 'You are a cookie on the landing now. Breakfast, lunch and dinner.'

I scurry down the corridor, still wiping the sleep from my bleary eyes. At the reception area I find Pung, Ismail and Goh.

'Welcome to cookie-land,' says Pung, enthusiastically. Goh and Ismail look away, as though bored or deaf to my arrival.

'This is news to me,' I say. 'No one told me I was working, until just now when Happy came knocking.'

Now Ismail is chuckling. 'Information, Peter. Need to know. Now you do!' Goh is staring at his fingernails, inspecting them with undue fascination. He hasn't spoken at all.

'What do I do?' I ask.

'Just watch what we do today,' says Pung, who is reaching into a box. He pulls out a large plastic bag. 'Why don't you start with collecting the laundry?'

Goh and Ismail have taken joint delivery of a large bucket of steaming brown. It could be tea, or it could be coffee—I still haven't worked out the odour—but it looks heavy. They are carrying it up the landing towards the cells. Pung has picked up another box, heaving with slices of buttered bread. He is signalling for me to follow them.

This is the morning food and laundry ritual that, until now, I have only heard from inside the cell. Goh is bending down to undo latches to release the trapdoors through which food and drinks are served. Ismail is pushing the heavy beverage bucket from cell to cell, filling inmates' cups. And Pung, having put on a caterer's plastic glove, is handing out the bread.

On cue, prisoners are pushing laundry out into the landing. It is my job to go from door to door, picking it up. I can hear expressions of surprise at my sudden appointment as a working prisoner. None of the comments are directed towards me—Goh seems to be in animated discussion on the topic with the Chinese inmates. I have heard my name amid long streams of twisted, twing-twang-sounding Hokkien dialect.

Breakfast chores for our landing take only a few minutes to complete. Now the cookies are back in the centre of the reception area, taking a communal breakfast. This is the first meal that I have eaten in company since the night before I was sentenced. I'm talkative. 'So, this is the life of a cookie? That didn't seem like a lot of work. What happens next?' I ask cheerfully.

'TV,' says Goh. This is the first sound he has directed to me since my arrival. He didn't look at me when he said it, so I get the feeling that I have caused some sort of unintended offence, perhaps merely by being here now. I'm choosing to ignore it.

'What? You are kidding?' I say to Pung and Ismail.

Ismail is laughing. 'No. We watch TV in the morning.'

'What?' I am shocked. This is like an induction into a secret society. Leaning in, I whisper, 'Do the others know?' I point back up the landing.

Pung leans in, mocking my conspiratorial tone. 'No, Peter,' he whispers. 'They cannot hear it. We don't talk about it in front of them either.' Sitting upright now, he adopts his normal tone of voice. 'And nor should you,' he advises, tapping his finger on my knee.

Goh leans over and puts two chocolate wafers in front of my breakfast sandwiches. *Silent rapprochement?* I wonder.

'From where?' I ask, adopting the Singlish form of rear-ended sentence structure. I find it easier to communicate with the Chinese in this way.

'Pay,' he replies. 'We buy canteen, for work. You have!' he says, pointing at the wafers.

'Thank you,' I say, fondling the wafers reverentially. Aside from the unusually tasty meals on Christmas Day, this is the first food item I have received that hasn't been boiled, baked or blanched to death by the prison kitchen. 'This job is looking pretty good,' I declare.

'Don't get too excited,' warns Pung. 'It's boring out here, and we're not allowed to sleep like you do in the cell, mister. Lunch comes at 11.30, and we issue that, and then there is yard, and after yard is finished we issue dinner at 4.30 or 5pm before going back to the cell.'

'Okay,' I say, mimicking Goh by folding the wafer in bread and dipping it into the mug of brown. But I am determined to be cheerful. 'It has to be better than spending all day in our rooms.'

The heavy blue door separating our landing from the rest of the prison complex is opening. Superintendent Nathan puts his head around the door and motions for me to come over.

'Mr Peter,' he says, handing me an exercise book. 'This is the notebook you requested.'

Two surprises in one morning, but I am unquestioningly thrilled about this latest development. 'Thank you. Thank you very much.'

'You know the rules,' says Nathan, waggling his finger at me. 'No security matters. Stick to your own personal thoughts. It will need to be cleared by the Superintendent of Prisons before you can take it with you.'

'Understood.'

When I sit back down, I see Ismail and Goh staring hard at me, like I just stole from them. 'What?' I ask.

They are silent. Nathan, tall and heavy on his feet, turns and leaves, clanking the security door behind him. It makes a sound that I have heard before. Laughing, as I remember when and where I have heard that sound, I say, 'Did you hear that? It's just like *Law & Order*. Bing, bong, clunk!'

Pung gets the joke, and laughs along with me. Ismail studies me with curiosity. Goh seems to have reverted to a look of irritation. Whatever offence I have apparently caused—firstly by coming to work, and then by getting issued a diary—is not my problem.

I have never been happier in Tanah Merah Prison.

• • • • •

A FEW DAYS LATER, in the exercise yard.

'Go, Skippy, go!' shouts someone sitting with the Chinese inmates. I am the only prisoner running laps, again. The rest are sheltering in the shadow of the building, as though exposure to the sun would shrink them into midgets.

I earned the nickname 'Skippy' during the screening of a movie called *Kangaroo Jack*. It stars Jerry O'Connell, who looks like the strange love child of Tom Cruise and Patrick Swayze. The plot was a little patchy—there were long sequences of the world's best-dressed kangaroo hopping through the bush—and it led to some odd exchanges in TMP.

'Do all Australians have pet kangaroos?' asked one inmate.

'No. We eat them,' I replied, a little provocatively. Non-Australians are always shocked these creatures are killed for food, or shot for recreation.

'Huh? How could you? They are so cute!' This remark comes from a Malay inmate covered in tattoos. I hear that he works as a pimp on the outside. He looks like an enforcer. 'Look at the movie, they're cute,' he cries again in protest.

'But I can tell you they don't wear sunglasses and hop around the bush with red jackets on. They're a pest—we shoot them.' I'm feeling intensely provocative.

The howls of protest erupt on cue. 'But they are a national symbol?' asks Heng.

'Yes. We eat the other one too. That's the emu.'

Ismail pipes up. 'Peter, what does kangaroo taste like?'

'Boring. It is the taste of nothing.'

Ismail is confused. 'Then why do you eat them?'

'I don't. Some people kill them and chop off their paws and attach them to souvenir beer bottle–openers.'

'Is that legal?' asks Marlboro Man, likely hatching a new import scheme.

'Legal? Yes, Marlboro Man. But in good taste? No.'

Pacing my run around the yard, I have worked out that every ten laps is one kilometre. I'm going to start off with five kilometres, and build up to more and more every week. Pilates is a good exercise routine, but nothing substitutes for the endorphin rush delivered by running.

Endorphins are making me happier, a hit lasting for hours afterwards. And compared to a lot of prisoners inside Tanah Merah, my burden seems fairly trivial. A few days ago I met an Indian-Singaporean serving a four-year sentence.

'Four years—what for?' I inquired, having completely abandoned my shyness at asking pointed questions of other inmates.

'I stole two bottles of beer.'

'And?'

'That's it. I stole two beers, and got two years for each bottle.'

'Come on, that cannot be true. Nobody goes to jail for stealing beer.'

At that moment, an officer passed by. The other inmate stopped him and said, 'Sir. Is it true that I am serving four years for stealing two bottles of beer? Tell him,' he says, pointing at me.

'What do you want me to tell him that for?' said the officer.

'He doesn't believe me.'

The officer looked back at me, shrugging. 'It is true.'

'And you want to know something else?' says the inmate, imitating a broad Aussie accent. 'It was bloody Fosters, maay-te.'

• • • • •

THE *STRAITS TIMES* newspaper carries an even more extreme sentencing story, this one involving another Singapore minority. An ethnic Malay named Mohammed Ismail was ordered to serve a whopping fourteen years by the Chief Justice of the High Court, Chan Sek Keong. The crime is weird and grubby—Ismail followed women into elevators and sniffed their armpits—but the penalty is outrageous. The Chief Justice not only jailed the man for years and years but had him beaten too, with twelve strokes of the cane.

According to the *Straits Times*, the judge agreed that the accused man had done no real violence to the women. And a medical report described his condition as 'a deviation from normal sexual preference'. So commonsense would suggest that a psychiatric response should be part of the court's responsibility. However, that is not how Singapore works. Instead, and quite cruelly, the punitive terms of Mohammed Ismail's sentence mean that he will not be entitled to early release for good behaviour. I have no doubt that the offence was indecent, but surely so is the severity of the punishment.

The other inmates don't seem to find heavy sentencing like this nearly as shocking. Pung is looking at me like I am the most naive man he has met. 'What is the breakdown of races in Singapore, Peter?' he asks, rhetorically. 'Three-quarters Chinese, roughly fifteen per cent Malay and the rest Indians, right?'

'Yes, I suppose so.'

'So, look around here,' he says, waving his arm at the rows of cells.

'What do you mean?'

'It is the reverse. Seventy-five per cent of prisoners are Malay and Indian. Maybe a quarter Chinese.'

'Are you saying the justice system is racist—the Chinese against the Malays and Indians?'

'I'm not saying anything. I'm just pointing out the facts.'

The facts show that race plays a big role in the Singapore story. Lee Kuan Yew is an unambiguous racist who considers Chinese racially superior beings. He also subscribes to eugenics. He went seriously off the rails after the 1980 census revealed that in Singapore it was the women with the lowest education levels and the lowest incomes who were having most children. For 'lowest' read 'Indians and Malays'. By contrast, graduate women (read 'Chinese') were not getting married, and those who did were not having enough children to replace themselves. Ever since, Lee and his regime have carried out an unambiguously race-based immigration policy aimed squarely at encouraging mainland Chinese and Chinese from Hong Kong to immigrate to Singapore.

Malays and Indians in Singapore complain increasingly about being effectively disenfranchised by the growth of the city-state's Chinese-ness. They feel insulted and left out when the regime talks about the importance of speaking Mandarin. And they get angry when entitled Chinese teenagers with dreadful spoken English are nominated to represent Singapore in the Miss Universe contest.

When I am running laps, I use the time to clear my head and sift critically the claims and comments of my fellow prisoners. It is true that the bulk of inmates are Malay. But I am not seeing the big picture, of other prisons. I'm seeing merely the Tanah Merah Prison population, and that may be misleading. When I put this to Pung he laughs, like I really am that naive.

•••••

I SEE KNUCKLES sitting alone, so I sense an opportunity to find out more of the story behind those scarred hands. 'That's five kilometres today,' I say, stopping before him.

'Too hot for me, lah.'

'Yeah, I have noticed that the Chinese guys don't like too much physical activity.'

'No. We take it easy. Like the Malays,' laughing at his own unintended, reverse-eugenics joke.

'What do you do, outside?'

'My office is in the street—Geylang.'

'What does that mean? I'm not familiar with Singapore.' I'm lying here. Geylang is the notorious red-light district on the island. Paul Theroux visited Geylang on his visit to Singapore for his book, *Ghost Train to the Eastern Star*. He confessed to having a penchant for pornography because, he claimed, it revealed an otherwise hidden truth of a place or a people. I think that's a cop-out. I think Theroux just likes porn and hookers.

'It's the red-light district. I look after working girls from Thailand.'

'Hard work?'

Laughing, 'Only when white guys like you refuse to pay.'

'Ah, so you are the Enforcer of Contracts, so to speak?'

'You could say that.' He's holding up his fists for me to inspect. They are an even bigger mess, close up.

'Looks like you have had a few contract disputes to sort out.'

'Yeah. I've had a lot of fights. Mainly drunk guys, a few Indians, sailors, a few Aussies who fuck the girls and try to get out of paying. Or try to fuck them without a condom.'

'How serious does the beating get?'

'Pretty serious. I've put a few guys in intensive care. I saw one guy kicked to death.'

'You *saw* it?'

'Yeah. That's what I say—I *saw* it.' Knuckles is silent. He is examining his hands, searching the contours of his broken knuckles, as though the cracks and warps are songlines, holding truths. Finally he looks up and says, 'You ask a lot of questions.'

'Professional curiosity. I'm a reporter.'

'I heard.'

'How does it work—the prostitution business?'

'Local girls mostly won't work. Too stuck up to fuck. The government turns a blind eye to the fact that so many Thais come here for "holidays" or to "study".'

'What sort of money do they make?'

'They charge fifty dollars for a fuck.'

'What is their cut?'

'Twenty.'

'That's not much.'

'Depends on the girl. Most of them work pretty hard and earn a lot more.' Knuckles is laughing now, I suspect at the image of 'work' that he has just conjured up in his mind.

'How many customers can they see in a day?'

'As many as they can take. Average, ten to fifteen. On a good day. But they have to pay off the mama-san who has set them up with a passport and visa, and they pay us for the accommodation that we provide.'

'How much is that, usually?'

'Around two thousand dollars.'

'Wow. So they have to see forty customers before they make any money?'

'You're good at this.'

Actually it is pretty easy to talk to a prisoner when you are one as well. I am trying to dismiss my horror that Knuckles may be a killer. Maybe I have asked too much. Maybe I should retreat.

'I'm going to take a few warm-down laps,' I tell Knuckles as I withdraw.

I'm struck by Knuckles' apparent honesty. Is it that, or his ability to weave a compelling and entertaining fabrication? On balance, I think the state of his hands suggest that the former is more likely than the latter. I am fascinated by the candour of prisoner-to-prisoner conversation. I am accessing an inside story that reporters never get to.

Apart from a few exceptions, like the sex offender who shares our landing, prisoners seem an unselfconscious community. Partly this is because there is an enforced egalitarianism about our current circumstances: we wear the same uniform, have the same hairstyle, eat the same food, sleep in the same sort of cell, have precisely the same worldly possessions and enjoy the same limited personal privileges and freedoms. Almost nothing sets us apart from each other. That would never be true or possible in the outside world.

TWENTY-TWO
Saving graces

ANOTHER DAY IS OVER, and I am back in my room busily scribbling into my officially sanctioned diary. I am pouring out six weeks of pent-up thoughts and frustrations and transcribing coded and shorthand unofficial diary notes which I have been quietly writing in my equally sanctioned copy of the Lee Kuan Yew memoir, *The Singapore Story*.

Apparently, I am a setter of precedents. Until I came along prisoners were not allowed to receive books in hard cover, since hard covers are deemed ideal hiding places for drugs and weapons or other items of contraband. That the authorities allowed me to have a hard copy of LKY's memoir suggests that the prison mandarins concluded that nobody in their right mind would dare attempt to smuggle contraband in the sacrosanct, untouchable book of the Singapore Almighty. Nobody seems to have considered the lending library corollary: smuggling *out* contraband, anti-regime thoughts.

This is too delicious. This is my private insurrection. Beads of salted sweat are dripping from brow to page, forming puddles, forcing my busy hand to pause or leap in the race to recall. I am reminded, as I write, of a Russian writer who remarked that it is easiest to bear something when you write it down.

I am lightening my burden with every stroke—sweeping away my shock and anguish at imprisonment. I am brushing off bloated self-pity and over-exaggerated hurt and anger at the missteps of my otherwise devoted partner, Mazlee. Nothing he has said or done is a hanging offence, so it is time to roll up the noose and call off the lynching party. Prisoners in glass houses cannot afford to fling stones at those who have stood by them. Perspective, at last, flows from the sharp end of my pen.

There is something, or rather someone, else who has gotten me to this point of acceptance and helped me maintain a positive outlook. His birth name was Tenzin Gyatso, but these days he goes by the more fancied name Dalai Lama. However, behind his back, I have always called him Dolly, because 'Dolly Lama' rolls off the tongue a whole lot more smoothly than *Dalai*. Australians can be lazy like this in matters of pronunciation.

All around the world, amongst different faiths and cultures, the Dolly is adored because he represents our better angels. He is a national and religious leader who espouses peace. And what is not to like about that? But, from a reporter's point of view, he is a bit of a nightmare. He does not fit easily into the contemporary sound bite-driven news paradigm, or make it easy to follow the fundamental journalistic K-I-S-S principle: Keep It Simple, Stupid.

The Dalai Lama is about as plain speaking as the Delphic Oracle, a saffron Yoda. And then there is that cackling, almost maniacal yet strangely infectious laughter. 'What's doing, Dolly?' I would think, when I saw him appearing on television from some corner of the globe, holding hands with an awkward-looking world leader like George W. Bush at the White House.

In March 2008, monks in Tibet began rioting and demonstrating against Chinese rule. The Beijing government blamed the Dalai Lama for stoking trouble. As the violence continued we flew to his hometown, Dharamsala in northern India, for another audience with the great man. And it was during our second audience that he made a statement that now resonates with meaning for me. He said that the world's problems would virtually disappear overnight if people stopped being angry and afraid.

Anger and fear—two potent emotions that poisoned my spirits as the year 2008 dragged on. It was only after my arrest and detention, and after months of focus on my own life, that I thought back to that statement. Then those words crystallised for me, and I vowed not to be either angry or fearful about the future. It is the key to attaining a personal state of contentment and happiness in life. Once you eliminate fear and anger from your thinking, anything is possible.

As we stood afterwards in his private audience room making our farewells, he grabbed my hand, shaking it vigorously. The urgent handshake lasted and lasted, until finally it became, for me, awkward. It was one of those moments that you imagine would be satirised in a *Seinfeld* episode: 'How long is long enough to shake a man's hand, before it becomes more than a handshake?' Jerry might say to George.

I can tell you exactly how long it lasted. One hundred seconds. Try shaking someone's hand for a minute and a half and tell me that the moment is not a little awkward.

Floundering, and in search of the fastest way out of this moment, I opened my mouth and spoke without passing my words through the usual mental channel for protocol awareness and self-censorship. Looking the Dalai Lama directly in the eye I said, 'Does this mean we are going steady?'

Stunned into releasing my hand by the barefaced cheek of my remark—possibly the first flirtation of this incarnation—the Dalai Lama responded with an equally shocking gesture: 'Not necessarily,' giggled the winner of the 1989 Nobel Peace Prize, before leaning in and pressing his clenched left hand against my chin.

It was the most enchanting uppercut I've ever received.

$$\bullet \ \bullet \ \bullet \ \bullet \ \bullet$$

I AM SITTING IN the shade, next to the basketball court, when I hear an order: 'Peter!' One of the older staff officers is summoning me. I like this guy—he's always smiling and affable. He is the antidote to Mr Happy—an actual, authentically happy man.

'Please, sit,' he says, motioning to the concrete bench at the side of the yard. We are well away from the other inmates, so I'm assuming he has something personal he wants to say. 'So. How is it going?'

'Pretty good, I think. Settling into the routine, the boredom. You know how it is, I'm sure.'

'Yes. The key to survival here, Peter, is the three A's: acknowledge, accept, adapt.'

'Well, two out of three, so far. I'm still working on "adapt". This is pretty foreign to me, you know. It is my first time in prison.'

'I know. I read your file. But if you have acknowledged and accepted already, you are a long way ahead of most of these guys, I can tell you,' he says, pointing at the other inmates. 'And I know that you might feel a grievance about being here at all, considering your PTSD issues.'

'Staff,' I say, addressing him, for this is how prison officers like to be addressed, 'I can't get hung up about that. It is what it is, and it happened in Singapore. I can't change that. And I'm not going to get past it if I don't let it go.'

'That's right. You have to let it go. The same with anything in life that goes wrong—we can't control the events, but we can control how we react to them.'

'That's where I'm at,' I am pointing to my head, 'up here. Now, at least.'

'If you don't mind me asking—why? What's made the difference for you? You looked pretty sad in December.'

'I was. No doubt about it. It was a tough month, getting used to being inside here. But I am working now, and I have the diary that I write in every day. That, I can tell you, makes a world of difference. Being able to write stuff down helps me make sense of the world. It's, well, therapeutic.'

'That's good. The work means you are out of your cell. That's much better, being busy. But, Peter, the diary. You must be careful. Don't put too much hope into it.'

'What do you mean?'

He is looking around, suddenly nervous. 'I am going to confide in you.'

'Confide what?'

'They are never going to let you—a writer, a journalist—walk out of here with a diary in your hands.'

'But they've told me . . . it will be screened and released. It's written on the front of the diary. Ricky Au, the supervisor, signed his name to it.' The staff officer is looking at me now, studying my face for some kind of recognition. He is silent. 'Are you saying that they lied to me? That they have no intention of letting the diary out of prison?'

'I'm not saying anything. Just think about who you are, what you do for a living. You just said yourself that writing stuff down is helping you get through this sentence. They can see that. That's all the diary is to them—a way of keeping you happy, for as long as you are here. They're doing you a favour in a way. But don't assume they are just as happy about you leaving the prison with it.'

I'm puzzled by this conversation. I'm studying the wall while I think of a way to react to what the officer is saying. Have I been naive in taking them at their word? They have set parameters for the diary and, as long as I stick to it, I can expect to take it with me, right? Or am I wrong? Are these guys that cunning?

Studying me, he says, 'Peter, remember you are in Singapore.'

TWENTY-THREE
Visit

MR HAPPY AND I ARE walking down a long and spotless hallway that serves as a spine connecting each of the five TMP prisoners' housing units. I'm reminded of a hospital or high school until I pass another heavy blue door, which brings me back to reality. This is a high-security prison.

The manner in which prisoners are escorted outside of housing units has been thought through fairly carefully. According to the rules, inmates walk a few paces ahead of officers and in a single or double line, so that we remain under constant visual supervision. It's a policy designed to protect officers from assault. There are closed-circuit surveillance cameras every thirty metres along the corridor, monitoring and, presumably, recording. Except for when I am in my room, I am under constant human and video surveillance. I find that reassuring. Prisoners cannot get away with anything untoward, but nor can officers; we are mutually accountable for our actions. Singapore prisons are probably cleaner and safer and more secure for prisoners than many penal institutions around the world.

I have been anticipating this day for more than forty nights—the day of my first visit. Mazlee wrote a letter dated three weeks after my sentencing hearing. It took another fortnight from arrival here for the prison authorities to deliver it to me. They say it takes that long because night-shift staff are responsible for opening the mail and verifying the safety of contents. Mail is then passed on to the inmates' housing unit, to be checked a second time by an officer who has contact with each prisoner. These multiple layers of censorship and verification mean it will take an average of two to three weeks for me to receive my mail for the rest of the sentence. At least I now know how the system works, and why it is so slow. Until now I just thought that nobody was writing to me.

Mazlee's letter was handwritten, which made it all the more personal, and therefore painful, to read.

'No, I have not forgotten you,' it begins. 'It's just that I've been waiting for three weeks for a letter of authority from the prison which tells me when I am able to visit you. The waiting game is unbearable for me because I have been depressed and sad not knowing how you are doing.'

The Singapore Prison Service is not geared for same-sex relationships. A few weeks ago I was asked to nominate one relative living in Singapore to be the holder of the visitor's pass, which entitles them to one monthly face-to-face visit. Since my family are all in Australia and my partner is here in Singapore, I nominated Mazlee as my family member. The officer paused, his hand hovering over the paperwork, before announcing, 'We don't have a category for that.'

'What do you mean by "that"?'

'For people like you,' he replied, shifting in his chair.

'Well, it looks like I just made history, pal—because Mazlee is my partner. And since the rest of my family aren't in Singapore, he is the one I want to see every month. It is him, or no one.'

The officer seemed genuinely surprised at this defiance. 'I will see what we can do. This is very unorthodox.'

A few days later I was told that Mazlee would be receiving the card that allows him to be a regular visitor. Other inmates told me not to get too excited about the supposed face-to-face visits. Apparently we will be sitting face-to-face but separated by a thick glass wall. I'm told that I am entitled to a second monthly visit via video link, like a live cross from studio to studio.

Mazlee's work flying in and out of Singapore with the airline means he gets to see my prison from above. In the letter, he says, 'Every time when my plane takes off or lands in Singapore, I peek out the window and keep a look out for Tanah Merah Prison and in my heart, deep in my heart, I send you my love.'

He does not mention the elephant that will be in the visitors' room—his decision not to accompany me to the sentencing hearing. From that day to this I have wrestled with my anger and hurt and frustration. Perhaps it is a good thing that the visit has been delayed until now, for I have gotten past the worst of my disappointment. In fact, I have had the time to 'game out' the whole episode and look at the events from his point of view.

But I am still human, and I am not sure how I will react when I see him. I'm nursing a stomach full of butterflies. This is an unusual sensation for me; I am not given to nervousness. I'm walking into a room to see someone I am missing, desperately. I want to hug him. Then I want to smack him across the chops. Whoever said love was logical?

'Where are we?' I ask as Happy orders me to stop in front of another of those blue doors.

'Visitors' Section,' he answers as he opens the door. 'Go inside and wait at cubicle number 1.'

Mr Happy leaves me to navigate down a narrow corridor that is startlingly familiar. It could be the Visitors' Room from Hollywood central casting. It is as though I have arrived on the dimly lit set of any of American cinema's prison genre greats.

If I step lightly and shut my eyes for a moment, I am a bit player in *Escape from Alcatraz*. Think Clint Eastwood, taciturn and ironic, in Alcatraz, with that unforgettable script, where less was more. (Prisoner: What kind of childhood did you have? Eastwood: Short.)

This passageway could be from Tim Robbins' *Shawshank Redemption*, a place where 'some birds aren't meant to be caged'. Or a scene from Penn's *Dead Man Walking*, a place where 'your mind does crazy things when you're locked up and surrounded by people who wants to kill you'.

I feel like a time traveller who has entered the time travellers' machine. No single feature in this room anchors me to the present day, to my present reality. This room has eight separate booths, all of which are unoccupied today. Each cubicle has a riot-proof, one-piece, hard plastic seat fixed to the floor by heavy bolts. Anger-proof seating. Each has a thick glass windowpane and a small desk, like a bank whose tellers have gone for the day after helping themselves to the takings.

There is one prop rudely absent. There is no bright-coloured telephone to yell into, or to smash in a moment of anger or frustration or despair. (Was that Burt Reynolds, in *The Longest Yard*?)

It is as though time has stood still in this strange little room, where life is imitating art. The only nod to the here and now, the only clue that confirms I am not dreaming, is a small microphone and speaker— a nod to modernity, an anchor that brings me out of this reverie and back to reality. 'Yes, this is a high-security prison.'

I sit myself down at cubicle number 1 and shut my eyes, feeling the thick glass with my hands. I am imagining myself as an astronaut on a 200-day space walk, still tethered to the mother ship of reality and freedom and my life outside—to my life beyond this room, this prison. I am so very close to it, but still so very far away.

Entering, from the left, I see two lead actors from my world: Mazlee and Karen Gosling.

'Hello,' I say, trying to cover my surprise.

'Hello,' they say in unison, trying not to notice that I am clearly not very happy about something.

Why have they come together? I think. This visit is scheduled to last for a mere ten minutes—precious time will be wasted if I have to pander to two relationships, being careful not to speak openly to one before the other. I am hostage to circumstance and now, having been relieved of the power to influence this arrangement, I feel myself shutting down.

I am angry and confused all over again. I need to talk to Mazlee, to hear him explain why he was in a coffee shop when I was being sentenced. I want to hug him, and shout out my disappointment and frustration. I do not want to feel this way any more. I need to let this go. But what can I say, for or against my partner, when there is glass between us and a guest alongside?

Disconsolate, I can feel myself falling into a dark and brooding silence.

I'm looking down. I'm looking to the left, and I'm looking to the right. I am looking anywhere but directly at Mazlee, and I can sense that my refusal to meet his eye is a cruel blow of disappointment.

Karen is filling the silence. 'How are you, Peter? You look like you have lost weight.'

'The food isn't so good.'

'What are you eating?'

'Fish or chicken—like aeroplane food, but much worse.'

My joke lands badly. Mazlee looks hurt by my remark, and I can see him searching its entrails for hidden meaning even though none was intended. That is the problem with slights—even imagined ones become real.

'I have been given a diary—at last.'

This is the information Karen wanted to hear. We spent a lot of time before I came to prison talking about how important it will be for me to write down my thoughts—and I had no idea how desperately I was going to need the outlet of writing.

Karen, looking slightly relieved, says, 'Oh, Peter, that is good news. I'm so glad for you.'

Mazlee is smiling too, relief expanding across his face, and I am smiling back, a tentative break in the ice. I think, *I love you. But I just can't say it yet. I need to be angry for a little bit more.*

'And I have a job,' I say pointing to my shirt, which has the letters CK emblazoned across the upper right-hand side, over my name, LLOYD, and my prison number, 12988. 'I am a cookie. That's what they call workers.'

'What do you do?'

I laugh, in anticipation of how they will react. They probably think I am going to say 'librarian'. So I just spit it out: 'I deliver meals.'

Mazlee and Karen both sit upright, in shock. They are probably wondering if this is a black joke, like claiming to be the proverbial guy in prison who does laundry or peels potatoes. Neither job, I must say, has the same languorous appeal as five minutes' work three times a day in return for the privilege of being released from my cell for ten hours out of twenty-four.

'Meals?' says Karen. 'Are you cooking?'

'No way. I can't cook for 800 men.' The mood is lightening. All of us are laughing now, and it is not entirely forced. A silent entente has broken out between Mazlee and me; on this visit he won't demand affection and I won't offer it. 'They deliver meals to the wing, and on each wing there is a work crew or, as they call us, cookies, whose job it is to hand out the meals.'

Karen is looking puzzled at my apparent enthusiasm.

'The perks are pretty significant: it means I am out of my room for ten hours a day. And the cookies get to watch extra television programs for the morning, between breakfast and lunch. It's not bad. Apparently I even get paid for this work, a grand sum of one dollar fifty a week.'

Mazlee: 'You get a dollar fifty? Are you kidding?'

'Would I make up something so fantastic?' I say, laughing.

'I suppose not,' says Karen.

Mazlee is talking, but I cannot hear him. It is like watching a goldfish. The audio link to the outside has terminated—it looks like my ten minutes is up already.

Mazlee and Karen are both mouthing words that I can no longer hear. Mr Happy is standing at the end of the corridor, hollering, 'Peter, come now! Time is up.'

How could he know that, I think, *unless he was listening. What a bastard.*

Mazlee and Karen are being ushered away from the window by an officer stationed on the other side. I'm waving. They are waving. The rope that tethers me to the mother ship has been severed. I'm being sucked backwards, into the deep black hole of space.

The time traveller's journey is over.

TWENTY-FOUR
Games people play

I HAVE BEEN SUMMONED to the prison administration section for an interview, about what I do not know. As I discovered when I was assigned to work as a cookie, prisoners are told only what they need to know, and mostly that is nothing. By this conscious omission, another layer of the Singapore criminal punishment regime—the denial of the right to the most banal information (to ask 'Where am I going?' and receive a courteous reply)—reveals itself.

Cedric the Surfer Dude is my escorting officer. 'So, how does prison in Singapore compare to Australia?' he asks.

'Um, strange as it may seem, Staff, but this is actually my first time in prison. As a customer, at any rate.'

Cedric is grinning, like he's just scored a goal or posed a long-planned 'When did you stop beating your wife?' question. I don't really mind. I suppose prison officers concoct distractions to alleviate the crushing boredom of their vocation, since they are largely professional key-turners and door-openers. Nothing too eventful—riotous assembly and the like—seems to happen in Singapore jails.

Still, I summon the temerity to launch a verbal counterattack. 'Have you ever wondered how many times you open and close a door each day?'

Cedric isn't smiling now. We have just arrived at a door marked 'Intelligence Unit'. Cedric knocks once, a little timidly I think, and then opens the door with one of his set of jingly-jangly keys.

239

'One hundred and one?' I suggest drily, looking from the keychain to Cedric's face.

'Ha. Funny,' he replies, stony-faced, pushing the door open.

From inside the office, a much older officer is gesturing for me to come in and take a seat in front of him. He has crab-shaped silver badges on his epaulettes, indicating a senior rank.

'Do you know who I am?' he asks.

'Yes. You are the Intelligence Officer.'

'Who told you that?' he demands.

'It is written on the door.'

Although Chinese, this guy immediately reminds me of the irrationally paranoid intelligence officer in the television series *MASH*, Colonel Flagg. After a few forced pleasantries—the awkward conversational equivalent of attempting to push out a turd while constipated—Flagg gets down to business.

'So you are a journalist?'

'Yes.'

He looks puzzled, like I am a creature who's just landed from another planet. 'Why do you do this job?'

'Come again?' I say, buying time before the inevitable authoritarian follow-up remark. *These bozos never let me down,* I think.

'Well, you stir up nothing but trouble,' he says, adjusting his pudgy waistline like a great white hunter going in for the kill. 'Journalists are so negative,' he adds.

Pausing for effect, I reply, 'Do you think so, Staff? I haven't heard that before.'

The impertinence of my response sinks in too slowly for an immediate counterattack. I call a ceasefire too—no need to provoke the prison natives.

The Intelligence Officer is giving me the 'I'm a busy bureaucrat' treatment, pausing in our getting-to-know-you chat to tap away at his computer, as though a public act of multi-tasking demonstrates his esteemed place in the authoritarian cosmos of Singapore. *Bah humbug,* I think.

I am taking the opportunity to read the paperwork on his desk. He probably hasn't encountered a reporter before, and has no idea that many of us have developed an uncanny ability to read documents upside down. Certain key words usually rise off the pages.

His desk is a disappointment, apart from the revelation of how much office time he seems to be devoting to planning a holiday to the Cameron Highlands, across the border in Malaysia. He has printed off page after page of tourist information and accommodation tips; he has circled a number of bungalows, indicating a preference for the cheapest housing. I can tell that the documents have been printed off here at the office, because they bear today's date and a time stamp at the top of each page.

After some self-serving chatter about prison needing to be austere, after my complaint about the absence of beds, for example, Mr Intelligence concludes by telling me that denial of material comfort is intended to remind inmates of their inherent character flaws.

At the mention of the name of my accuser, Saini bin Saidi, he waves his hand as though irritated by an insect, declaring, 'Malays are nothing in this community.'

'Pardon me?' I say. 'You know that my partner, my boyfriend, is Malay-Singaporean.'

His expression remains as blank as that of the sphinx. He is clearly unembarrassed by his racial faux pas. Then he leans in: 'I said they are nothing,' he repeats.

His tone is final and emphatic, as though Malay 'nothingness' does not require explanation. It is obvious to him, and it should be obvious to me too.

• • • • •

OUT IN THE YARD, it's Culture Swap Wednesday. Knuckles, Heng and Ismail have been trying to teach me how to play sepak takraw. This game resembles volleyball but with a rattan ball, and players are only allowed to use their feet or head to touch the ball.

I've seen this played on television in Thailand, but Ismail reckons the Thais stole it from the Malays. 'Yes. This is our game first. It was played in Malacca, then Thais took it to Bangkok.'

This could provoke a war, but I'm going to say it anyway. '*Takraw* sounds Thai, if you ask me.'

Ismail is considering this point. '*Sepak* is Malay. It means "kick".'
He is ignoring the rest of the argument.

Heng has his back to Ismail but is looking at me, laughing. '*Takraw*
means "woven ball" in Thai, but he is never going to admit that.'

Ismail is my age, but has the agility of a man in his twenties. He
has played sepak takraw all of his life, and it shows. 'Ha! Ten nil!' he
shouts, as the ball eludes me one more time. I haven't managed to reply
to a single serve, and the enthusiasm of this old dog to learn a new trick
is waning.

'How about we try my game?' I suggest.

'What is that?' asks Heng

'Australian football,' replies Knuckles.

Ismail points out the obvious logistical problem. 'No ball.'

'Let's use the sepak ball,' I suggest.

Before anyone can object, I grab the small, ultra-light ball and run
to the far end of the yard. I turn and kick in the direction of the other
inmates, thirty metres away. Much lighter than an Australian football,
and round instead of oval-shaped, the sepak ball takes greater flight
than I anticipated when I punted it as hard as I could.

It is sailing over the heads of Ismail, Knuckles and Heng, and over
the idlers sheltering from the sun. It hits the prison wall with a heavy
bang, and then plinks and plonks its way across the guardhouse roof,
tumbling and rolling here and there before coming to rest atop a sharp
upturned spike of freshly laid razor wire, like a gruesome ornament in
a primitive tribal village.

'Holy shit!' I mutter.

Ismail is staring in disbelief. Heng and Knuckles are looking at each
other, as though seeking a second opinion on how to react. Is it funny,
or serious?

Marlboro Man, standing now, raises both arms over his head, like
a cricket umpire.

'Shut up! I can fix this,' I say.

Running the length of the yard, I survey the guardroom to see if
officer 'Colonel Blimp' or any other guard is aware of the rooftop ker-
fuffle. Nobody seems to have heard it. Leaning on Knuckles' shoulder,
I reach down and peel off my right sandshoe.

'Don't do it,' he urges.

Ignoring him, I reply, 'Watch this!' Holding my shoe up for inspection, I add, 'Just like a boomerang.'

Eye-hand co-ordination is not a quality for which I am famous. However, this is not the moment to hesitate, and I am left-arming the shoe with as much force as I can muster. Inexplicably, the shoe finds its mark, striking the sepak ball hard enough to set it loose. It falls softly to the ground. The shoe, however, does not follow—a lace seems to have caught on the edge of the razor wire. Now my shoe is dangling from it, like a hostage swapped in a prisoner exchange and then killed by angry villagers.

'Fuck!'

All I can hear is the laughter of inmates, no longer able to contain their mirth. Everyone is laughing. Knuckles, Ismail and Heng are laughing so hard they need to support each other to stop from falling down. The prisoners who are sitting down are falling sideways.

'Nice. Thanks for your support!' I say.

Marlboro Man is up, dancing like an ostrich, making loud whooping noises.

'Whooping? Really? Are we whooping now?' I inquire.

'Whoop, whoop!' he cries, rocking his head back and cackling.

'Fuck.' It's all I can say. 'Fuck!' I'm tugging at my lower lip, the way I do when I am nervous. Here comes trouble. It's Mr Nathan, the superintendent. He is entering the yard, hands on hips, in that 'Hello, hello, what's going on here?' pose.

'What is the meaning of this?' he demands.

'Meaning of what, sir?' asks Marlboro Man.

'Why are you flapping your arms in this manner? Are you poultry trying to effect an escape?'

Now I'm laughing. 'Very good, sir!' Nathan possesses the driest wit of any officer in the prison. His deadpan expression is hilarious. Sometimes I'm not sure he even knows how funny he is.

'Humm,' he says, looking my way and then down at my feet. 'Mr Lloyd. Where is your shoe?'

'Ah . . .' I'm going to have to confess, I think. 'My shoe is . . .' And just as I am about to give myself up, the lace breaks and my missing shoe falls off the roof and lands just behind Nathan's back, narrowly missing his head.

I can hear the sound of air being sucked between the teeth of Heng and Knuckles, who are standing close enough to Nathan to see how near he came to being brained by my size 44. Blinking, I continue. 'My shoe is right behind you. It flew off when I kicked the ball,' I say, as I run over and collect both the ball and the shoe.

Nathan seems to know that he is being had. He's giving me the same eyeballing he gave me when he locked me up back in December. Licking his lips, he says, 'Indeed it did. Perhaps less force next time?'

• • • • •

HALF AN HOUR LATER, I'm sitting quietly in the corner of the yard when the friendly staff officer comes over for another chat.

I'm torn. This man may be a Deep Throat informer, or at the vanguard of a Singapore Prison Service mind-control unit. I sense that he wants me to ask questions, so I do.

'Do they execute people here in Tanah Merah?'

'No. That's across the road, in Cluster.' Cluster is the name of the giant prison complex across the street. The outside world calls it Changi, but in fact Changi prison no longer exists.

'When do they do it?'

'Fridays. Wednesday if the prisoner is a Muslim.'

'Really? They make concessions for religion?'

'Some.'

'Have you done it?'

'Me? No. I didn't sign up for such a duty. My role is here, helping prisoners become better people. That is not for me.'

'Who does it?'

'ASPs, usually—Acting Superintendents. Some officers want to do it—they believe in capital punishment. Why are you asking about this?'

'It's been in the papers.'

'You know that?' He is surprised.

I'm not going to volunteer to Staff how I know this, but I have been quietly applauding the boys in the censorship room for going easy on the black paint again. It seems that the Law Society president, Michael Hwang, has set a cat among the pigeons in the regime by publicly questioning the effectiveness of capital punishment, caning and some jail sentences.

Emboldened, I ask, 'So are most of the people who get executed Malay and Indian?'

'I think so,' he says.

'Is it quick?'

'When it goes right.'

'What do you mean?'

'I hear stories.'

'What kind of stories?'

'That sometimes there are problems. You see,' he is sitting forward, explaining with his hands, 'they make the noose according to the height and weight of the inmate. It is called the long-drop method. If they get it wrong . . . well, you saw what happened in Baghdad at the execution of Saddam's brother.'

'Do you think people struggle? Is there time?' I say.

'They can't. The doctor slices open the tendon at the back of the ankles just before they drop them.'

'Oh God!' I exclaim. 'That is way too much information.'

Laughing, 'You asked, man. You asked, remember!'

'I've heard that the tongue swells up. Is that true?'

'Yes, I hear that too. They place a bag over the head, and draw it tight around the neck. It protects the execution room staff.'

'From what?'

'Eyeballs.'

'Eyeballs?' I say, not following this line of thought.

'Yeah. Eyeballs. Sometimes they explode out of the head.' He's using his fingers to illustrate. 'The face becomes engorged, and turns blue.'

I feel ill. 'Okay. That really is way too much information.'

'Change of topic then?'

'Sure.'

'How is the diary going?'

'Fine—why are you asking?'

'No reason,' he says, leaning forward to inspect his shoes. 'I plan ahead.'

Again, I am not following this turn of conversation, so I echo his comment. 'You plan ahead?'

'Yes,' he replies, 'and I always have a back-up plan.' Looking at me, he asks, 'Do you?'

That night I am in my room. The lights have gone out and I'm lying in the semi-darkness, weighing up the meaning of today's conversation with the staff officer. I think, *Is this guy setting me up? Is he baiting me? Am I being fed some lines that they think will end up in my diary?*

This is a mind game, all right. I'm just not quite sure where Staff is coming from. Deep Throat, or deep trouble?

$$\bullet \ \bullet \ \bullet \ \bullet \ \bullet$$

I DID NOT SLEEP well again last night. My first worry was that remark about back-up plans from Deep Throat. I am not sure exactly where I can back up my diary in an austere prison where I have no possessions, no access to computers or telephones or even paper. Even loo paper is rationed to one roll per fortnight.

Prisoners are issued one local blank pro-forma letter per month for sending out of the prison—strictly to friends or relatives. With just forty-six lines of available writing space, that meagre piece of paper offers too little space and too little frequency to attempt sending out diary content in letter-form, however coded the language might be.

I could relate stories of prison life to Mazlee during our twice-monthly visits in the hope that he goes home and writes it down, but then that implicates him in my scheme. In Singapore, that is a very bad idea. Whatever I come up with has to be my own secret arrangement, with no one else involved. This could backfire spectacularly.

My sleep was interrupted by another anxiety, my still unresolved 'Mazlee issue'. We had our second visit two days ago. This was our first tele-visit, with both of us sitting in front of cameras in soundproofed rooms. Mazlee said he was in the TMP admin block a few metres away, but he could just as easily have been in a television studio in Sydney, such is the sterile formality of a tele-visitation.

I could hear him far better than during the face-to-face interview, when we were separated by a glass wall. But that does not mean we were communicating any better. He was trying hard—but I am just not ready for easy conversation or eye contact.

I do not feel comfortable saying private things during visits which are probably monitored. So I have decided to put my frustrations to bed in a letter. Almost certainly this will be scrutinised too—but at least at some distance from me. This is how it begins:

Let me give you immediate relief by saying I love and miss you. That is not to say that I am going to gloss over the hurt and disappointment at the choice you made. Being in a coffee shop while I was being sentenced is a wound that will take time to heal. So often now I lie awake and punish myself by thinking back to moments of happiness; lying arm in arm and feeling you breathe slowly and surrender to sleep, safe in my embrace and the knowledge that you have my enduring love. On these nights I weep, and wonder whether things will ever be the same again.

I feel like a walk-on character in a Jane Austen novel, quaintly conveying affection—and frustrations—via long-hand letter writing. With no email, no telephone, no mobile phone and none of the intimacy of genuine face-to-face meetings, this is how it is to be. Let's just hope my Mr Darcy is still waiting in the wings when this is all over.

TWENTY-FIVE
Famine to feast

AFTER THE LETTER DROUGHT, now comes a proverbial deluge of correspondence. I am receiving a regular flow of letters from my family and friends—some of whom I have not seen or spoken to since I was in high school. One of them sent me a copy of the school newspaper from 12 March 1982—the day I committed my first act of journalism: 'Activities began for the year recently and with a wide range of choice offered, 1982 is shaping up as the best year ever. The year began well with the purchase of gym equipment and guns.'

Not only did I embrace cliché-writing from an early age, I also demonstrated an alarmingly wide-eyed lack of curiosity as to why my school was offering recreational activities involving weapons. North American–style school massacres had not been invented back in 1982.

From my time living in Bangkok there is a stream of amusing letters. One came from a writer friend who knows of my fascination with all things to do with the monarchy—can there be a more outmoded form of government? In her letter she relates the protocol for a meeting with Cambodia's former King Sihanouk, who does not approve of two-toned outfits on men or women. In a Court Circular, his former majesty says, 'when one is received by the King, it is not correct to show up in front of His Majesty in "two-tone" costumes, for example, a dark jacket and light pants. And do not forget to button the jacket.' The fashionable former king helpfully suggests two-toned outfits may be worn 'when one goes to a club, a casino, for a stroll or a commercial movie theatre'.

There have been letters from ABC colleagues too, including from Virginia Trioli. A year ago we barely knew each other, but then the ABC decided that we'd be ideal co-hosts for a new television breakfast news program they were planning. I was uncertain about the project until I met Virginia in person, and got to know her over martinis in a chic Melbourne bar. After that meeting I had no doubt that we'd work well together. Now she has written me two long and amusing letters, with often scandalously funny notes, which remind me that, although our professional association is on hold, she has become a devoted friend.

A crisis of the kind I have been going through tends to sort out the men from the boys in your life—the friend from the not-so-friend. Virginia is firmly in the camp of journo friends who rose to the occasion, like Tim Palmer and Sarah Stewart. There were others too, like Sonia Zavesky, who dropped her work and flew to Singapore to see me during the week of my collapse and admission to the psychiatric wing of the Mount Elizabeth Hospital. And of course there is the dearest friend of all, Kirsty.

From the mother of my boys, I am now receiving a stream of witty tracts about what is going on in her life. In her first letter, she tells me that in December people were wrongly informed that I could receive only two letters a month. That explains the initial drought. I am an enthusiastic convert to the most mundane detail of other people's lives—since none could be more mundane and routine than mine.

'I need to share,' begins one letter from Kirsty. 'I was just cleaning up the kitchen when Tom comes up to me and asks whether Dad will be out of jail when it is his birthday. I say yes, and he says, "Good, because this is what I want him to get me," and shoves a Big W brochure in my face. God forbid, beware direct-mail marketing.'

It is not always entertaining news. Kirsty reports in a more recent letter that Jack had a seizure in a swimming pool that led to the ambulance being called to make sure his airways were fluid-free.

This is sobering and frustrating. I am not allowed to make or receive phone calls. I cannot Skype. I cannot email. There is no way to relay my shock or support to Kirsty, beyond writing an impersonal form letter that will take around four weeks to reach an overseas destination.

This is the bittersweet aspect of prison life. I receive unlimited mail but have strictly limited opportunities to respond, given that I can send only two letters per month and only one of those can be international mail. The other must be to a Singapore address. I am engaged in a one-way conversation with the world. Communicating with a prisoner in Singapore is the sound of one hand clapping.

I don't talk about either of my children to other prisoners. That is one area of my life that I keep fenced off against trespassers. My behaviour was different when I was working as a correspondent. Back then I paid particular interest to the issue of children's welfare, especially the disabled. Journalists walk a tightrope—we need to sense and feel the emotion of any given situation in order to convincingly convey the events to an audience. To feel too much—to become too involved—is a danger that can blur our ability to objectively tell a story.

I walked that tightrope in Thailand when reporting on the despicable treatment of HIV-positive infants orphaned after the death of a parent who had been living with AIDS. Bangkok authorities kept the HIV kids in separate rooms, forced them to sit in colour-coded chairs and forbade them from playing with other, uninfected orphans. These kids were institutionalised and stigmatised.

And it happened too one day in Sri Lanka a few years ago, when our journey on an assignment for *Foreign Correspondent* brought us to a refugee camp on the outskirts of Batticaloa, a large town on the east coast.

· · · · ·

I COULD TELL FROM the transfixed smile and the naive, limpet-like way that he attached himself, clutching my left hand and grabbing hold of my left wrist, that this little boy who had wandered out of the curious crowd of onlookers was determined. And the way he insinuated his way into my zone of personal space, without any apparent hesitation or fear, gave me pause to suspect something else.

'I think I have a son just like you,' I said, looking down to examine his face for understanding. He stared back with an absent expression, saying nothing. He put his smile on high beam and pressed his hand further into mine.

'You're a quiet one, eh?' I teased. 'Can you take me to Mummy?'

There was still no sign of cognition, so I looked around for a carer, somebody to step forward. No one did. So I asked out loud if anybody knew his family. No one replied. No one seemed to want to reclaim the child who had just claimed me.

Over the years of the island's civil war there had been a series of pitched battles for this strip of territory. By early 2006, the government had the upper hand and was already predicting the total military defeat of the Tamil Tigers. Decades of conflict had caused the displacement of hundreds of thousand people.

Before I travelled to Batticaloa I had drinks with an aid worker in the capital, Colombo. I asked her what sort of atmosphere I could expect to find in the camps.

'Silence,' she answered, almost conspiratorially. 'It's hard to describe until you see it. But there's just a kind of silence when you go to these places.'

'Silence like church? Or silence like traumatised people who can't speak?'

'Definitely the latter. People in these places hardly talk about the things they've witnessed—the tit-for-tat violence and the like. And, of course, intimidation still goes on inside the camps.'

My cameraman for this assignment was, as usual in South Asia, Wayne McAllister. The quintessentially Aussie actor Bryan Brown would have no trouble playing Wayne McAllister in the movies. But that's the superficial stuff. Wayne's also a witty and sentimental guy; a thinker and philosopher; a gifted, if not eccentric, artist; and one helluva talented stills and video photographer. At the camp, I watched as Wayne disarmed the apprehensive-looking refugees by kneeling down and asking permission to record the frugal circumstances they had found themselves in. By rights I should have been by his side, assisting him by holding the microphone. *Foreign Correspondent*'s producers are sticklers for getting good-quality sound to enhance the pictures.

Normally I'm on my game, but on this occasion my hands were already full. And there wasn't a producer around to see me slacking off with the kid who had stolen my hand and won my heart.

'Let's go outside and see who's there,' I said to my mute young acquaintance. Happily, he trotted along by my side. I was deliberately trying to remain in full public view with the kid, lest anybody raise a false alarm that a western man was trying to abduct a disabled refugee. Foolishly, perhaps, the fear of that awful accusation kept running through my head. I was also worried that it wasn't safe or appropriate for me to be seen holding a stranger's hand, but every effort I made to unlock his grip failed, and all of the tricks I normally use to distract my own boys' attention—those 'Oh look at that!' moments—seemed to have the reverse effect here, making him grip me that much harder.

It was as though the little mite knew exactly what I was thinking, and he wasn't having a bar of it. After a few failed attempts to get the guards at the front gate to take over, I gave up trying to offload the kid. 'What the hell,' I thought. 'He's not doing any harm to me, and I'm not doing any harm to him.'

And then I got mad at myself. What's happened to me that, when a disabled kid seizes on a new face to get some harmless affection, all I worry about is whether someone might think I'm a creepy sex offender? I'm in broad daylight, surrounded by people, doing a public filming assignment for the Australian national broadcaster.

'I don't suppose you can understand a word I'm saying,' I said, staring down at my companion, 'but you've got a tough gig here.' I looked around. It wasn't the worst refugee camp I'd seen—nothing compared to the squalor of Bangladesh's southern camps. But my heart sank at the thought of the life this little boy led here. For the able-bodied, refugee life is a misery of material deprivation combined with boredom and then moments of pure terror. Armed thugs aligned with one side or the other routinely enter refugee camps to engage in the recruitment of child soldiers, or carry out extortion, abductions for ransom or political assassinations. A lot of parents take turns staying awake at night, to make sure their children aren't taken.

Of course nobody actually starves in these camps, which exist under the umbrella of the United Nations High Commission for Refugees.

But there usually isn't enough food for more than one proper meal a day. Add mental disability to the roster of challenges and you've got a kid with a future filled with even more uncertainty than most.

After another hour I finally had to say goodbye to my dogged little companion, easing out of his determined embrace and handing him over to a guard when Wayne had finished filming the sequence.

The boy cried when I walked away. I could hear him sobbing heavily and making a whimpering sound, the first attempt at verbal communication that he made. I couldn't turn back because, if I did, I would have cried too. And I didn't tell Wayne because I knew he would be upset as well, in that taciturn Bryan Brown kind of way.

Someone much smarter than me once said that a society ought to be judged by the way it deals with its weakest members. I thought about that idea a lot afterwards.

How would Sri Lanka deal with the lost boy of Batticaloa? I will never really know. But because I have my son Jack, I will always worry about it.

TWENTY-SIX

Beyond Everest

LOVE BEGINS IN THE IMAGINATION.

Last night I dreamed of the day *after* prison. Mazlee and I are sitting at the edge of a steep cliff overlooking a vast sea. Hues of brilliant orange tickle and dance on distant clouds, resting on the faraway horizon. Nature has framed an end-of-day spectacular. We are sitting alone in a state of contented silence, telegraphing unspoken messages of relief and amity and love. This is a tender reunion. The harmony we previously found in our togetherness is being restored. We have granted each other release from old agonies in the room of sorrows.

If my nightmares were signals of torment from the past, then this dream must be a glimpse, of sorts, for a wished-upon future—a future that begins in the imagination.

The Austen-era romance-by-mail continues apace. After I expressed my hurt about what happened back in December at the court, 'Mr Darcy' replied with a simple apology. That is enough for me, and now it is time for both of us to move on from that moment.

And it seems that I am not the only person having to be patient with the slow pace of communication. 'I received an email and SMS from Kirsty the other day,' says Mazlee in another letter. 'She was so glad to finally receive your letter. Isn't it amazing and frustrating at the same time to know how much time it takes for a letter to arrive to any one of us? I guess we are spoiled by progressive new technologies.'

Such dreams and letters are a tonic for days that seem to pass with crushing monotony. I measure out small milestones that mark the progression of my sentence, like an antidote to poison administered in very small doses. I mark small periods on a makeshift calendar: so many days until my next visit from Mazlee (tomorrow), or so many days until the Ides of March, and so forth. It is easiest to bear a prison sentence when it is consumed in bite-sized chunks.

For some inside this jail, where there is so little to do and so much time in which to do it, clock-watching is a dangerous habit. Pung is among those fixated in this way. It strikes me as being psychologically self-harming, since this practice borders on an obsessive-compulsive addiction to the lacerating tick-tock of yet another hour, in another day, in another month, of just another year.

I am reading, so I can occupy my time quite productively. By sentence end I aim to have read eighty books. I offer my private books to Pung but he refuses: 'I am too lazy to read,' he says, as he dozes and daydreams next to me during the daytime hours when we are idle between meal service.

I am looking forward to the halfway point of my sentence. After climbing the first Mount Everest of psychological recovery, and then the Second Everest—the despair that followed my sentencing—this looming milestone seems like the beginning of the end, the final track down the side of the highest mountain climb of my life.

• • • • •

LATELY I HAVE BEEN trying to deal with my present circumstances as well as plan for my future under the influence of a self-help book that I found in the library, *The 7 Habits of Highly Effective People*. I am usually allergic to self-help publications, sensing snake oil somewhere in the mix. International success, for example, does not dilute the shabbiness of a crappy little book like *The Secret*, which amounts to little more than a grand con tailored for the needy and greedy.

But the *7 Habits* book really is different. The author, Stephen Covey, sets out seven guiding habits which are basically principles of ethical behaviour. Most of them centre around having a positive attitude, and then being organised and thoughtful about what it is you want to achieve. My favourite 'habit' is No. 5—'seek first to understand, then be understood'. Covey calls this 'the principle of mutual understanding'. In a way what Covey is telling us is that listening to the other point of view, in any situation, is the first step towards finding common ground.

This Covey book, plus my mantra from the Dalai Lama (to abandon anger and fear), are giving me a new lease on life. So what's new?

I've stopped directing my frustrations at these circumstances onto Mazlee.

I've pledged not to be bitter about the past.

I've decided that life after prison will be less about work, and more about family and friends.

And I have realised that, rather than being a failure, I am in fact a success story. I am far more resilient than I ever imagined. Post-traumatic stress disorder of the kind I experienced has led some sufferers to take their own life, or broken them irretrievably. I have not submitted to this condition. I took back control of my life. In prison, I have been using my time to rest and recover, and to accept my circumstances and adapt accordingly. I have used this time to consider the past and forgive myself for making mistakes.

With around a hundred days left of my sentence, I am determined not to waste the opportunity presented by the crisis. I am going to document the prisoner experience. This place is a goldmine for a journalist. All I need to do is listen, and learn.

• • • • •

MY DAILY ROUTINE is settled into a fixed pattern that never changes. Where once I abhorred the monotony of routine I now cling to it, as I would to driftwood in a tempest. Up at seven, at work by half past. As the newest recruit I am the lowest ranked cookie in the invisible hierarchy, so I oblige Pung and Ismail and Goh by collecting the laundry or closing hatches or running errands at their suggestion. Accepting with humility a menial workload is the only real exertion. Once that pride barrier is smashed, playing fetch-and-carry is an easy task for a prisoner with nothing but time, endless time, to occupy.

After breakfast we cookies sit on the floor in the reception area of our landing and watch a light entertainment DVD compiled by an audio-visual department in the prison. Stripped of news or current affairs programs that may fill our heads with information and, more scandal-ously, ideas, the disc is a daily pull-together of pop culture programs screened on Singapore terrestrial television and provided as a privilege for all of the prisoners with work responsibilities.

The shows include *Don't Forget the Lyrics*, *American Idol*, *Ninja Warrior*, *America's Funniest Videos*, *Mr Bean*, Attenborough nature documentaries, *Hell's Kitchen*, *Cooking in the Danger Zone* and a series of terrible made-for-television movies. Many of the movies chosen involve animals and children. These are recorded from the local children-friendly channel and star a monkey or a chimp, invariably named Jack.

Lunchtime in prison occurs at what is morning tea time everywhere else, 11.30am. The opening of what I have dubbed the '*Law & Order* Door' on the landing signals the commencement of lunch duties. This is the door through which baskets of food are dragged by other cookies in charge of prison-wide distribution. That is the beauty of cheap labour—you can employ a lot of prisoners to dole out the dishes.

Every day there is a piece of fruit to be distributed. This onerous duty mostly falls to me, being at the bottom of the cookie pecking order. There are only three types of fruit in prison: bitter oranges, browning bananas and soft red apples. They rotate each day. I walk up the landing, placing a piece of fruit before each of the twenty odd cells. Next comes Ismail, sliding a large delivery box containing trays of meals. Food service in prison is colour-coded. Blue is 'soft diet', a mulch of pureed rice and gunk for edentulous inmates. Yellow is for the vegetarians. Red is non-spicy, and blue is for regular meat-eaters.

Lunch is invariably the most complained-about meal. It is a culinary doomsday of the disagreeable, distasteful and indigestible. Soggy rice is the centrepiece, generous portion sizes of which contrast sharply with the meanness of anything else on the plate. The 'anything else' part is hard to describe, but rarely does a day pass without the appearance of cabbage in some form or another. I marvel at how the kitchen can invent, and re-invent, the humble cabbage. I have seen it fried, baked, boiled, braised, blanched and raw. I have seen cabbage fly solo, or matched with corn. I have eaten cabbage and curry. I have even had it pickled. Yes, cabbage is a truly versatile vegetable.

After lunch, we four cookies trundle back up the landing and collect the food trays. Between one-third and half of what went into the cells comes back out, thrust onto the landing with a flick of disgust. We make a joke of the obvious waste in front of officers, to drive home the point that the prisoners are not satisfied with these meals.

'Oh, they're off the carbs again,' Pung says, as he empties an inmate's heavy tray into the bin. There is only so much rice a man can eat in one sitting.

Dinnertime is a preview of our future lives as senile senior citizens. It arrives before five in the evening, two hours before sundown. It is issued, eaten and trays collected by 5.30. Meat-eaters can reliably predict a choice of fish or chicken, accompanied on every occasion by too much rice, cabbage du jour and an assortment of other vegetables robbed of all colour, texture and identifying flavour. In prison, you eat to live; nobody lives to eat.

It strikes me as nonsensical to keep inmates locked up when they eat. These are just more rules and regulations created to exercise custodial control, and yet they create a larger problem down the track: prisoners who have simply stopped thinking for themselves.

Denial of liberty is merely the first layer of punishment. Then there is the denial of choice—over what I wear, where I live, with whom or how I spend my time, what I eat and even the question of when. These are matters of trivial daily importance, decided for me and other prisoners by the authorities. In this way, prisoners are structurally disempowered from making simple day-by-day decisions for themselves; as a corollary, they become dependent on others to do the mundane thinking for them.

How then do prison authorities expect inmates to return to society fully functioning? When people are stripped of the power and responsibility to make decisions, they are less competent and capable. It is beyond my understanding why prisons go out of their way to drum this capacity out of inmates. The inmate and society must be diminished by this policy.

· · · · ·

IN THE YARD MY afternoons are spent running in circles on the jogging track. Sometimes I keep running to avoid conversations with the voluble Superintendent Nathan. Today he is waiting at the finishing line. 'I went to the movies recently.' He has me cornered at the water bubbler.

'What did you see?'

'A wonderful movie from your country—*Australia*.'

'What was it like?'

'Excellent. Very, very good acting by the lady, Nicole Kidman, and the man, very handsome. Jackman. Huge Jackman.'

Nathan's accent, being distinctly Singaporean English, produces a heavy cadence on the 'u' sound. So the pronouncement of Huge Jackman sounds profoundly, well, huge.

'Huge?' I repeat, examining Nathan for any hint that he has heard the mistake.

'Indeed, a very talented man, this Mr Huge.'

I am using every ounce of self-discipline not to fall down laughing at this mispronunciation of Hugh Jackman's name.

'You are in this line of work,' says Nathan. 'Do you know him?'

What is it about Australia, I wonder, that reduces us, in the eyes of people who live north of the equator, from inhabiting the largest continent in the world to huddling together in a community of simpering inbreeds? I'm in a playful mood, so I'm going to take this conversation out for a run of its own and see where it takes us.

'No, I don't know Huge,' I say, 'but I do know his sister, Enorme.' I am stealing shamefully from an episode of *30 Rock*, but I am gambling that Mr Nathan, being an authoritarian's authoritarian, is not a big fan of that show.

'Ah, an actor as well?'

'No. A singer.'

'Really?'

'Yes.'

Mr Nathan seems lost in thought about this actor-singer family nexus. 'What kind of singer?' he inquires.

'Show tunes,' I say, digging myself into a deeper hole.

The Super muses over that reply for a moment, taking a drink of water from the prisoner's bubbler. *Surely,* I think, *he's run out of questions. This is getting awkward—if he goes into the security office and brings up the Jackman clan on Google, I think I am in big trouble.*

Finally Nathan draws himself up, wipes his mouth, and asks, 'What type of show tunes?'

'The usual—you know, "happy people songs",' I say, waving my hands in the air to underscore my *happy* euphemism.

'I see,' says Nathan. I think I have strayed close enough to the topic of sexuality to make him uncomfortable. *What a relief.*

'I must make my rounds,' he declares. 'Good afternoon.'

• • • • •

LATER IN THE WEEK another karaoke singer arrives on the landing. He lives next door. Knuckles was my neighbour but he was released two days ago, having served out his two months for stealing a bike. By now, I imagine, he's back on the streets of Geylang, keeping the johns and girls tidy.

His replacement is this skinny Malay guy. To my horror, he likes to whistle pop tunes; at lights out a few minutes ago he started crooning love ballads, beginning with Billy Joel's signature hit 'Piano Man'.

Oh Lord, here we go again! I think. *He's another Goh.* In fact, I can hear Goh singing too, in really bad harmony.

Laughter and applause are greeting this unlikely duet—a double murder of a popular classic. Skinny Guy and Goh are stoking some sentimental fire on the landing, for now everyone is shouting the chorus.

I can hear more whoops and jeers and applause. Some of it seems to be coming from the landing below, which houses a large number of transsexuals, who are catcalling for attention: 'Wait, lah. It is our turn, darlings.'

Our landing has fallen into silence, in anticipation. I'm taking a leak, during the intermission, when I hear the familiar lyrics about Lola, the showgirl.

More whooping and applause now as the inmates on my landing catch on that here is the Barry Manilow classic 'Copacabana'. Anybody over the age of twenty-five knows the chorus and, one floor down, the boys who want to be girls take up the slack on the verse that nobody can remember unless they are drunk.

This carry-on is all the proof I need for an emerging thesis on imprisonment: lock a man up long enough and he will do anything for entertainment. I have surrendered to reading the *Twilight* series of vampire books, chick-lit of a kind I swore blind that I would never read.

On nights like this, I see Tanah Merah Prison as an all boys' boarding school. There are no bars and shadows and the corridors, although antiseptic and long, are open and clear. Inmates refer to rooms, not cells. When I am outside, enjoying yard privileges, I can see the sky and feel the rain and catch the breeze. Officers are more guardians than guards. Their mantra: 'Behave like an adult, and you will be treated as one.'

Singapore's laws have not been kind to me, but the penal system, at least, is a more forgiving place where I am safe and secure and oddly entertained. There are no fights and brawls, at least not amongst the inmates on this landing. And that is all that I will ever know, since no two landings ever mix together. I shower and shit in the privacy of my cell, so my modesty remains intact. There is a kind of social harmony too, despite Malays and Chinese living together but separately.

TMP is a strange place, but it is not a dangerous place. My fascination with it grows by the day. Incarceration is an opportunity to learn more about people I would probably otherwise never meet, and to hear stories I would almost certainly be excluded from hearing. I did not choose this turn of events in my life, but I am embracing this experience for all that it offers. Even Barry Manilow.

TWENTY-SEVEN
Corporal punishment

I'M NOT ALONE ON THE running track, for today I have been joined by Diva, a new inmate with every reason in the world to be bitter about his imprisonment. He is the owner of a public garden maintenance contract company whose 'crime' was to hire two foreign guest workers whose visas had expired. Doubtless he was exploiting their situation to lower their remuneration but, all the same, Diva is now serving a year in prison as punishment.

'This bloody government is so *stew*-pid!' he exclaims, as we round the bend on another lap. 'They throw people in jail for most minor infraction! It is *cray*-zee!'

Diva is an ethnic Tamil-Singaporean, and his exaggerated Singlish emphasis at the end of sentences makes me laugh, no matter how serious the topic he ruminates on. That's already his nickname, the 'Ruminator'.

'Look, man,' he says, mid-stride, 'I was a soldier, an elite soldier, and this is what they did to me!'

Diva's story—and I suspect it may have been renovated and embellished for my ears—is that he was once a member of the elite Singapore Armed Forces Commando Formation. Its existence was never even acknowledged until the dramatic hijacking of a Singapore Airlines Airbus A310 in March 1991.

'I was in that operation,' says Diva proudly, when I mention my knowledge of the crisis. 'Those fuckers hijacked the plane after it left

Kuala Lumpur, and threatened to start killing hostages,' he explains. 'They were as good as dead after that.'

'What do you mean, "as good as dead"?'

'We had them park the plane in a hangar, away from the terminal building. A team of negotiators kept them busy while we planned the assault.'

'So the negotiation—that was a ruse?'

'Basically. They may have surrendered, but we weren't planning on taking prisoners. When the Special Forces team goes into a job like that, it is only to take out the fuckers, plain and simple. We go in to kill.'

'How did the operation play out?' I ask, mid-pant. Diva has an uncanny knack for talking and running at the same time. I have to admire that sort of fitness level. *Maybe he's not bullshitting me,* I think.

'We stormed the plane. How, exactly, I can't say. I signed an Official Secrets Act, and I have to abide by it. But I can tell you that I went in the main left doorway, behind my chief. He and I took out two hostage-takers—right between the eyes.'

'No chance of surrender, then?'

'We didn't ask, man!' he says, with horror at my naivety. 'And the bullets, they are a special type—designed to explode once they hit you. Anti-terror ammunition isn't intended to wound, I can tell you, Peter,' he laughs.

We're silent for a while. I'm fascinated by the idea that even a loyal citizen, who has served his nation, can be shit-canned and jailed on a first offence. Diva was pensioned out of the army after a near-death experience: a parachute failed to open and he barely survived the impact, which left him with a metal plate in his head and another, with pins, in his leg. I'm wondering if all these events challenge Diva's sense of national loyalty.

'Too fucking right it does!' Diva shouts, when I pose the question. 'I'm done with this whole fucking country. These bloody buggers can get fucked! They can get fucked!' he repeats, with unnecessary emphasis. The whole yard has heard him.

Diva's ambition—such as this is a statement of ambition—is to retire to Australia and grow leeches for medical services. 'I'm already leech farming on a plot in Malaysia,' he says, 'and man those fuckers are gold. They are easy to grow and fetch a very tidy price from hospitals and research facilities. *Cray*-zee!'

Diva's ruminations on the regime make other inmates roll their eyes, as if to say 'We've heard it all before.' But his yarns intrigue me. He insists, for example, that the social elite in Singapore receive not only special attention, but also special protection. Every Singaporean citizen over the age of twelve is issued with a photo identity card, or IC. It is mandatory to present the IC to police or other officials of the regime. According to Diva, the identity cards of the elite have on them a stamp of a small white horse. It is an old Chinese code, says Diva, to indicate elite status. 'Those fuckers with the white horse never get arrested, no matter what they have been doing. I swear man,' says Diva. 'This is fucking true. I swear!'

•••••

IN THE YARD, CONVERSATION is running short. 'Are you a cat person, or a dog person?' That's Andy, a lanky Chinese inmate. He's cheerful, but guarded, like someone withholding a terrible secret. Prisoners wear an identity strap around the right wrist with their name and prison number. Andy's is the colour of an inmate on special watch, usually indicating past attempts at self-harm. I sometimes see him holding onto the strap, self-consciously covering it with his left hand.

'Cat,' I reply.

Andy gives me a knowing look, like he always knew I was a cat person. 'Of course you are,' he says.

'Okay, mister,' I challenge. 'So what am I—a Coca-Cola or Pepsi person?'

Without a moment's thought, he says, 'That's way too easy. You're Coca-Cola.'

'Wrong,' I declare proudly.

'Am I?' he insists. 'Or are you just ashamed of admitting to drinking Coke?'

'Wow, Andy, that's really deep,' I say. 'But I have to disappoint you by saying that I drink *both* Coke and Pepsi. It's only dogs and cats that I am adamant about.'

Goh is standing in the middle of the yard, vaporising about something in his dialect to the other Chinese. He has this habit of standing in front of the Chinese group *sans* shirt and holding forth on some topic while simultaneously stroking his biceps. During a lull in the monologue, Goh dips to the ground and performs a series of push-ups for the crowd, who mostly sit in embarrassed silence wondering, like me, what on earth Goh is trying to prove.

When a staff officer walks past, Goh yells a phony and provocatively loud welcome: 'Hello, Sir! Good afternoon to you, Sir!' he says. The officers usually grin and bear it, knowing that to respond would only encourage this childishness to continue.

• • • • •

AFTER YARD TIME, inmates strip and are searched before returning to the housing unit. This involves queuing up to enter a room where we remove our shorts and T-shirt in front of a duty officer. Each of us has to open our mouth for inspection and whirl around, performing a nude pirouette.

Most inmates carry out this task with the usual prisoners' unselfconsciousness, since refusal is not an available option and one comes to accept and adapt to the indignities of prison security regulations. The one exception to this rule is inmates who carry scars of the caning punishment.

Goh, Ismail and Pung have all been caned and carry permanent scars. Pung received five strokes of the rattan after he was convicted for trafficking and brought to jail. His scars are three years old, and still appear pink and tender. When he strips for the after-yard inspection Pung performs the obligatory moves in a hurry, like a man late for an urgent appointment. It is the same with Goh and Ismail. Public nakedness must be a sobering reminder of being flogged, since no one present seems to even try to disguise expressions of fascination and revulsion. Getting caned makes a man an unwilling, walking billboard for tough-love law and order.

Walking back up to the landing, I pluck up the courage to ask Pung about being caned. 'How soon after you came to prison did the caning happen?' I say.

'A few weeks. They don't give you any warning. They just come to your cell one day and say, "Follow me." '

'What happened next?'

'I was taken to a room where some officers and a nurse were waiting for me. There was this padded A-frame in the middle of the room,' he says, making an A-shape with his hands. 'They ordered me to strip naked, and bend.'

'It's set up like that? Permanently?'

'Yes. I think the room is soundproof. It is just over there,' he says, pointing in the direction of another landing on the opposite side of the prison.

In Singapore, caning is mandatory for scores of offences—from rape to robbery, vandalism to drug trafficking. In a majority-Chinese community—the culture that invented fireworks—caning is also mandatory for importing and selling fireworks, such is Lee Kuan Yew's Talibanesque bent against innocent fun of just about every conceivable kind. The only up side for a prisoner sentenced to death is that they are not caned as well. It is compassion of a kind, according to the strange moral compass of the PAP-controlled Singapore judiciary.

Perhaps the meanest judge in Singapore's history is Lee Kuan Yew's old Cambridge University classmate, Yong Pung How. Ruthlessly tough, Yong remarked in 1996 that, 'Rehabilitation is something I have never understood. Compassion went out the window a long time ago. Now I just deliver justice.'

Lee Kuan Yew introduced mandatory caning in 1966 for vandalism. His rationale had nothing to do with justice or deterrence. It was a punishment designed to shame and humiliate.

For Pung, 'justice' was five strokes delivered in the most feared room in the prison. Selfconsciously rubbing his behind, Pung says, 'It feels like a real whipping.'

'I thought they used a bamboo rod?' I say.

'No. It is made from rattan. They wet it, and it becomes flexible, bends easily.'

'How big is it?'

'I didn't see how long it is, but the scars on my arse are half an inch wide,' he says, pulling down the side of his shorts and exposing the scars on his left flank.

'They still look sore,' I observe.

'No. It's just how it looks. The pain went away—after two weeks.'

'Two weeks! Jesus Christ. How hard do they hit you?'

Laughing, he says, 'Hard.'

According to the law, the cane is mandated to be a diameter of 1.27 centimetres. I have read accounts that describe how prisoners are restrained during canings, echoing what Pung says. When the inmate is bent over the A-frame their wrists are locked down in handcuffs. A similar technique is used on the ankles, to ensure the inmate holds still during the beating. I cannot imagine how anyone would not struggle after the first stroke is applied.

The Singapore Criminal Procedure Code says: 'The punishment of caning shall not be inflicted unless a medical officer is present and certifies that the offender is in a fit state of health to undergo such punishment. If during the execution of a sentence of caning a medical officer certifies that the offender is not in a fit state of health to undergo the remainder of the sentence the caning shall be finally stopped.'

I would have thought the 'do no harm' section of the Hippocratic oath would prevent a doctor from even participating in such a barbaric form of punishment. The medical community in Singapore could, should it find the wisdom and courage to stand up to the regime, stage a collective walkout. Refusal to attend canings would force the government to suspend this form of punishment.

'What did the doctor do for you?' I ask Pung.

'He applied iodine, to stop any infection. And they gave me a paracetamol for the pain.'

'That's it?'

'Yes.'

'Some house call!'

'Yeah. They don't really do anything for you. You are bleeding when it is over, and they make you pull up your pants and walk back to your cell,' explains Pung. 'I had to lie face-down for two weeks. The sores kept cracking and bleeding, and then scabbing over again. It was agony.'

'Does everyone bleed?'

'Of course. That's the idea.'

'What do you mean?'

'Peter!' Pung punches me in the shoulder, as though to get my attention. 'They *aim* to cut your arse open!' he says. 'They try to hit the same mark and open the skin, so that you bleed. It's their way of making sure you get a scar, something to remember the punishment by.'

'Nice.'

'Yeah. Bad for me, worse for others. I only got five. They can do twenty-four strokes on some guys. Imagine that!'

Talking to inmates about caning is a sensitive topic of conversation. Every inmate who speaks about corporal punishment seems to relive the trauma of that dreadful moment. Shamsudin tells me his story, which is even more harrowing: 'I was in Subordinate Court, facing trial for theft,' he says. 'I didn't want to come to jail. They were going to put me in here for eight years.'

'What did you do?'

'I threw myself off the sixth floor, into the garden in the atrium.'

'Jesus Christ—you tried to kill yourself?'

'Yes. I broke my leg and smashed my hip.'

'That's all?'

'No. When I got out of the hospital, they charged me with attempting to escape.'

'You are joking? Suicide at the court qualifies as an attempt to escape?'

'That's the law. They gave me an extra five years on my sentence and eight strokes for attempted escape, on top of my sentence for theft.' Shamsudin is shaking his head in disbelief. 'I'm here for thirteen years, no remissions.'

'Do you remember the caning?' I ask.

'I will never forget it.' Shamsudin's eyes are filling with tears. 'I cannot stop thinking about what they did to me . . .' His voice is trailing off and he is staring over my shoulder, at some imaginary point on the wall behind us. I see him fighting to re-exert control, trying not to break down and lose face.

'There is nothing wrong with feeling this way,' I say, trying to comfort him.

'I am Muslim. I am so ashamed—I was tied, naked. The officer who did this to me just whipped me and whipped me. I was screaming, I was begging for mercy. They just kept beating me and beating me. I could feel blood trickling out of my buttocks.'

'Afterwards, what happened?'

'They untied me, and the nurse put something on my wounds to stop infection. They offered me a pill for the pain. That's all. I went back to my cell and lay there for a week. Every time I moved or rolled over, the scab would break and I would bleed again.'

'This is exactly the same story I hear from everyone else.'

'That is because it is the same for everyone. Nobody gets a bandage, or any medical treatment. The nurse carries around a box, a medical kit. Do you know what they call it?'

'What?'

'"The Caning Kit."' He is laughing now. 'Can you believe this? Here in my country a nurse has a kit for caning. Cruel people. I live in a cruel country. Doctors and nurses are supposed to help us? Big joke, lah. Big joke on us,' he adds bitterly.

'What do you think you will do?' I ask.

'When?'

'When you leave here.'

'I don't think that far ahead. I have years and years left on my sentence. My life is over. They may as well kill us. Because they don't want us around.'

'Who doesn't want you?'

'The Chinese.'

TWENTY-EIGHT
Deep throat

DEEP THROAT IS ON MY SIDE. He has been venting to me about Singapore Almighty's daughter, Lee Wei Ling.

At fifty-four and never married, Wei Ling is a doctor with an important job in pediatric neurology, but she does not feel the need to restrict herself to her area of obvious expertise. Obligingly, the *Straits Times* newspaper provides her with a weekly column in which she sets the world to rights, like an old-fashioned preacher with a bully pulpit.

Lee's first contribution of 2009 was a startling assertion that Singaporeans are guilty of becoming too soft and comfortable in their affluence. Deep Throat says the column is provoking fury on the Internet, leading one critic operating under the pseudonym 'Patriot' to fire off a letter of complaint to the *Straits Times*.

The *ST*, unsurprisingly, declined to publish a letter critical of the First Daughter. Apparently Patriot's letter was published on a blog instead. Deep Throat says Patriot excoriated Lee for attacking Singaporeans, demanding to know what moral authority she possessed to talk about suffering and deprivation to a community that had suffered decades of suppression and intimidation at the hands of her father.

Changing the topic, I say to Deep Throat, 'Have you been following this story about the Thai navy letting refugees drown, rather than allow them to reach Thailand?'

'Yes,' he says. 'It a disgrace, isn't it? They ought to be ashamed.'

Hundreds of people called Rohingyas—a Muslim ethnic minority from an area in Burma—had drowned at sea when the Thai navy turned

270

them back after their failed attempt to reach the Thai mainland. But their makeshift craft were not strong enough to sustain a return journey. It was left to the Indian coast guard and Indian navy to pick up the 500 survivors, many of whom were suffering acute dehydration.

In 2007 I spent an unforgettable few days in the makeshift camp these refugees escaped from, filming a report for the ABC's *Foreign Correspondent* program. I have seen impoverished living conditions in Africa and across Southeast Asia, but nothing prepared me for the horror of the Rohingyas' refugee camp, situated along a narrow mudflat between the Teknaf River and a busy road. It was as if the hand of God himself had come down and swept the planet's most desperate people to the edge of existence, and challenged them to live there or die. Death came swiftly for some, through disease or hunger or drowning, when the river rose in unexpected moments of flash flooding, or horrific traffic accidents, when trucks and cars hurtling past knocked down and killed children playing on the road.

The proverbial will to live—powered by faith or good fortune or good genes—kept most refugees alive, and trapped in a place that is quite literally a hell on earth. When we arrived the assault on our senses was shocking and profound. Death aside, I cannot remember smelling a more foul odour in my life. The camp was beyond the description 'squalid'. The ground was a soft mix of water, human faeces and mud.

During a walk-around, we found a woman named Gulzar Begum picking weeds, the main ingredient in her family's one daily meal. Her journey into misery had begun just over the border in Burma. After their land was confiscated, the Burmese army forced her and her husband into slavery. Gulzar watched as soldiers beat him to death for dropping a heavy sack of rice. While we filmed Gulzar preparing the day's meal, the mathematical impossibility of her dead husband fathering so many young children became apparent. When we quizzed her, Gulzar revealed a predatory truth of being a woman refugee. She had been raped, repeatedly, since her husband's murder. She pointed at her children and declared, 'I have six daughters and one son—but I am not sure who fathered them.' Even when her husband was alive, Burmese soldiers raped her. It's a pattern of sexual abuse that continued in the camp. Local men frequently snatch refugee women, taking them away in cars. Because of her experience, Gulzar forbids her eldest daughter to leave the shelter. 'The local men come here and eye her up,' she said. 'They come here and demand her, so I have to keep her out of sight.'

The appearance of a visiting foreign film crew in a refugee camp raises expectations that someone, somewhere, might finally pay attention to your plight. It was our hope too. But sometimes we seem to make almost no difference at all. It is true that the media can be powerful, but it is also true that the media can be ignored and be rendered impotent. Despots who don't need to soothe public opinion or run in real electoral contests are the least likely to be moved to humanitarian action by media pressure, however sustained.

Burma is a topic on which the meddlesome Dr Lee Wei Ling has been fulminating in her *Straits Times* column. She reveals a truly hard heart by telling readers that, when Cyclone Nargis battered the Irrawaddy delta, her reaction to the tragedy was 'only moderately emotional'. Lee defames the entire population of Singapore by claiming, without any supporting data, that the rest of the community feels the same way as she does. She claims, incredibly, that Singaporeans care more for their own kind (*Does she mean the Chinese kind?* I wonder) and for their dogs than they do for foreigners.

What shocks me, aside from Lee's outrageous thinking, is that the *Times* is allowing this rubbish to be printed at all. The Lee family really ought to steer clear of vaporising on Burma, because doing so only exposes the moral black hole in which the state of Singapore finds itself. On the one hand, it takes the high moral ground on heroin—tut-tutting disapproval at poor souls trapped in the grip of addiction, and hanging them too—and yet, on the other hand, it names orchids in the state-run Botanic Gardens after visiting dignitaries from the narco-regime of Burma. Singapore's foreign and domestic policies could not be more compromised, confused or contradictory. If drug pushers are bad, then so are their enablers. Perhaps hanging the next Burmese government official to visit Singapore would resolve the inherent hypocrisy, and the obvious contradiction between their foreign and domestic law-and-order policies.

I can thank Deep Throat for pointing out to me the madness of the orchid-naming ceremonies. The most recent beneficiary of this botanic absurdity, he says, is Thein Sein, the number-four 'goon' in the junta's hierarchy. Thein Sein's visit apparently inspired a rare act of public protest: three Singaporeans tried to present a bouquet of orchids to the man from the tyrant-state, only to be detained by the police. Deep Throat says the flower is called *Dendrobium Thein Sein*.

'If you happen to pass by,' I suggest, 'can you pee on it, or tear it to shreds?'

Roaring with laughter, DT makes an exit. We've been chatting for fifteen minutes and, I suspect, he's being careful not to be seen with me too often, or for too long.

TWENTY-NINE
Lessons learned

'SO WHAT SORTS OF PRESSURES create stress for prisoners?'

It's me asking the questions. I am standing in front of a white-board, pen poised, before an audience of half a dozen mute and smiling prisoners. The level of obedience is assisted by the fact that a burly prison officer is sitting just off to the right, observing this absurd pantomime.

When I arrived in prison the superintendent in charge said that he wanted to put my writing skills to some sort of use. That was five months ago. I never heard another word about that project. Now, with just a few weeks left on my sentence, I have been summoned to work: as a teacher running a class on stress management.

'Why me?' I complained, when the instruction was delivered by a senior officer.

'Because we have seen how admirably you have dealt with your problems before you were a prisoner—and afterwards when you arrived.'

It is also true that the officers of TMP have been reading my incoming and outgoing mail, monitoring my visits with Mazlee and routinely checking my diary for subversive content. They know exactly what I am thinking, and feeling. But I have to invoke the saffron Dolly on this particular breach of privacy—letting go of anger and fear. It's their prison, and I'm just a visitor.

So here I am, conveying my self-help tips to some emotionally raw inmates, a few of whom are at the commencement of their sentence.

'For me, writing is a key,' I say, before sharing my favourite quotation from a Russian writer, that 'it is easiest to bear something if you write it down'. Of course, nobody is writing that pithy line down.

I decide to tell them a story about stress involving someone else. And how letting go of anger and fear helps the individual overcome whatever stressful situation they may find themselves in.

• • • • •

THE STORY HAS BEEN in the newspapers lately. The UN-backed genocide tribunal is underway in Cambodia and the man in the dock, Kaing Guek Eav—better known as Duch—is appearing for his role in the Khmer Rouge regime between 1975 and 1979. The KR killed millions of people, including the wife of an extraordinary and inspiring man I met in Cambodia in early 2004.

Bou Meng was imprisoned and tortured, and he watched as his wife was killed. And yet he is a model of dignity and compassion rather than bitterness and revenge. Bou Meng personifies the kind of courage and humanity that will help Cambodia endure and prosper as a nation. In every posting, a journalist develops a favourite nation. Mine was Cambodia; my first to Southeast Asia and, in part, Bou Meng is the reason why.

Between 1975 and 1979, 16 000 Cambodian people were herded into Phnom Penh's notorious Toul Sleng prison, codenamed by the regime S-21. Prisoners were tortured and starved, or beaten to death. Most inmates were trucked to the outskirts of the city for execution, a sentence carried out by young cadres wielding farming hoes. Of the handful of survivors, only three men are still alive; one of them is Bou Meng.

On a sunny day in the courtyard of the prison-turned-torture museum, the diminutive but spirited 62-year-old Bou Meng told me his extraordinary tale: 'A guard came around and said, "Can anyone paint?" I said, I can. So they stopped torturing me and handed me a pencil and piece of paper. The guard shouted at me, "Draw something. If it is no good, we will kill you!"'

The guards liked Bou Meng's work so much that they ordered him to paint a portrait of Pol Pot, the regime leader. It was enough to save his life. But bitter tears flowed soon after as Bou Meng described something else: witnessing the torture and murder of his wife some weeks before his miraculous reprieve. The old man's grief was visceral; time had not lightened the burden of events that took place more than a quarter of a century earlier. He slapped his hands to his head, as if he was seeing visions of the murder. He clawed at his skin, as if to wipe off the spray of blood and gore. And he clutched at my wrist, conjoining us in the contagion of human grief and sorrow.

I held back; fearful of getting involved, fearful of what to say or do next. And fearful too of being in the cameraman's way. This was an emotionally gripping piece of television and I didn't want David Leland to miss a moment of it. When Bou Meng emerged from twenty years of isolation, most people had given him up for dead. But the painter was very much alive and anxious to speak to the media, to set the record straight about Toul Sleng and volunteer as a prosecution witness at the Khmer Rouge tribunal.

After recording the interview at S-21, we drove Bou Meng home to a small hamlet in the province of Svay Rieng province. On the way he sat and chatted in Khmer, describing the countryside, acting as a tour guide. He was charming and funny and full of forgiveness for the countrymen who tore his life apart. He said that he wanted justice for the surviving members of the regime, but of a legal kind. Bou Meng wasn't the type of man who believed in witch-hunts and torchlit search parties and mob justice. Bou Meng was at peace with his world.

We wanted to film a sequence of Bou Meng at work as a painter, surviving on the skills that saved his life. The piece he created for the story used to hang on the wall of the ABC bureau in Bangkok. It is gripping—and horrific. On a red backdrop, Bou Meng painted a grim, naive-style vision of the torture and murder of his wife. It may not be the best work of art ever created, but it has an authenticity that is hard to go past without pausing to consider, as someone else once said, man's inhumanity to man.

For proof and posterity, I had David take a photograph of the artist and me squatting together holding the painting. As we stood and said our goodbyes, I proposed for Bou Meng a new assignment.

'What's that?' he asked.

'I want you to paint Pol Pot for me.'

Bou Meng paused for a moment, scratching the ground with his bare feet. I felt a twinge of guilt, like I had just asked a rape victim to draw me a picture of the rapist. I wondered whether I had just crossed a line. But my guilt edged back when Bou Meng looked up, smiling, and said, 'It would be an honour to remind the world who Pol Pot was.'

I went away convinced that Bou Meng would produce something dark and sinister, that Pol Pot might well appear on canvas with pointy ears and a devil's tail. David and I talked for days about the way he remembered Pol Pot, as a wizened old man laying on a straw mat. That was how the old communist warrior looked during his last-ever television interview, a journalistic coup by Nate Thayer from the now defunct *Far Eastern Economic Review*.

In that interview Pol Pot was a human in serious decline and decay, in urgent need of oxygen to keep breathing. He was said to be (mildly) apologetic about the murder and starvation of nearly two million Cambodians under his watch, but not exactly repentant. Most of my stories in Bangkok were filmed with the same camera that had filmed that interview, and that just creeped me out.

A few weeks later a friend delivered the hugely anticipated Pol Pot portrait to me back in Bangkok. When I unrolled the canvas and held it up, I was astonished. The ogre I had expected was not there. Instead the painting depicted a cherubic-faced, happy-looking man with a rich crop of jet-black hair, standing proud and tall. I had urged Bou Meng to paint Pol Pot as he remembered him. And he did just that. That's when I recalled—and fully understood—Bou Meng's parting words: 'It would be an honour to remind the world *who* Pol Pot was.'

Bou Meng had taught me one of the greatest lessons of my years as a correspondent. All of the pejorative journalese terms that we use to describe the bad guys—the Khmer Rouge leader being chief amongst them—merely demonises the subject, putting unnecessary distance between them and us. That's a big mistake. Because when you stand back and look closely at the Bou Meng portrait, what you see is that Pol Pot is just another man. He's just a human being. He's one of us. And that is the thought—not of butchers and madmen and psychos—that really ought to keep the rest of us on our toes.

The inmates thought the story of Bou Meng was fascinating too.

'There are a lot of things we can take out of his experience, but the one I want to emphasise here is this,' I say, hoping to build up to a climax that might get these guys' attention. 'Don't be a victim,' I pronounce.

• • • • •

I AM FIGHTING UPHILL in prison against the victim mentality. I see it every day with most of the inmates on my landing. A few days ago I was reading. Next to me Pung was staring at the wall.

'Would you like one of my books to read?' I asked.

'No,' he said, with irritation, 'I told you before—I don't read.'

'But you've been here for three years, and you still have six months to go. Don't you get bored?'

'Yes, but I'm too lazy to read.'

Pung turned away, fixing his stare at the wall opposite. This was his way of telling me to drop it.

Heng is the same. Not long after I arrived, back when I believed stories that he was smart and clever and educated, I lent him R.F. Delderfield's classic *To Serve Them All My Days*. I had thoroughly enjoyed this story of the life of a schoolteacher, which begins at the end of World War One. Heng lasted a day before handing back the book and grunting his disapproval with a two-word review: 'No sex.'

This is how it is with most prisoners: they are incarcerated, incurious and selfishly uninvolved in anything but their own lives. Sometimes I wonder if I have ever come across such a concentration of so many profoundly self-obsessed people. That's usually when, with an ironic titter, I remember where I have spent most of my working life—in the profoundly self-obsessed world of television.

Heng sits in his room all day, alone, until emerging at yard time, where more often than not he sits alone again, obsessing over the monotonous certainty that tomorrow will be identical to today. He has no interests, and no distractions. Prisoners like Heng and Pung are self-petrifying. Chemically speaking, they are as inert as nitrogen.

I suspect that the Singapore regime is not particularly interested in countering this creeping, prison-induced social dysfunction. Vocational training seems non-existent, bar a few courses in computer skills which have limited places. Opportunities to work have virtually dried up. Prison workshops have been mothballed because commercial demand for goods has dried up, and this is due, say prison officers, to the global economic crisis. Heng says the closure only reinforces suspicion among inmates that these workshops only ever existed as a means to exploit cheap prison labour. If they were intended to help prisoners improve their skills and experience, he argues, they'd still be operating.

In conversation with my fellow cookie Ismail I am left wondering whether he prefers prison to freedom, because he speaks of prison life with sentiment and enthusiasm. And I also wonder whether the public would be better off for him to remain here, given his penchant for guiltlessness and thoughtless self-absorption. To hear Ismail speak he has never done anything wrong, and yet the world has dealt him an endless series of grave injustices.

'You see,' he explains, 'the police, they always disturb me. When I am not in prison they follow me—they always ask me questions, where am I going, who am I with, what am I doing.'

'But you were guilty?' I ask. 'Every time?'

'Nothing,' he protests, not answering the question directly. 'These charges are nothing. Always nothing.'

Psychologists talk of 'injustice collectors'; these are people who are convinced that they are never wrong, but are frequently wronged by other people. Prison is their natural home. Inmates like Ismail, Heng and Goh are adamantly certain that they are without fault, and are entitled to certain privileges as a result of being jailed. Goh is to be released a few days after me and argues that the prison authorities, having held him in prison for four years, are responsible for finding him a job immediately upon release.

'What do you want to do when you leave?' I ask, playing along with this injustice-collector logic.

'Ah,' says Goh, laughing and rocking in his place. 'I want to go your country and make drugs! No executions, lah!' he says before rewarding himself with an affectionate pat on the stomach. His shirt, as usual, is off, and he is performing his push-up regimen for the crowd.

'No, really—what is your job on the outside?' I persist.

279

'I sell drug!' he says, after a quick set of five. 'You want me to come to Sydney? I sell drug to your friends.'

For Diva, the perpetual injustice of prison life is the slow delivery of mail.

'Man, I tell you,' the Ruminator bellows, as we take another turn on the running course, 'these fuckers deliberately go slow on giving us my mail.'

'Why do you think they are holding up your mail, rather than anyone else's?' I ask Diva.

'Because, man, I am the only one who complains.'

I know for a fact that Diva is not the only inmate who complains about the slow mail service although, knowing Diva as I do, I can easily understand how he would think this way. He is king amongst injustice collectors.

I'm reminded of the warning by the superintendent of the prison when I arrived: 'These people are not your friends.' He was right. I can see, looking back, that none of the inmates formed friendships. They talk, but the conversations are banal and shallow and mostly limited to mutual venting of perceived injustices.

And there is something else that I have noticed. Cookies sit on the floor in the reception area of the landing close to the doorway that leads to the main administration block. Prisoners on their way to being processed for release use that door. For all the chatter and bravado and game playing, none of them ever looks back.

THIRTY

Sentinels

PRISONERS KEEP SECRETS.

Most people keep some aspect of their story to themselves, fenced off so no one will trespass. Some tell false or fanciful stories as a ruse, to distract. Others choose silence. In prison, I have noticed that this pattern of behaviour seems amplified. And for one man it is motivated by the desire to cheat death.

James and I are sitting side by side on the floor of a holding room in Cluster Prison, across the street from Tanah Merah Prison. I've been for an x-ray to screen for TB, a routine health check for all inmates, and I am awaiting transport back to TMP. James, I presume, is here from another prison and has been brought in for the same purpose. I haven't seen him before.

'How long?' he says, posing the shorthanded question that begs to be asked amongst prisoners of recent acquaintance.

'Ten months—I'm about to be released. End of June,' I say, smiling involuntarily at the idea that my prison experience is coming to an end soon. 'You?'

He is sighing. 'Life,' he says. And then, after a long pause, he adds, 'Or death.'

Before I can ask what he means, James explains, 'I am on death row.'

'Sorry to hear that,' I say, scrambling to adjust to the confronting revelation that someone I have known for less than thirty seconds has revealed something so private and shocking—that he is to be hanged by the Republic of Singapore. James and I are sitting so close to each other in this crowded room that I can feel the heat of his body. I can see his chest rising and falling as he breathes. I can see the beads of sweat forming on his forehead. I can see the small scar on his left knee—a fall from a bike as a child, perhaps.

And already I know this stranger's fate. I know that he will hang from a rope whose length was chosen for James's weight and height. I know that in the final moment his head will be covered in a suffocating bag, that he may whimper and beg for mercy and shit his pants, and that piss will run down his leg and over the Achilles tendon that has been sliced open by a doctor who has taken the Hippocratic oath. I know all of this and I feel a pit opening in my stomach—a wave of nausea and an urgent compulsion to say something comforting to a condemned man.

'How did this happen?' I ask, preferring to encourage him to tell me his story rather than me pouring out empty platitudes of the type he has probably heard a million times.

'I was a courier—I drove four kilograms of heroin across the border from Malaysia. I had to deliver the stuff to a place at Bukit Timah,' he says, referring to a well-known road in Singapore. 'The police had been following me from the border. And they knew I was coming,' he adds.

'Why did you do it?'

'I needed the money—I'm Malaysian,' explains James. 'I knew the risk, but I don't have a job. I thought that one time'—he shrugs—'who would know?'

James's reward for risking his life was to be $400. He never received the pay-off—police arrested him as soon as he arrived at the destination. His trial is underway but he has no illusions about the eventual outcome—a mandatory sentence of death. Given that he will appeal, James estimates that he has roughly a year to live. But he is not surrendering to his fate.

'I'm HIV-positive,' he whispers, careful not to be overheard by other prisoners, 'and I have gone off treatment since I was arrested.'

'Why are you telling me this?' I ask.

'Because you are a foreigner—and you are about to leave Singapore.'

I am puzzled by the connection between James's health and impending execution. 'So what has that got to do with the case?'

'I am trying to develop full-blown AIDS before my execution—you see?' James is tapping my arm, as though waking me for a revelation. But I'm shrugging my shoulders, a silent gesture of query.

'I still don't get it,' I say.

'If a prisoner is dying, he can receive a compassionate pardon and release from prison—even a prisoner on death row.'

'Let me get this right,' I say, adjusting myself to face James. 'You are going to try your hardest to get so sick that you are dying from AIDS to stop them from executing you?'

James is nodding. 'You see, I can go back on treatment when I am released.' He must sense that I am not convinced by this bizarre plan. 'It's a risk—but I would rather die at my own hands than let them execute me.'

'So you're committing suicide, in a way?' I say, characterising James's plot as self-harm, not self-help. I can see that he is bristling at my use of the word 'suicide'.

'At least I am in charge,' he says, defiantly. A little desperately too, I sense.

• • • • •

JAMES IS KEEPING A secret from a state that wants to kill him. The lies and deceptions of most inmates are far less grand in their motivation. Some, like Heng, the youngest inmate on my landing, weave fabrications simply because they can. They manufacture stories as a substitute for entertainment. And maybe because, as he keeps saying, 'I am a little bit crazy.'

When I am jogging around the yard listening to Diva's fantastic stories, I sometimes wonder whether I am in step with Walter Mitty, the fictional book character with a vivid fantasy life of himself in heroic roles. So far, Diva has told me that he was an elite soldier, a crack paratrooper, an anti-terrorist marksman and a personal protection agent once responsible for the safety of the current prime minister, Lee Hsien Loong. But my suspicion is mounting.

As we come to a halt after another fifty-second lap, he is telling me again about his terrible accident. Panting, and talking, he says, 'We were doing a night jump, very dangerous, you see. My chute failed, and I crashed into the soft ground next to the runway. I nearly died.'

'And then?' I ask, trying not to betray a gently mocking tone.

'I tell you—I nearly died that day. They had to revive me then and there in the field.'

'Remarkable. You managed to land in a field and not on a runway!' I add.

'Yes,' says Diva, 'it is a miracle. I could have landed a few metres to the left and hit the runway, and I would have been killed instantly. *Cray*-zee!'

'What injuries did you have?' I ask.

'Well, I cracked my head open, I can tell you,' says Diva. 'And I have a big steel plate in it now. And this leg,' he is reaching down and rubbing his left leg, 'I have a huge plate here also.'

'So they got rid of you, for being an invalid?'

'Basically. There is no room in SF for wounded men. It's a young man's game. They pensioned me off.'

The Ruminator does indeed have a long surgical scar on his leg, but this says nothing about the provenance of the injury.

Other inmates raise the drawbridge simply to forestall strangers. Because my case attracted so much publicity I did not have the opportunity to 'spin' a prison story, reinventing the exact nature of my offence or tales of my past life. And my foreign nationality meant that I could not easily blend in. I am both noticeable and known.

Contrast that with the inmate here who is a convicted sex offender—he is a local who is not well known, and thus is able to go about his business largely unnoticed. We were talking in the yard some time ago, before I knew the truth, when he told me that he had been sentenced to almost a year in jail for a white-collar crime involving accountancy fraud. It seemed a harmless enough case of incompetence or avarice or, considering the fact that he was caught, an unfortunate combination of both.

'I was working in a small firm here in Singapore,' he lied, 'and I will be out in a few months.'

He said he was planning on moving back to Australia, where he worked for a number of years. Whenever we spoke he shifted the conversation away from himself—out of shyness or a rightful claim to privacy, I thought. I had no suspicion then, as I do now, that he was diverting questions of a biographical nature that might identify his offence, a predatory and unwanted sexual advance.

THIRTY-ONE
Please, just leave

MY DIARY HAS BEEN OFFICIALLY cleared for release according to the boss of the housing unit, Ricky Au. This is welcome news after Deep Throat's months of hints that they'd refuse permission and that I needed to have a back-up plan, just in case.

I am due to leave tomorrow. The Intelligence Officer, 'Colonel Flagg'—the bozo who doesn't approve of Malays—has called me down for a pre-release interview.

'So you have served your full sentence, and tomorrow you will be released into the custody of the Immigration Department and deported from Changi Airport,' he says.

'Yes, that's how I understand it,' I say.

'I see you are going to Thailand—not Sydney?'

'That's right. I'm going to Koh Samui with my *Malay* partner'—a quick pause for ethnicity to sink in—'for a few days holiday before I head back home.'

'Huh,' he says, with a look of disapproval. 'All right. We anticipate media tomorrow, here at the prison. But you will be driven straight out of the jail and taken to the Immigration Centre, where you will be kept in custody until your flight. There will not be any opportunities for you to talk to the media. Understood?'

I'd like to wind him up and give him cause for moral panic, about me heading off to the beach for a holiday with my boyfriend. But I am feeling sentimental, so I button my lip and say, 'That's fine with me.'

Back in my room, I consider the benefits of a short stay in custody. In a fast-paced digital world prison in Singapore is, unintentionally, one of the last bastions of the slow-time, analogue world. For the past two hundred days I have been adhering to the rhythms of life as we once knew it. Life before the bleating, 'look at me, look at me' mobile phone. Before the burden of the portable computer, which burgled our private time in a way we never quite anticipated. And before the breathless, 24/7, gadget-obsessive lifestyle that so many of us slavishly embrace. I arrived here with a raging case of 'digitalitis', but I have gradually overcome this particular nasty.

Of my material possessions, I have missed the sum total of nothing. Not the perpetual logging on and checking of emails, only to find an inbox full of fluff and nonsense. Not the relentless calls from fifteen different editors insisting on more stories, more often for them and for no one else. And not the fear that I may have neglected to bring along the right power adaptor and chargers on the assignment to keep this whirling, dizzying frenzy of digital stuff powered and perpetually controlling my life.

Instead I indulged a guilty pleasure called reading, devouring nearly eighty books in those two hundred days. After years of chastising the women in my life for a fawning adulation of Jane Austen, I finally relented. Jane and I have been spending quality time together in my room. And while I humbly acknowledge that I was wrong—that there is much to be admired in the prose of Austen—I could still happily throttle some of her sillier characters, namely *Northanger Abbey*'s Catherine Morland. As a self-obsessed teen, she's only recently met her match in the fictitious Bella of the *Twilight* vampire series, a frowning brat undeserving of a prom date with any creature, let alone a vampire. For sharp and tight writing my greatest pleasure has been reading Hemingway. I have one literary confession: James Joyce's *Ulysses* is still in the corner, and I am still happier communing with ants.

Goh is confined to his room for the remainder of his sentence. The closer he gets to release, the more disturbing his behaviour becomes. I think he is frightened of freedom. A week or two back, he started acting more strangely than usual. In the yard, he sat on a bench hunched down like a bird and began flapping his arms. Later that day, he removed his prison identity wrist-strap and threw it at an officer. For that he was sacked from working as a cookie and sent to his room pending an investigation of the incident, which qualifies as an assault according to the strict rules of the prison system.

Before the case could be dealt with, Goh staged an attention-getting collapse in his room, claiming he was suffering a heart attack. I saw him carried away, one hand over his forehead and the other placed, theatrically, over his heart. Half an hour later he was sent back from the infirmary with strict instructions to lie down and allow the gas to pass.

$$\bullet \bullet \bullet \bullet \bullet$$

IT IS A BUSY last day. I should be eating lunch but I am with the Superintendent of Prisons, the SOP. It is his turn to interview me.

'So you have finished your sentence, I see,' he says, sounding remarkably like Colonel Flagg. I'm wondering what is the point of two farewell interviews. 'Any complaints?' he says, studying my file intently.

This is my favourite prison protocol—offering the captive the right of complaint. *I will hold my fire until I have cleared Singapore airspace*, I think. 'No,' I say, 'I have nothing I want to say here.'

'That's all then,' he says, closing my file. As he rises to leave it occurs to me that the boss has not looked me in the eye once during this extraordinarily brief encounter. Suddenly, I have a bad feeling. Something is not quite right here. He couldn't wait to get out of the room.

$$\bullet \bullet \bullet \bullet \bullet$$

AFTER LUNCH, AND OUT IN the yard for the final time, I'm running my last laps with Diva and listening to his latest ruminations on the injustice of his captivity. 'I tell you, man,' he says, 'this fucking place is driving me mental.'

The source of today's grievance is food quality. Diva has a point—lacklustre is the kindest description I can offer for the slop that is served up to inmates. In its defence, the prison says all meals are designed and supervised by a dietitian. So is processed dog food, but that doesn't make it appetitising to humans.

'These people serve us rubbish,' ruminates Diva. 'And they expect us to be happy!'

Happiness is optional in prison. I told myself that I was happy, long before I actually was. It's hard work being positive, especially in the face of a personal crisis, but eventually it stops being a self-help benediction and becomes a self-fulfilling prophecy. Eventually, I became happy. The worst thing a prisoner can do is to allow the negatives of incarceration to occupy all of the available space in their mind.

That's how I was at the beginning, until I found a balance of positive activities, my personal three R's: 'riting, reading and running. Everyone has to find his or her own way, but wallowing in melancholy is the *least* helpful state of existence. And collecting injustice, ultimately, does no justice to your own cause. It holds you back, when the only way out is forward.

Off to the side of the yard I see Heng, sullen and menacing and alone, as usual. 'Do you still hear him complaining about the quality of fruit?' I ask, teasingly. Diva's room is next to Heng's.

'My God, man!' says Diva. 'He's gone mad about it. He was shouting and yelling about the bruises on the bananas. He says the cookies are deliberately damaging his fruit.'

'All of the cookies?'

'Yes.' Diva is laughing and trying to maintain the pace. 'He says Pung gives him bad apples on purpose.'

I haven't had any direct contact with most inmates since I stopped being a cookie. According to the regulations, all prisoners must cease their work activities just prior to their release. But Pung is still working and, it seems, is now the fruit-wrecking culprit. It used to be me. Pung has a few months left on his sentence before he will be released and deported back to Malaysia.

Ismail's time is almost up too. We are sitting in the yard, and he is telling me about his plans for life after jail. 'I am going to get a wife,' he says, with his usual flair for certainty. 'She will look after me, and make me meals and keep my house.'

'Seems like you've already found one,' I joke.

'No,' says Ismail, perplexed by my comment. 'I have not. But this is how it will be.'

'How do you know you will ever meet the right woman?' I ask, trying to tease out some final titbit of Ismail logic. I'm wondering if he has plans for some kind of arranged marriage. 'What about love, eh?'

'What has love got to do with it?' Ismail replies, frowning at my apparently absurd sentimentality. 'I just want a woman to cook and wash my clothes and have sex.'

'Sounds like you could do with two women, Ismail,' I say, pausing for effect. 'A maid and a prostitute.'

A bell is sounding, saving me from the temptation to mock Ismail's certitude any further. As I approach the room where the prison officers supervise inmates in the yard, Colonel Blimp summons me. *Another insincere farewell,* I think.

'I am to inform you,' he says, with more formality than even he usually exhibits, 'that the decision has been made not to allow you to remove the diary from the prison.'

'What?' I say, completely stunned. I am not sure that I have just heard that right. 'I can't have the diary?'

'That is correct.'

'But it was cleared—I was told already by the officer in charge of this section, Ricky Au.'

Blimp is sitting back, enjoying the moment. 'Indeed, but, on referral to higher authorities, the decision has been revoked, I am afraid.'

'What higher authority are you talking about?' I demand. On the verge of my release, I am abandoning the requisite *please-sir, yes-sir, thank-you-sirs.*

'HQ,' he says.

I'm boiling with fury. This is a last-minute U-turn. I have been the subject of a two hundred day 'bait and switch' operation.

'You're a bunch of liars!' I am raising my voice now. 'And you've just blown your credibility with me, and EVERY PRISONER WHO CAN HEAR ME NOW'—and I am yelling, so they can—'BECAUSE YOU LOT LIE TO PRISONERS!'

With that satisfying outburst I turn and walk away, leaving Blimp stunned at my audacity. Then I stop. Emboldened, I return to Blimp to make one final, incendiary remark.

'I construe this as an act of political censorship,' I begin. 'Other inmates are released with their diaries,' I say. Blimp is speechless, so I press on. 'If you do not give me back my diary, I will refuse to leave the prison tomorrow morning. You lot can explain why a foreign prisoner who has completed his sentence is refusing to leave the prison.'

Blimp is perspiring. 'You must leave tomorrow,' he says. 'It is required.'

Steadying myself now I say, 'I am not leaving without that diary.'

•••••

BACK IN MY ROOM, I am pacing the floor. This is what Deep Throat said would happen. Happily, I took his advice. For the last four months I have been openly writing in the prison-issue diary by day, while at night scribbling in pencil the important and more controversial remarks into the inside pages of my library books as they have rotated in and out of prison.

I began writing diary notes in my copy of the Lee Kuan Yew memoir before I was issued with the diary. That was an act of necessity. It was only after the warning from Deep Throat, and after the Lee memoir had been sent back out of prison, without complaint, that I realised library books were a vehicle for my literary contraband: a hidden diary.

I have to maintain the façade of outrage, otherwise these officers will suspect that I have been up to no good. I still have here in my room three books with pages of pencil-written diary notations.

'I'm going to enjoy these last few hours,' I say out loud.

It's dinnertime. I don't have any further appetite for prison food, and I am fuelled up on the faux outrage of being denied my diary. It is, of course, not entirely faux—I really would like to take the diary with me, if only as a souvenir item.

I suspect the root cause of the diary's seizure is the inclusion of numerous observations on the Lee clan: founding father Kuan Yew; current prime minister Hsien Loong; and newspaper columnist and doctor daughter Wei Ling. I did this deliberately—to bait the authorities of this supposedly democratic republic, to test their ability to tolerate foreigners making critical observations about the Lee family and about the fawning, unchallenging coverage it receives in the local news media. Of course, the regime is falling for the bait and behaving like a panic-stricken, autocratic regime.

What's the big deal? Arguably, perhaps the most sensitive observation I make is not an observation at all. I simply noted the existence of a rare political confession. Lee Hsien Loong, in the *Straits Times*, conceded that he was brought into politics two decades ago to be groomed for the prime ministership. 'In Singapore we've been fortunate to have had a very long process of grooming and preparation before people take over in positions of responsibility.' He said that he was a PM identified '20 years in advance'. In other words, Lee the younger concedes there was a master plan for him to take over as PM. Now readers are free to draw their own conclusions without any interpretation from me, since the Lee family are fond of suing anybody who infers that Lee Hsien Loong did not achieve his position through merit.

The door is swinging open, and two officers are standing before me.

'Peter,' says Officer Happy, 'are you going to leave tomorrow?'

'No,' I say defiantly. 'If I don't get that diary, you are stuck with me. I'm not going anywhere.'

'You cannot say such things about the first family of this country,' says the other officer, confirming my suspicions.

'Peter,' pleads Happy, 'you have to go—you cannot stay in prison. It is against regulations.'

Laughing at the absurdity of that statement, I say, 'Forget it. Lying to me, telling me that the diary is cleared for release, then telling me at the last minute that it is not—that's not just a lie. In my case it is a pretty clear act of attempted censorship. You guys are treating me like a political prisoner all of a sudden, so I will start acting like one.'

'What do you mean?' asks Happy.

'I'm not eating your food'—this is fun, I think—'and I am not leaving.'

NEXT MORNING.

I slept heavily, nourished by the pantomime of my diary outrage and my empty but thoroughly entertaining threats to go on a hunger strike and refuse to leave. Maybe my ludicrous threats will rewrite the manual for releasing a prisoner from custody, with a new subsection, 'Things That Can Go Wrong'.

'Peter.' The door has swung open. Officer Ricky Au, the boss of my wing, is standing before me. 'I am begging you, please, just leave today, eh?'

I'm not going to let Ricky get away without a scolding. 'It seems to me that you guys have undone six months of goodwill. You had my respect, and my support, until now. I was quite happy to go out and tell the world what a safe place this is—but it isn't really, is it?'

'What do you mean?'

'Singapore. It isn't a safe place to *think*. It isn't a safe place to write, or question. A sign of a mature democracy,' I lecture Ricky, 'is one that allows people to say and write what they think—no matter what. But you guys see a diary that talks about one particular family and you run scared like little rabbits.'

'You can't say these things,' he pleads, adding, 'Besides, it wasn't my decision. I was overruled.'

Of course Ricky was overruled. The People's Action Party is nothing if not in firm and absolute control of the Republic. The bureaucrat who allows a reporter to leave prison in possession of a diary that includes reflections on leadership and power and freedom of speech is the bureaucrat who has lost his mind.

The collective consciousness of party-cum-family loyalty—the hive mind—rules supreme in this city-state, and today is to be no exception. I don't need the diary to prove my point. The authorities' refusal to hand it back speaks volumes.

Epilogue

WHEN I LEFT TANAH MERAH PRISON, like all of the inmates who had left before me, I did not look back.

I was reunited with Mazlee at Changi Airport and we flew together to the Thai resort island Koh Samui for a long overdue holiday. That first night I took five showers and brushed my teeth with real toothpaste for the first time in more than six months. On Samui, I found the amity and love of my prison dream. The future began again during that retreat, and today Mazlee and I are together and committed to building a future in Australia.

The Chinese word for crisis is a character that combines two words, danger and opportunity. Businessmen in western culture have a saying based on the same idea: 'In every crisis there is an opportunity.' Post-traumatic stress disorder, PTSD, was my crisis. I didn't see it coming. I often call PTSD 'mental cancer': its presence is not known or acknowledged until after the diagnosis, and until after the damage is done. Like cancer, it is a pernicious condition. But the good news is that, like many cancers, it can be treated and eventually cured.

I survived the crisis of PTSD because I had a network of supportive relatives and friends and, most notably of all, an extraordinary and patient partner in Mazlee. When I was barely able to put one foot in front of the other, they showed me the way forward. I survived the crisis because I wanted to. Anyone who has suffered a psychological disorder or illness will tell you that, at some point, they made a conscious choice to pick themselves up and start getting well again.

'Wellness' is not a passive concept—it is a conscious decision. And I survived this crisis because I had the inner resolve and capacity to stand on my own two feet. I critically examined the entrails of my life. It wasn't always a pleasant thing to do, but I did it because I knew that I had to confront the past in order to build a new and sustainable future. Our friends and family get us only so far on any road to recovery. At some point, we really are on our own. It is up to the individual to draw from his or her inner reserves and undertake the last, really hard work.

I took responsibility for myself and confronted my PTSD crisis in the long hours I spent talking to counsellors like Karen Gosling and Dr Ang Yong Gong. Since my return to Australia I have carried on that dialogue with the wonderful and insightful psychologist Deborah Vertessy.

And I took legal responsibility for the errors of judgement that happened during the crisis. I was guilty of the offences for which I was sentenced. It was my bad luck that the offences occurred in a country where there is virtually no regard for clear and extenuating circumstances.

At no point did I ever buy into the ridiculous idea that the regime was prosecuting me because of who I was. At the same time, I can tell you that there were no favours done either.

So what was the opportunity in my crisis? I learned that family comes first. I learned that my friends are my greatest assets, and that my life is worthwhile. I also learned that flying around the world to dangerous places did not make me remotely happy. But there is much more. Two hundred days in prison was an opportunity to sit and think, to review and consider and plan. It was a mid-career sabbatical of a most unusual kind.

After some soul-searching about whether I even wanted to rejoin the world of journalism, I returned to work at the Australian Broadcasting Corporation, in Sydney. After everything that happened, I remain a 'believer'—I believe that journalists play a critical role in maintaining a free and open society. I believe that journalism is not so much a career as a vocation. And I believe that I still have a role to play.

I do not blame the ABC for what happened to me, any more than I would blame my parents if I developed a genetic illness. That's life. Embracing the Culture of Blame is a fool's errand. There is no percentage in being backward-looking.

That is not to say that there are not lessons to be learned about the handling of PTSD. But these lessons are complex and nuanced, and must be applied almost entirely on a case-by-case basis. There is no one-size-fits-all remedy to the threat it poses to media professionals. Every correspondent is different. Every situation they find themselves in is different.

The best that an employer can do is manage the known risks thoughtfully, and create an environment where correspondents feel safe and supported when talking about stressful situations. On reflection, PTSD became a massive crisis in my case because I did not 'download'. The 'mental bucket' was never emptied, and eventually it overflowed. Hindsight, though, is a wonderful thing.

My crisis has been a catalyst for change. There is more space opening in the Australian media—internally as well as in published form—to talk frankly about stress and reporting. It was already happening, but the magnitude of my troubles has given the issue a real momentum. This can only be for the good.

My return to work at the ABC demonstrates something, too: that a workplace crisis does not have to end in adversarial conflict, with two parties lined up behind lawyers. I have learned from long experience in journalism that becoming a 'victim' or 'the angry litigant' serves no meaningful end. In the case of the ABC, managing director Mark Scott demonstrated admirable ethics and compassion, for which he deserves plaudits. It would have been far easier to say 'man overboard'.

But this, ultimately, is the message that I want the broader public to hear. The 'P' in PTSD does not stand for permanent. My crisis is over. Like countless others who have experienced a mental health illness, I made a full recovery and returned to work. Stronger, more self-aware and happier.

23091403R00178

Printed in Great Britain
by Amazon